My Father | Married | Your Mother

My Father | Married | Your Mother

Writers Talk about

Stepparents, Stepchildren, and

Everyone in Between

Edited with an Introduction by Anne Burt

W. W. Norton & Company   New York   •   London

For information about permission to reproduce selections from this book, write to
Permissions, W. W. Norton & Company, Inc., 500 Fifth Avenue, New York, NY 10110

Manufacturing by RR Donnelley, Harrisonburg
Book design by Chris Welch Design
Production manager: Andrew Marasia

Library of Congress Cataloging-in-Publication Data

My father married your mother : writers talk about stepparents, stepchildren, and
everyone in between / edited with an introduction by Anne Burt.— 1st ed.
p. cm.
ISBN-13: 978-0-393-06088-1 (hardcover)
ISBN-10: 0-393-06088-8 (hardcover)
1. Stepfamilies—Case studies. I. Burt, Anne.
HQ759.92.M92 2006
306.874'7—dc22

2005031832

W. W. Norton & Company, Inc., 500 Fifth Avenue, New York, N.Y. 10110
www.wwnorton.com

W. W. Norton & Company Ltd., Castle House, 75/76 Wells Street, London W1T 3QT

1 2 3 4 5 6 7 8 9 0

Contents

Introduction | ANNE BURT   13

My Father's New Muse | DANA KINSTLER   27

Le Beau-Père | PHYLLIS ROSE   34

Losing Janey | JACQUELYN MITCHARD   41

On Having a Stepmother Who Loves Opera |

ANDREW SOLOMON   50

My Father's Chinese Wives | SANDRA TSING LOH   61

Infinite Family | LISA SHEA   74

My Mother's Women | DAVID GOODWILLIE   81

A Package Deal | KATE CHRISTENSEN   98

Wicked | ROXANA ROBINSON   118

My Papa Married Your Mama | TED ROSE   127

My Wedding Presents | STEPHANIE STOKES OLIVER   134

A Good Man Is Hard to Find | SASHA TROYAN   143

On the Uses of Animals | SHEILA KOHLER   150

My Room | ALICE ELLIOTT DARK   155

A Trickle of Talk | LINDA PHILLIPS ASHOUR   164

Stepmother | SUSAN CHEEVER   174

Advice to New Stepmothers: On Undertaking the
   Stepfamily Vacation | LUCIA NEVAI   180

Infidelities | ELIZABETH POWELL   189

Dogs and Daughter | D. S. SULAITIS   196

Broken | S. KIRK WALSH   207

Diana's Child | MAURA RHODES   218

My Fairy Stepmother | LESLIE MORGAN STEINER   227

Step Shock | CANDY J. COOPER   234

Learning to Pray | MIKE DOLAN   245

The Mrs. Davises | SUSAN DAVIS   256

Stone Soup | BARBARA KINGSOLVER   265

Contributor Biographies   277

For Delayna, Tessa, and Craig

Acknowledgments

My heartfelt thanks, first, to the writers in this book for their insightful, brave, and beautiful essays. I am enormously grateful to Jill Bialosky and Beth Vesel for their guidance and wisdom, and to Susan Davis, Gina Hyams, Christina Baker Kline, and S. Kirk Walsh for their generous ideas along the way. Thank you to Evan Carver, Elizabeth Kadetsky, Sarah Mahoney, Karyn Marcus, Yona Zeldis McDonough, Elizabeth Pierson, and Steve Romagnoli for their excellent work on behalf of this book. Finally, thanks to my family and friends for their patience and love throughout this process.

My Father | Married | Your Mother

Introduction

Craig's online dating profile appeared on my computer screen with the irresistible opening line: "I have the most amazing three-year-old daughter."

I thought "Oh, so do I!" and clicked over to his information. He lived five minutes away from me. His picture was one of the few in black and white, but instead of a studied arty look or an attempt to show off an aquiline nose or a full head of hair, he looked unselfconscious, caught in a moment of surprise. I'd never seen a photo register so much honest emotion. I was in conversation with his face as well as with his words by the time I got to his second paragraph. So I wrote to him—something incautious, something completely out of character: "Call me. Here's my number."

In twenty seconds the phone rang. We talked for two hours. And thus my story of Happily Ever After began. The only catch: it was Happily Ever After Divorce.

The spring I met Craig, my freshman literature students at Fordham University in New York City were reading the novel *Mrs. Dalloway* by Virginia Woolf. I'd read it at least five times before, including back in graduate school, the year I met my first husband. Whenever I come back to Virginia Woolf, I see something new. This time, alone and mourning the bitter end of my marriage, I was brought to tears by her bird's-eye view of the random intersections between people over a single day. She would take us deep into the thoughts of Clarissa, who obsessed alternately about the table settings for her party, her own mortality, and roads not taken in her romantic life. Then Clarissa would hear the bells of St. Margaret chime the hour. Then Rezia, a stranger to Clarissa, would hear the same bells and we'd be deep in *her* fears that her husband was crazy, her regrets that she left Italy for England, and her love of decorating hats with stuffed birds.

I was teaching *Mrs. Dalloway* while pretending to my students, many of whom had taken classes from me in my married past, that my marriage hadn't exploded. They were eighteen, nineteen years old and saw me as a well-read fossil, unchanging for all eternity. But inside, I was roiling. My trust in my husband has thoroughly eroded when I realized at last that I was living with a man whose definition of a faithful, intimate marriage differed wildly from my own. I could have been a character in one of Woolf's novels. To distract my students from my frequent tears and shaking hands, I sent them outside with their notebooks to observe people walking by Lincoln Center, randomly intersecting for a moment, then going about their separate, unknowable lives. I had them report back in class. I was reeling from my own sense of loss and disconnection and found great comfort in absorbing myself in the ways strangers connected—including these relative strangers, my students, with whom I connected through teaching *Mrs. Dalloway*.

Concerned friends convinced me that writing an online personal ad no longer held the stigma it had a decade ago, the last time I played the dating game. The screen name I chose for my

Internet dating profile was VWCD1925, which stood for Virginia Woolf, Clarissa Dalloway, and the year the book was published. It was my bid for connection with other random souls. I wrote my profile in ten minutes, talking mostly about my daughter, Tessa, and about my delight when three of my students tried to convince me that *X-Men* had a lot in common with *Mrs. Dalloway*. I never thought of my screen profile as anything but an opportunity to window-shop. I was alone in the suburbs with Tessa, I commuted to New York once a week to teach, and I wrote freelance magazine pieces. The computer was a revelation. I could spin imaginary relationships from the comfort of my own home while my daughter slept, and I didn't even have to put in my contact lenses.

Then Craig appeared, and my imagination seemed paltry by comparison. Everything about his work and hobbies was new and exciting to me. He built cabinets for a living. He surfed—waves, not cyberspace. He bought a ramshackle 1979 sailboat with sleeping room for five without ever having sailed a day in his life, and taught himself to sail at the same time he figured out how to fix the faulty inboard motor. Then he taught himself to sew in order to update the twenty-five-year-old moldy upholstery.

Later Craig told me that he knew we would be serious at the beginning of that phone call. "How did you know?" I asked. "You just sounded so right," he said. I understood, because he sounded right too. But all I knew at this point was that I liked him and that even if we turned out to lack any physical attraction, I still wanted to meet him with our daughters at the playground to commiserate about being single parents in the suburbs.

I had only one doubt: he told me that after he sold the house he and his ex-wife shared, he bought a BMW convertible. Red flag. Was he a player? A midlife-crisis fancy car driver? Was this

his idea about how to wow the babes? My fears were completely alleviated when he pulled into my driveway for our first date. The scary BMW convertible was a decade old and covered in deep-crusted dirt. I loved it on sight, because it confirmed my instinct that this wasn't a man who wasted his weekends cleaning and polishing his car. The tan leather seats were cracked and faded. And the best sign of all: in the backseat was strapped a neon blue child's car seat, complete with five-point restraint system and twisted nylon bands. He was my kind of guy, and the roof of his car was wide open to expose the truth of his life.

I started to fall in love when the car pulled into the driveway; I was head over heels by the time he opened the door and stepped out into the light spring drizzle. The grace with which he swung his legs around, his gait as he walked, his craggy face, his smile, complete with crooked bottom teeth, his bright hazel eyes, sent me into a flutter. By the end of the date we had already planned our next two.

When I told my closest friends and relatives about Craig, they were thrilled. I was no longer sobbing; I was beaming. But when I started telling people that Craig and I were serious, I began to hear a hundred versions of doubt. "Rebound" flashed in their eyes—and fear that I was setting myself up for another broken heart. In theory, they were right. In their shoes, I'd be thinking "She must be afraid to be alone," and "So fast—is she settling for Mr. Right Now?" After all, I couldn't believe it myself. After years of misplaced trust in my marriage, how could I so readily trust again? I was not supposed to be this happy. I was supposed to curl up in a corner, rend my garments, and ululate: my daughter was a child of divorce, I was a wronged wife. I lost the future I had planned for, my financial security, an extended family I had embraced and who had embraced me too. And yes, I still wept over the pain and disappointment—but Craig and I could talk about it, because he had suffered disappointment too. I was truly in love.

Finding each other was incredible—but we were sane enough, despite the speed and surprise, to grab each other and hold on tight. Craig became essential through the whirlwind of upheaval that followed: selling my house, moving to two different apartments in three months, going back to work full-time, quitting my job after only four months. I knew I wanted to date a man who was already a father. To fall in love with someone who also provided a built-in play date for my daughter was an unimaginable bonus. Tessa and Delayna, Craig and I bounced together on a giant trampoline; we sailed around New York Harbor in Craig's aptly named boat, *The Second Wind*. We were on the best extended double date in history.

IF I STOP the tally sheets, total the columns, close the books right here, the big bell in the winner's circle would ring. Here is our Happily Ever After, well earned. The numbers all add up to a better life. But I can't stop; nor can I keep going at this crazy speed. I have to slow things down now because Tessa is watching me do the math. She huddles in the pillow-and-blanket fortress she's built on the living-room floor of our unfamiliar new apartment, her big eyes peeking over the sign she had me write in red magic marker: WICKED WITCHES STAY OUT!

And at the marina, Delayna jumps up and down on the deck of *The Second Wind* while her father furls the jib and says, "Daddy, I'm your first mate, right? I'm still your first mate!"

I come from a long line of people who never divorced—neither my parents nor any of their parents split up, and I always assumed I'd follow suit. I used to speak confidently of how my marriage would never end and how I'd always put my daughter's needs above all else. Craig and I can rationalize—and believe, for we truly do—that our happiness is good for our daughters. Yet I must ask myself in the middle of my joy: Whose needs are we putting first now? What else are we bringing into their lives?

EIGHT P.M. on a Monday. I'm bathing Tessa after a typical long day of push and pull. She is screaming because a soap bubble touched her eye, and rather than let me rinse her face, she paddles her arms wildly in the water, soaking me, the towel, my clothes, and the bathroom floor. My patience is gone and I'm counting the minutes until she goes to sleep. Then I hear the doorbell; it's Craig, stopping by to pick up his wallet, which ended up in my handbag after the weekend.

"We're up here!" I call, suddenly lighthearted and calm. I'm thrilled to see him, even for ten minutes—after a year we still don't spend the night together if either of us is with our daughters. When I kiss and hug him, he doesn't mind the bathwater at all.

Then I hear a little quavering voice from the tub: "Mommy, do you love Craig more than you love me?"

I practically trip Craig in my haste to push him away and embrace Tessa's wet, nude, tiny body. "No, of course not, Sweetie," I say. Good Mommy Me wraps her in a warm fluffy towel, sets her on my lap, and explains about all the different kinds of love. Does she think that Craig loves Delayna any less because he loves Mommy? No, she admits. (Despite my soothing words, I think secretly and angrily about the recent night when Delayna asked me to read *Cinderella* to her and Tessa. After I said "And Cinderella lived happily ever after," Delayna announced, "With no sisters!")

Good Mommy tells Tessa about the special places we have in our hearts for so many people, and reminds her that just as

Big Nut Brown Hare loves Little Nut Brown Hare in her bedtime story, Mommy loves Tessa all the way up to the sky and back. Craig, a Good Daddy himself, nods and reassures. Tessa is appeased, at least for the time being, and falls asleep immediately.

Another Saturday I take Tessa to see a marionette show of *Hansel and Gretel*. We sit on the floor of the darkened theater with other parents and children; she crawls into my lap and hides her eyes with nervous anticipation. I lean forward to brush a strand of light brown hair off her face.

"There's a witch in *Hansel and Gretel*," I whisper, to prepare her for the character that frightens her more than any other. Wicked witches loom in every unfamiliar corner of our new apartment: under the couch, behind the cabinet doors, inside the barrels of the stackable washer and dryer in the kitchen. Little ones in pointy hats scamper out of the oven when I open the door; huge ones with blue faces and long sinister fingernails wait in Tessa's bedroom closet for me to kiss her good night and leave the room so they can swirl around her bed in the dark.

Tessa, still burrowed in my lap, thinks for a while.

"Is the witch a stepmother?" she asks, her whisper tickling my ear. It's a logical question, given that in the fairy tale she loves and fears the most, *Snow White*, stepmother and witch are interchangeable.

"Not all stepmothers are evil," I offer. Even as I say the words, I remember that in the show we are about to see, a woodcutter's children are sent off into the forest alone by their evil stepmother, who hopes they'll be eaten by wild animals so she and their father don't have to share the meager supply of food with his children.

The curtain rises, and there is no stepmother puppet: just a regular mom and dad and their two adored, if malnourished, children.

"Ooooh," squeak the unseen grown-ups manipulating the Hansel and Gretel puppets. "Mommy and Daddy love us so much that they are going to sell our only cow at the market tomorrow so we can eat. But we love *them* so much that we are going to sneak out tonight and search for food in the forest."

I breathe a sigh of relief. This version is family sensitive; nothing to fear but a witch puppet who is most decidedly not a stepmother. If Delayna sees this show, she won't have to worry that the equivalent of me would banish her to the woods.

But the sanitized, politically correct version of the tale haunts me anyway. Is it impossible to imagine that the children could love their stepmother enough to go into the forest to bring *her* food? If the archetypes presented by fairy tales represent our deepest wishes and darkest fears, maybe the fairy tale opposite of Good Mommy isn't Bad Mommy: maybe it's Evil Stepmother. I recall with shame my anger at Delayna's "no sisters!" declaration: does my reaction mean that I will be an Evil Stepmother too? I've grown to love Delayna, and I know she loves me now too. However, she also knows that I'm Tessa's mother, not hers, and Craig is her father, not Tessa's. Tessa leaves *Hansel and Gretel* calm and happy; I leave it scared to death.

MY CHILD COMES from my body; more than that, she *is* my body. She smells good and feels good and folds into me like skin. When she feels my breath against her neck, she is calm, comforted—all's right with the world. This I can do: I can breathe, I can hold. I truly have the power to make wicked witches go away. But what about another mother's child? I can reassure Delayna when she's upset, but I can't make her world right by breathing.

The task of becoming someone Delayna can trust seems Herculean; when she is afraid of evil stepmothers and stepsisters, she knows—and I know—that I am powerless to keep them at bay. And this is how I finally realize, on the brink of becoming a stepmother myself, that the myth of the blended family is a lie.

Parenting any child is a terrifying prospect; there are days when the only way I can get through is because of my physical connection to Tessa. She belongs to me, so even when she acts horrendously, my basic need to care for her overrides my impulse to walk away and never come back. I belong to her, so even when I discipline her, her basic need to hold on to me overrides her fear that I might harm her. When Tessa is afraid, I'm overwhelmed by a primal desire to protect her from everything frightening, even her own imagination. My heart screams at me to make it all better. I want to protect Delayna too, but without that primal connection, can my hugs and kisses possibly make her whole world safe again? Will Craig's hugs and kisses save Tessa? We can mix our family, but we can never blend. This is the situation that Craig and I are walking into, and there is no way it can be otherwise.

OUR APARTMENT IS growing more crowded than ever: sharing space with the Wicked Witch of Tessa's imagination now is the Evil Stepmother of my own. No matter how rational and careful I am in the daytime, the E.S. comes roaring out of my closet at night with a vengeance. She has an arsenal of weapons on her side: Snow White, Cinderella, angry children, bitter ex-wives and ex-husbands. She could turn me—or just as easily anyone in the new family Craig and I are cautiously assembling—to the dark side. A sign written in red magic marker might work as a talisman for Tessa, but I'm terrified that all the love and good intentions in the world can't keep my nemesis away.

Who will look at me and see the Evil Stepmother first—
Delayna? Craig? Tessa? Or will I look in the mirror one day and
see her myself?

Craig's and my Happily Ever After is Delayna and Tessa's
Once Upon a Time. Once upon a time, two little girls realized
they were about to become stepsisters. Once upon a time,
Delayna's father met a new love to compete with her for his
attention. Once upon a time, Tessa's mother found someone who
made her happier than Tessa could by herself. Both girls have
been banished to the metaphorical dark woods; their stories will
have to be about finding their way out despite the wicked
witches and evil stepmothers who lurk behind each tree.

In my own story, the Internet is both a wicked witch casting
an evil spell on my marriage and a fairy godmother waving her
wand and transforming my life. Computers have brought me the
beautiful opportunities I felt were inherent in *Mrs. Dalloway*;
people who once were strangers now affect each other's lives in
powerful ways. It's what I cried for and craved when I was teaching the book, and what I was subconsciously hoping I'd find
when I signed up as VWCD1925 on the Internet.

Well, I found it and I want it. But for each new happiness is a
new complication. Tessa, Delayna, Craig, and I: each of us has
squared the number of intimate relationships we must navigate.
This was not a choice for Tessa and Delayna, nor was it for our
ex-spouses. But strangers do meet: that's what can happen when
you release yourself into the ether, or take a walk down Colum-
bus Avenue with a notebook.

I'm on the precipice right now, staring at all the myths, good
and bad. This is the moment before I take one more giant leap,
bringing not only Tessa, but Craig, Delayna, our exes, their
future partners, our friends and our acquaintances, with me. In

this moment before I must settle in, close down, make things work despite my fears, I need to look the Evil Stepmother right in the eye.

IT WAS WITH Tessa and Delayna's yet-to-unfold stories in mind that I began my research for *My Father Married Your Mother*. We hovered at the precipice of this new, mysterious set of relationships. My perennial instinct when approaching any unknown is to seek out the stories of others who have been there and who have the sensibility and skill to share the true meanings of their experiences through honest and original writing. According to the United States Census Bureau, one out of two marriages ends in divorce, yet seventy-five percent of divorced people remarry. When stepchildren enter the picture, the marriage failure rate jumps: two-thirds of all remarried or cohabitating couples with children break up.* In the groundbreaking book *The Unexpected Legacy of Divorce*, published in 2000, Judith Wallerstein and her coauthors found that the adult children of divorce who had the hardest times were those from blended families. With such dramatic evidence, I decided that I couldn't possibly be alone in my quest for the truth about stepfamilies, so I headed for the bookstores.

Everything I found was wrong.

Shelves of self-help books proclaimed that by following ten cardinal rules, filling out twenty forms in a workbook, or reciting reassuring mantras about putting the children first, I could avoid the pitfalls and create the perfect blended family. Even with my limited experience, I already knew that the conflicts inherent in

* U.S. Census, 1990 and 2000. From the Stepfamily Foundation (www .stepfamily.org).

the very concept of the stepfamily were bigger and more complex than this. Even respected psychology books about divorce and children avoided the point I found so powerful: pretending that children can simply live happily ever after in a blended family will cause more permanent harm than divorce itself. Children have one mother and one father, and no amount of storytelling can make it otherwise.

I finally found a glimmer of truth when I looked to the word "stepmother" itself. According to the *Oxford English Dictionary*, the origin of the prefix "step" comes from the Anglo-Saxon "steop." It means "bereaved." Of course, I thought: I wasn't about to become a stepmother because I would "step" in to parent Delayna, nor would I be a "step" removed from her. The archival meaning of the word "stepmother" addressed the grief inherent in our situation: why, then, didn't any of the books? I had found the Evil Stepmother at last, only to discover that she had been buried under mountains of sunny advice on the blended family and finger-pointing at the nature of divorce.

When Tessa was born, I read every memoir on the complicated emotions of motherhood that I could find. The writers became like trusted friends, confessing in print the anger and fear I was afraid to confess to myself. Now I wanted the same brutal honesty about stepfamilies. What I found instead were impossible promises to children made by parents about what their "blended" family was supposed to be. Since I couldn't find the kind of truth-telling, soul-baring community in print that had sustained me in those early, confused days and nights of new motherhood, I decided that I wanted to build it myself.

Literary writers have the ability to render the truth about psychological issues in a way that stays deeply with readers; it made perfect sense to me that *My Father Married Your Mother* should be in the form of essays by writers with no agenda other than telling the truth. I began to contact writers I knew, who told me that they had always wanted to write about their step relationships but had never had the opportunity. As word about my project got out, writers I didn't know began to contact me, bursting with stories to tell.

The collection began to take shape. Each essayist in *My Father Married Your Mother* examines step relationships directly and honestly. Lisa Shea muses about the impact of bringing a stepfather into her teenaged son's life when she still grapples with the impact her own two stepfathers had on hers. Roxana Robinson wonders about lost opportunities for a better relationship with her adult stepdaughter. Jacquelyn Mitchard mourns the choice that her adult stepdaughter made to cut off contact all together. Andrew Solomon explores the impact of a new stepmother even though he and his brother are grown when she arrives. David Goodwillie examines the myriad complexities of a mother who left his father for another woman instead of another man. *My Father Married Your Mother* also includes essays from writers in the same family, each with a different take on his or her postnuclear situation. Phyllis Rose discusses her second husband's qualities as a stepfather while her son, Ted Rose, writes about his tumultuous relationship with his stepbrother from his father's remarriage. Sheila Kohler and Sasha Troyan, mother and daughter, write about Sheila's remarriage and second family. And married couple Mike Dolan and S. Kirk Walsh write of the effect that rotating stepparents and constant instability had on their own, distinctly different, childhoods.

Rather than separate the writers into two corners of the boxing ring—stepparents on one side, stepchildren on the other—I chose to organize *My Father Married Your Mother* as a series of conversations I wished that I could sit in on, conversations I imagine having someday with Delayna, Tessa, and our friends. *My Father Married Your Mother* is the book I was looking for but couldn't find when Craig and I fell in love: each of the writers in this collection seeks nothing less than to transform the way we talk about stepfamilies.

My Father's New Muse

I feared she'd rob me of my creative role, and of my
power in the family.

P emerges from my father's bedroom in our Santa Fe vacation house in a pink nylon negligee, its low V neck
trimmed with lace. At the bottom of her bare legs, her toe-
nails are painted fuchsia.

"Put some clothes on," I hiss. She looks startled. At the table,
I stick my face inside the *New York Times*. Moments later, she
reemerges from my dad's bedroom in a pair of running shorts, a
white T-shirt, and sneakers. Although in her mid-forties, she's got
the body of a twenty-five-year-old, looks foxy in sweats. With her
upturned nose and alert, clear blue eyes, P. could be my mother
twenty years earlier, except she has short, dark brown hair. My
mother is blond, and was never allowed to cut her hair, not while
she was living with my father, a portrait artist, who requires a
clean forehead for the three-quarter presentation from his
women. One of the things my mother did right after she left my
father was to lop off her gold tresses into a vicious bob.

I've complained for twelve years about the added responsibilities of being my dad's stand-in wife, but I'm not prepared for my
replacement: a stepmother in the making, albeit one who still
wears short skirts, runs two miles every day, and owns a small
publishing company. This is day three of our vacation in New

Mexico. September in Santa Fe is almost nirvana. P. runs every day, under skies clear and blue as her eyes, the pioneer woman exemplified. I follow suit, only never, despite her invitation, running with her. I take my own path since I never want to talk while I run, especially not to her.

P. and my dad share a bedroom, while I sleep solo in another. At night, my father takes her to cocktail parties, which I decline, finding myself suddenly busy on dates with a local photographer, after months of being single. When I do join them for dinner, she's at his right at the dinner table, an art student to his left. She and I order the same meal almost every time, as if sharing an astrology sign and an alma mater means we're driven by the same desire. Oh, and we are: the race to love my father more. My dad rarely asks about my meal, unlike the nights at home in New York when he takes me out for intimate dinners. And my sense that our life is not going back to how it was deepens with every bite of grilled salmon in roasted piñón-ancho chile beurre blanc.

My dad is a guest teacher with the Santa Fe College of Art, and as usual, a dozen vibrant, adoring students flank him all day long; they leave early in the morning to catch the clean light and paint out-of-doors. Primarily a portrait artist, my dad prefers, deep down, to paint landscapes in warm climates. He's also frequently asked to judge shows, which is how he met his girlfriend. P. runs a small art magazine which she started with her husband. While reporting from Denver, she met my dad, who was guest judge for the show. Their long-distance relationship, which started when I was thirty, has lasted two years; once a month, my dad flies from New York to Casper, where P. lives with the youngest of her three children. Then she comes east to visit my father and her two eldest children, who attend East Coast colleges. She is waiting for her youngest son to finish high school before she settles down.

When my mother left, I was a first-semester sophomore in college. Back in our apartment during a break from school, I pulled open my mother's dresser to borrow a scarf and discovered she'd packed all of her belongings. Closets were empty. My father's sorrow was so compelling that I temporarily left college and moved back home to stand in as *hausfraulein*. He said I had a good eye; I offered feedback on his paintings in progress. I was surrogate model for his portraits, the ones that line every wall of his Manhattan apartment. I was his date to bars, restaurants, and weekend homes outside Manhattan. We crossed Fifth Avenue arm in arm, going up the stairs of the Metropolitan Museum like a May–December couple. My dad murmured in my ear, "They'll think you're my date." Or he introduced me this way, waiting to see if anyone caught on. If I wore a form-fitting dress, my dad admired me, especially if I was in heels. He paid the coat check, holding my coat out. Wearing a fedora and a Burberry, very much the 1940s romantic, long-handled umbrella under his arm, he only dropped my hand to insert both index fingers into his mouth and whistle for a cab.

Immediately after graduating from college, I moved back in again, this time for two years. But as the years proceeded, I began to feel burdened. I found a studio apartment ten blocks south in the East Village. Still, he called too much. "He always wants me to go to openings," I moaned to my sister, who moved overseas when my parents split up. "Just don't go," she always stated from her faraway perch, exhaling Gitane smoke into the phone. But it always seemed utterly natural, for he needed a date, and for a while, so did I. Then I read Henry James's *Washington Square*, and started to worry. Could this relationship proceed indefinitely? Sometimes, I felt the urge to move back into his apartment and stay forever, especially with rents in New York skyrocketing as they did in the 1980s. For a while, I didn't have a boyfriend; then, when I was twenty-seven, I met T. and my dad found P. The first time we were all together was at a small night-club in Greenwich Village, where my dad knew the band and singer. It was loud. I watched my father gaze nonstop at P., stroking her hand, while they listened to the ballads of his era. Afterward, on the walk to T.'s loft, I stomped down Seventh Avenue South.

"Ooh, I *know* why you're so mad!" T. laughed, jumped his legs apart like James Brown, and started howling near Canal Street, "Papa's Got a Brand New Bag!"

How I denied it. But on vacation in New Mexico, I began to recall his words, and wondered how I'd be able to free my dad from her hold.

BACK IN NEW YORK, pictures of P. start to appear: charcoal drawings, watercolors, photos, and oil sketches. My dad pins them everywhere. When my dad loves something or someone, it becomes apparent in exactly this way: paintings cover the walls in his bedroom, photos are taped above his desk, even tucked into the mirror where he shaves. This is how he begins to show his devotion.

When I was a child, he'd draw compulsively on surfaces, at restaurants, sometimes on the back of a menu. He'd usurp it, winking at the waitress, or if necessary, drawing right onto a cloth napkin with an ink pen he'd extract from his inside jacket lining. Once he drew me as our dog, which I adored, my long ponytails transformed into wavy, silky ears. But P. seems to have skipped the napkin phase and been bumped right up to watercolor: vibrant hues of brown for her hair, cerulean for her eyes, the Maine shore behind her, her pursed lips ready for a smile. My father and P. begin to take trips, and with each one he returns with rolls of film, new sketches, watercolors, and then, the first oil portrait.

This is when I know they are in it for the long haul.

He never paints her in a widow's black veil. She doesn't want to be seen that way. But I remember the story, and it haunts: how her husband slumped over the wheel next to her, leaving her to raise their three children on her own. And I understand how my father fits in. With a nurturing soul and fingers twisted from years of gripping a paintbrush, he was rendering her as he knew how: swaddled in light, his love object supreme, a creature to admire and adore.

WHEN I WAS three, my father painted me in watercolor; this portrait has shown a dozen times, won awards, been cataloged in books. The painting reveals a dimple in my chin, hazel eyes, and fine, light-brown baby hair. More recently, he painted me in oil, while I was asleep. In it, I appear awake, although I could never get up early enough to sit for him in person. He painted it from a photo. It had been twenty years since he painted me, and now I resemble a cameo ring, head in oval presentation. In the painting, I look just like my mom.

There's a portrait of my mom that my father painted in the 1950s, when they first lived together in the studio which is still his home. "B.C." my mother called this era, with a secret curl to her lips. Before Children: before darkness and culpability and burden and consciousness. Before responsibility. My father painted her in a tight, paisley, scooped-neck cotton dress. Pouty lips, soft hair, blue eyes full of desire, still wild from wandering through forests with him. There's another, later profile of my mom, with her hair piled up high; both these portraits are hidden in his guarded studio closet.

If you put the oil portraits side by side, my mom's and mine, you'd see a triptych of one woman from different phases of life. That's how I experienced my role during the years when my dad was single, as if I were temporarily my own stepmother, all grown up and standing in my mother's black pumps. I resemble my mother so closely that I am never surprised when other family members call me by her name.

I believed I might not exist unless my father saw me and drew me in his style, his signature adorning the lower right-hand corner; then, I'd be mounted on a wall, facing out, caught in time, any time prior to the present. The portrait would steady him, hold his focus, so that he, my dad, chronicler, storyteller, magician, might keep me in his collection, keep me alive.

Portraits sit on easels in my dad's studio, lit by north light that falls through twenty-foot-high windows. He takes three rolls of film for each sitter, dozens of which he studies to discern the right expression. My sister and I always called this face "the moment of truth." My dad prefers smiles; he studies these to finish a portrait. When I lived with him, he'd call me over to the sitter's chair, his pointy eyebrows raised. "My next victim," he'd drawl in his Dracula voice. I'd unclasp my hands and sit completely still, while he finished the other sitter's portrait using my wrists and elbows, thumb joints, bent fingers, the light going through my cupped hands.

NOW P. ASSUMES my father's name, sorts his mail, bakes him bread, and organizes his documentary film screening. Is it a coincidence that I marry the same year they tie the knot? Or that I finally write again, preparing for graduate school after years of feeling blocked?

She appeared like a storybook animal whose bright eyes and cheerful demeanor mark the opportune, narrative shift: the bunny escorts Snow White into the dwarves' cottage, leading her to a new life. I feared she'd rob me of my creative role, and of my power in the family; but I was set free, to move over and focus on myself. I would finally shed my status as *Hausfräulein* and let her magic work.

So perhaps I might borrow her from my dad for a minute, let her be backdrop and north light, let her be my next portrait, as I write this down now.

When I get pregnant, she takes me shopping for baby clothes and a crib. When we finally buy a house, P. drives up to advise me on where to set up my office. She worked at home too, when her kids were small. She donates an old computer and printer when we're too broke to buy a new one. When I visit their house, she scoops up my daughters, takes them for a swim, entertains with a cookie-baking spree.

At family events, I bristle when asked to pose for a "family portrait." Seated together, we are clearly two clans, not one. Her children and I nervously sniff around each other, seeking the corresponding empathy to that between P. and my dad. A half-generation younger, they appear with new tattoos, belly piercings, and just-out-of-college stories. They're the age I was when I slept through the sittings for my dad's portrait. And so I understand their fascinated nonchalance toward my dad's art.

SOMETIMES I STOP to study P.'s portrait, try to comprehend her as my father does. Her lips are soft, ready to speak or kiss; he paints her sharp, blue eyes gazing out to a place I'll never see; it's him she's seeking, of course, her portraitist. It's their intimate connection he captures. I sense I can never really know her; I can't really see her separate from my dad or myself. Sometimes, I think I've gladly handed him over, but I regress. She is the love object, she'll never stop reminding me, just as I'll never stop wanting to be painted by my father again.

Le Beau-Père

PHYLLIS ROSE

*Stepfamilies may be beautiful families, offering second
chances, the possibility of improving on the originals.*

When my son was thirteen and I had been divorced
from his father for eleven years, I installed another
man in our house. Laurent did not become Ted's
official stepfather for another five years; he had to get divorced
before we could marry. But for all practical purposes, he was the
stepfather. He was always in the house with us. The three of us
ate dinner together every night. We used the same bathroom, the
only one in the house. Ted and Laurent shared a phone line and
took messages for one another. Laurent and I cheered from the
bleachers at all of Ted's high-school swim meets. We traveled to
family weddings together, usually had Thanksgiving together,
and took vacations together. We were—and have been since
then—a family.

Laurent arrived at a good moment, just as Ted was about to
enter adolescence. Ted had been a gallant little boy, with a strong
sense of responsibility for my welfare. This was no doubt another
burden that the breakup of our original family had imposed on
him: he was the man in charge of Mom's well-being. Laurent's
arrival let him off the hook. Someone else was there to take care
of me. Not that I needed much taking care of. I wasn't an invalid
or an alcoholic. I had a full-time job as a professor at a university,

and we lived on the college campus, where things were pretty easy to manage. But I've always felt—and Ted confirms—that it was a relief to him to have me hook up with someone just then, so he could devote himself full-time to his teenage years. In the deep dark reaches of the psyche, he could stamp an upper case "Not My Problem" on Mom, which is as it should be.

Physical spaces within the house had to be redistributed when Laurent came to live with us. He is an artist, works at home, and needs a studio. Ted's bedroom and mine had been across the hall from each other, with my study and the bathroom on the same floor, the second floor of the house. Upstairs in the attic was another finished room, a guest room, largely unoccupied. This might have become Laurent's studio, but instead, Laurent moved into Ted's bedroom and Ted moved up to the attic. By leaving his childhood room behind, he gained privacy as well as the chance to play music as loud as he wanted. We both recall his move to the attic as a happy thing. Laurent made a sign to hang over the knob of the door to the attic stairs, saying TEDDY IS IN or TEDDY IS OUT, so when his friends called we would know his where-abouts without shouting up to the attic. This somehow made it seem all the more that Ted had a kingdom of his own up there under the eaves.

By the time I found Laurent, Ted and I knew pretty well what a bad stepfather was like. A bad stepfather would come into our household and want to change things. He would have strong feelings about everything and want to be obeyed. He would espe-cially want Ted to conform to some image he had of what a child should be and do. He would weigh heavily. A bad stepfather would have some image of fatherhood in his mind that he was trying to fulfill, and to do so he would need Ted's cooperation. At his parodic worst, he would call Ted "young man" and slap him awkwardly on the back. He would try too hard to have a relationship with Ted, although Ted knew very well that the guy was not there for *his* sake, however much he might pretend to be. We both remember "the man with the chemistry set" as the epitome of the bad stepfather, the man bearing gifts that were really directives: "this is how you should be spending your time."

Tobias Wolff created a great portrait of the bad stepfather in Dwight of *This Boy's Life*, a memoir of Wolff's years with his mother after she and his father split up. Dwight is always trying to shape Toby up. "Dwight made a study of me," Wolff wrote. "He shared his findings as they came to him." The list of Toby's deficiencies went on so unendingly that it lost its power to hurt and merely seemed like "bad weather" to get through. Dwight set Toby tasks, ostensibly because he needed discipline, really because Dwight himself was such a loser that bullying a kid was his only way to experience power. He made Toby take on a paper route, a low-paying, endlessly penitential paper route, whose proceeds he claimed to be saving for Toby but which he ended by confiscating. He made Toby—bizarre detail—shuck horse chestnuts every night after dinner and then let them rot in the attic.

Ted suffered nothing like that in the years before Laurent. The worst improvement he had to endure was the chemistry set, and what scorn the giver has since received for the gift. Pity the poor man who tries to insinuate himself between a woman and her son who understand each other and know which side their bread is buttered on—the side of their continued partnership. Pity the poor son who never knows what schlemiel his mother is going to fall for and bring into his life, adding to the wound of losing his father the wound of an impossible new person to deal with. Pity the woman trying to find a guy who suits both herself and her child.

Laurent proved to be an excellent stepfather, the very opposite of the man with the chemistry set or Tobias Wolff's Dwight. I don't believe in twenty years he's ever once told Ted what to do. He's never rebuked him in the slightest way. He's never suggested paths, implied direction, exerted pressure. He never imitates someone he thinks he should be, which makes him very cool. Children pick up on pretense and insincerity. In Laurent, there is none. He does exactly as he pleases and allows everyone around him to do the same. Perhaps because he is an artist, he is wholly self-contained. He doesn't need validation from anyone else. He has an inner life. He *is* someone. He never looked to Ted to complete him. This quality of his Ted calls "spaciousness."

If he is spacious, it must also be said he's a little spacey. He is a children's book illustrator, the world's leading expert on drawing elephants who stand up on their hind legs, wear clothes, and act French. He lives in never-never land. He's about as effective a manager as Snoopy. A moral dilemma for him is whether humanoid elephants can be depicted with animal pets on a leash or eating a hamburger. (The answer is no, after much inner debate.) Because he is French, many aspects of American life bewilder him. I once saw him hold a fast-food hotdog on a tray and try to figure out how to make the mustard in the plastic pump descend to it. What kind of authority figure could he be to an American lad who had worked with the mobile hotdog vendor across the street on football weekends and who had been taught the proper sequence of condiments in the most complicated order? The answer is, none. As an authority figure, Laurent was nonexistent. He was Consort. He was Ornament. He was not a substitute father. And none of his Magoo-ishness made him any less splendid a member of our new family. In fact, it was largely responsible for making him the perfect stepfather. His haplessness—his instinctive belief that the world will take care of him—is part of his immense appeal. People flock to take care of him. People tend to see him as something rare and precious, which he is. His reluctance to impose himself on anyone else comes across as delicacy and grace, an ultimate tact. But I wonder if precisely the qualities that make him so appealing a human being and such a splendid stepfather aren't those that would have made him a frustrating and difficult father.

Laurent's children are grown and I didn't watch him fathering them, so my observations are based on his treatment of our dog. This is admittedly an undignified and perhaps meaningless sample population. Still. The aloof self-containment and reluctance to direct that were so wonderful in him as a stepfather were less useful as we tried to turn a puppy into a responsible, self-confident, and independent dog. Laurent's deeply egalitarian nature refused to accept that Vinny, our Yorkie, was really the ignorant and untrained animal I knew him to be. In Laurent's view, when Vinny misbehaved it was because he was justly angry at us and needed to punish us. Therefore, it was up to us to treat him better, for example, by giving him scraps from the table so he would be "happy" and stop whining for scraps as we ate. When Vinny interrupted our conversations with friends, demanding attention by placing a tennis ball in our laps, Laurent would offhandedly throw it to him, hoping to keep him amused for a while and then being surprised when Vinny himself didn't know it was "time to stop." When he takes Vinny for walks in the city, he returns home exhausted because the dog stops so often to sniff that the shortest walk seems to last forever. "Pull his leash," I say. "Say, 'heel.' Don't let him get away with it. You are supposed to take the lead, not the dog. Who's walking who?" What is a father if not an alpha male, whose strength and competence let children feel secure, whose directions provide children with structure and something to rebel against? But Laurent as father offers no directions, sets no standards, and demands nothing. Vinny loves him, of course. How could he not? But I can't help thinking Vinny would be a better Yorkie if Laurent had exerted more authority, in a way that would have been disastrous if he had tried it with his stepson.

The French word for "stepfather" is *beau-père*—literally, "beautiful father"—so much more appropriate for Laurent's relationship to Ted than the harsh-sounding English word, which emphasizes the marginality and sideway-ness of the relationship. In French there is no distinction between new family members acquired by one's own marriage, which we would call father-in-law and mother-in-law, for example, and those acquired by the remarriage of a parent, which we call stepfather or stepmother. In French, all these variations on the original nuclear family have the same name; *beau-père* means father-in-law as well as stepfather. Perhaps the language is onto something. Stepfamilies may be beautiful families, offering second chances, the possibility of improving on the originals. Those of us who were not so good the first time round have a chance to be successful the second time, in the beautiful version of our role, because of the very features, in some cases, that made us not so good the first time. Weak fathers can be effective stepfathers. The negligent can be enabling. The remote can weigh lightly. The cold can be cool. The other side of that coin, of course, is that we may be worse. The qualities that made us good parents, for example, firm control, loving supervision, may make us intrusive, unwelcome stepparents. To my mind that is a risk well taken in the interests of making the nuclear family a more flexible institution.

I'm with those who see the traditional western bourgeois family as potentially a breeding ground for neurosis (Freud went into this) and overwork for women (Margaret Mead and more recent feminists took this one on). Mead introduced twentieth-century Americans to the idea that "primitive" societies, with their extended families and cross-family living arrangements, had something to teach us. She pointed out the burden that the nuclear family and the traditional division of work placed on a mother, isolated from supportive women of another generation, with too intense a focus on her husband and children. The intensity, Mead felt, was not good for parents or for children. But the high-pressure, lifelong, isolated family she wrote about turns out to have occupied a rather fleeting moment in social history, created by the combination of improvements in health care and increased life expectancy with a lingering Victorian social rigidity. In the nineteenth century and before, death kept rearranging families. Even in the developed world, in the very seat of Empire, women died, especially in childbirth, much younger than now. Their husbands remarried, often widows with children of their own from a previous marriage. What mortality did then, divorce has been doing for decades. It works toward expanding the nuclear family and decreasing its inherent pressure. Families enlarge. Intensities dissipate. Responsibilities get spread. It's hard to tell a little boy who has lost his father in a divorce that his suffering is for the larger good of western civilization, but when he's grown, in retrospect, he may see the ways in which his life was enlarged and made beautiful by the precious possession of a *beau-père*.

Losing Janey

JACQUELYN MITCHARD

She had a mother in full. She didn't need another. And yet,
perhaps because she and I were both so young when we were
thrust together, I didn't know what else to be.

Janey was the first child I loved, though never really my own.
She was my little girl, and then she was my big girl, then my
lovely grown stepdaughter. And then, she was gone from my
life. As the old rhyme goes, one day she stepped on a crack and
broke her stepmother's heart. She didn't mean to hurt me with
her choice. It wasn't because her father and I divorced. It wasn't
because she and I had a gigantic fight. It was as if, for many reasons, our time together was held in an hourglass, with only so
much golden sand.

Janey is not her real name. Hers is a fairy-princess name,
the name of a beautiful village in Europe. And beautiful is how
she always looked; sun-streaked hair tumbled over her face as
she ambled downstairs to watch cartoons every Saturday morning, for twelve years, when she woke up in our house. We wore
out eight one-thousand-dollar cars, heaps we used for nothing
else but to pick Janey up on Friday nights from her mother's
house, several hours away, and bring her back again on Sunday.

My husband—and I, certainly I, too—wanted Janey to be
more than a tiny part of our lives. But her parents' parting had
been bitter, and the sharing was not much easier. Each time she
left, her mother wept until she and Janey were weak with grief.

Each Sunday night, her father stormed and I cowered. There were battles over precise hours at which the precious cargo must be delivered, over the exact moment when summer began and ended. There was even an objection that nearly went legal over my taking a shower with a sand-encrusted five-year-old.

I was no help.

I didn't see it this way back then. I saw only my own need to feel wonderful, kindly, useful, and treasured.

Knowing (or believing) that this would be the only child with whom I'd ever share a parentlike relationship, I wanted it all, to the fullest. Younger perhaps in experience than I was in years, and having no mother of my own to teach me, I tried too hard to dazzle Janey with stories and adventures. I tried to nurture her, forcing her to finish the healthy messes I concocted, even when they made the poor kid gag. And instead of wisely and gently turning away from her mom's obvious resentment, I tried to combat it. When Janey had tantrums, I tried to discipline her, while her poor pop rushed to the rescue. And then we tussled over Janey, too much.

My hormone faucet seemed to have no "off" switch. It made me a fool.

SHE WAS A folded bud, six weeks old, when we met. Her father and I were then just coworkers, but he trusted me to take care of his firstborn while he and his wife went out for a night on the town. I remember the exaltation and fear I felt, being alone with this morsel, rocking and changing her, feeling, for the first time in my lonely young womanhood—for my mother had died several years earlier—the possibility of real connection with another needy being.

Not until a year later, when her parents were talking separation, did my relationship with her father deepen. Green in that department as well, I listened only to my own hunger, not the mayhem that satisfying it would cause. The marriage would have ended anyway; it had shallow roots. But I was the proximate cause. When Dan and I married, Janey held a bouquet of wild-flowers in her small fist. We called her that, *chicoria*, the Italian word for wildflower.

As the years progressed, we found ourselves at the perhaps inevitable crossroads: I wanted a child of my own.

I could no longer bear the nights when Dan held Janey and told her that she made his life worthwhile. What about me? Did I want all that made life worthwhile denied me?

We had furious confrontations over this, and they spilled all over the map of our lives. And Janey witnessed them. Finally, my need won out, only to begin a long struggle with infertility culmi-nating in a terrifying ectopic pregnancy. Janey was scared to pieces. Just months later, we adopted, at his birth, a baby son. Her brother became the star of Janey's life.

For Janey's mom, our little boy, like our big dog, was another enticement, another sweet to lure her sweet away. Yet, dearly as I loved my son, there was still plenty of room for my Janey. We had our own secrets and covenants she shared with no one else on earth. But we also had conflicts. Her mom's style and ours dif-fered. We limited TV at our house, but Janey had access to her own set at home. I foolishly believed I could bend her to schol-arly pursuits by force of will; Mom wanted her little beauty to watch her weight.

"I am not *you!*" Janey would shout at me, with all the ferocity she could summon. And it was prodigious.

Kid stuff, I thought. She'll get over it.

Instead, she got over me.

———

THE CASTLE, PERHAPS always mostly pretend, began to crumble when my husband died from cancer, just four months after his diagnosis. Janey was barely seventeen, and Dan in his early forties. By then, Dan and I had given birth to or adopted three little boys. In his heartbreak at leaving all of them, but especially his Janey, Dan asked that most of the relatively small sum he left behind be set aside for his daughter. His first wife, he told me, was more fragile. I would be able to take care of "my" children. Another wrangle. Misplaced, ill-timed, and one too many. None of it mattered. But I didn't know that then. I was wild with grief and fear. I was angry that Janey could flutter with excitement over her senior prom while her dad lay dying. She couldn't understand why I didn't get the reason that *any* girl would climb through *any* window to flee the silent dirge that played throughout our home.

At Dan's funeral, she sat with her brothers and me, her mother and stepfather a few yards away—all of us, for one moment, united in grief.

THEN, TWO YEARS later, flushed with what seemed a fortune after a delightful reception of my first novel, I took all the children to Europe—in part to see the village for which Janey was named. But instead of being thrilled, Janey was morose: she and her best friend, whom I'd invited too, spent most of their time trying to find telephones to call home, Janey trying to reach the sweet boy she would later marry. One raw morning, when the girls were locked in their room in our villa scribbling letters home and I needed help with the children, I erupted.

"If you don't want to be here, you should go home," I told both of them in a too-cold voice. Janey was twenty. She asked for her plane tickets. I handed them over.

And I didn't see her again for six months, not until we met at a Chinese restaurant where I begged her, after an exchange of letters both pitiful and acrimonious, to come back into our lives. The children missed her. I missed her. I tried to explain that she was not an artifact of my past, but someone I would always love, personally.

"I don't know what you mean," she said prophetically, "by love."

She did agree to give "us" another chance.

But she had given me something to ponder. What *did* I mean by my love for her? Was it simply sentimentality? Did I love her as I loved my own, my full-time brood?

Yes. And no.

Was what I felt need? Or pride? A sense of something broken, a set of china missing the tureen?

I don't think I was then, or that I am now, so shallow as that. But I had begun to see how my immaturity, during Janey's child-hood, made her feel like a bone over which three selfish adults fought like junkyard dogs. I had begun to see that, for most of my adult life, I had worried about how she fit into *my* portrait, not how I could help her paint her own. I wanted to buy her a mock-ingbird; but I never considered that it might be the last thing she wanted—from me. She had a mother in full. She didn't need another. And yet, perhaps because she and I were both so young when we were thrust together, I didn't know what else to be.

Even then, there were moments of pure joy.

We all cheered at her graduation too. She graduated with hon-ors: she had become a scholar after all, but in her own way.

There was her wedding day. I watched her brother, only four-teen, walk her down the aisle in the place of her father, while she wept glorious tears, the most beautiful bride I've ever seen. And I wept, as the two of them danced to "In My Life," the song played at her dad's memorial. I'd married again, and my little daughter, just two, was Janey's flower girl—just as Janey, so many years ago, had been my flower girl. The picture of the two girls together, my little one's beatific face upturned at the sight of her sister, "a real princess," all in lace, is still the most important object on my daughter Francie's bookshelf.

Two years later, Janey's mom opened her heart and let me join her and the in-laws at the window of the nursery to see my not-quite grandchild. I was swept away by pride and tenderness.

We seemed, then, to enter a period I found particularly satisfying, a communion between a younger and an older woman. She came to my side in a tender vigil when her youngest brother lay near death from a ruptured appendix. I never loved her, or anyone, more.

· But Janey was slipping away.

When I hugged her, she seemed to stiffen. When I told her that I loved her, she said "Thanks." She had grown to a place in life in which she wanted to acknowledge her own very missed feelings, instead of caretaking the feelings of parents. Seeing in her own marriage what a family and home should be, Janey could analyze in retrospect what her childhood had lacked—not love, but sense and consistency. She could see how her father's and my battles, mostly over Janey's mother and Janey, had scratched us, but torn at the vulnerable little girl she'd been.

Her visits to my home became fewer, and dutiful. Cards replaced telephone calls. The cards that came were signed "From," not "Love."

When we came to admire Janey's new home, I felt as though an invisible fence had been drawn around us. While I was often on the road for work, and busy with the younger children, Janey's mother, now a young widow, and Janey's in-laws had developed a culture of their own, with jokes and rules and memories. When I complained to Janey that I had no part, she told me sadly, "You never tried. Not really. You always left as soon as you could."

She was right.

I left because it seemed that only when we were gone could the gathering really begin, that everyone could relax. I felt that I was the spider in the punch bowl. But I'd also tried, while Janey's friends gave me puzzled looks and her mother sat in silence. I thought Janey's assessment wasn't entirely fair. Hadn't I hung in there, trying to keep the daughter Dan loved so extravagantly together with the siblings she, in turn, adored?

I had tried. But also, I had been missing in action, drawn away by my own new love, my accelerating career. It all seems so unnecessary now. For irrefutably, whatever I meant by love, I always cared. I should have shown how much, more.

But Janey was no longer a little girl or sulky teen I could send to her room to cool off. I protested, but she lashed back, bringing up all the tears and fears of all the years I'd been indifferent to her mother's emotional suffering and to Janey's confusion and mangled loyalties.

"You could be one of the kindest and most inspiring people and one of the cruelest," she said. Cruel? I was aghast. But I realized that she was still seeing my pettiness, my sharp words of wounded pride, as a mouse sees a giant, through the eyes of the child she'd been. How could she see them otherwise? As study after study has shown, in divorce it's not really fair to try to "share" a child. The parents may each get half, but the child never gets a whole. She was fed up, Janey told me, with pretending things she was supposed to feel but didn't, with hiding the old, cold anger to which she had a right.

Don't, I begged, in phone calls and letters, don't let this be a breach that ends one day in a hospital room. Think of the kids, I pleaded.

"I'll always want to see them," she said, and added that they would understand more when they were older. She told me not

to bother with a guilt trip. She'd been subjected to enough serv-
ings of guilt for several lifetimes.

She was right, again.

THERE FINALLY CAME a day, just before last Christmas,
when I phoned Janey's husband to ask if I might send Christmas
presents, even though Janey had said she would no longer come
to our Christmas Eve dinner. In a voice tinctured with pity, anger,
and confusion, he said, not unkindly, "Don't make me decide that
for Janey. Don't make me a part of this."

And so, I wrote a final e-mail. And opening my hand, I let her go.

I told her that I would never fully understand her grief and
anger, but that I believed it was real. Withdrawing from her life
was the least I could do for that once so-conflicted child.

Her gratitude was heartbreaking. No longer would she have to
battle her mother to give me my slice of "family" time. She could
see her siblings, and she was still child enough to believe that
twice-yearly visits would bear blossoms of a bond with them.
Finally, I was the adult I should have been, but couldn't be,
twenty-five years before, when she toddled ambivalently into my
life. I wept the rest of that day, and on and off for the next several. There are very few times I can think of her without crying.

But I no longer intrude.

A FEW WEEKS ago, sorting pictures before a move, I accidentally let slip the antique frame that holds Janey's wedding picture. Behind it was her high-school graduation photo. Behind
that was a photo of her, still with a smile full of metal, her
chubby little brother at her side. And still behind that, a picture
of her as a wispy-haired little girl, wide-eyed with joy, holding
that brother in his swaddling blanket. Briefly, I thought I should

send all but the wedding photo to Janey. These were memories she ought to be allowed to keep.

But I found myself replacing those layers of life back in order, into their rightful casing. Those memories may not ever have been what I believed them to be.

Still, they are mine.

Leave her alone, and she will come home, my friends tell me. When will we see Sissy, asks my littler daughter, now eight, as her memories dim. I try to be reassuring. But I know my Janey. She came to this decision hard. It cost her. She may never forget me, but neither may she ever forgive me. It is to her mother that she owes her best and first allegiance. She cannot be angry with her dad, ripped untimely from her life. That leaves me, a lightning rod like every other stepmother, one who thought that by some luck or wisdom, I could escape the storm.

One of the last things I told Janey was that I would always be there. More misty meaningless words, I'm sure she thought, that would vanish like steam once I'd written them. But there may come a time when Janey needs to reach for me in the room where I've left a light on for her. I wish, sometimes, I could erase her smile from my mind. But that time passed long ago, when my heart fell open as I wriggled free the first loose tooth, as I wrested a cigarette from her clenched teenage hand.

Our future may travel on parallel roads; but our past cannot be unbraided.

And so, I have no choice. I will be there, as long as I *am* here, waiting for the chance to try again, waiting—whatever it means—to offer my love.

On Having a Stepmother Who Loves Opera

ANDREW SOLOMON

Family is not a zero-sum game. Having more of it
does not reduce the key connections.

When my mother was dying, she said that it would be terrible to grow old alone. "Don't think you're paying me some kind of tribute if you fail to remarry," she said to my father. "The thing I hope for most is that you will build a new life for yourself." She told my brother and me to welcome whoever came along. "She won't be me," she said, "but you should make every effort with her, for my sake and for Dad's." It was a wonderful thing to say, a guilt-reducing formula that would smooth the awkwardness of transition. Judging by how awkward the transition was anyway, I hate to think what would have happened had my mother's take been less generous. My anxieties about the topic were matched only by my brother's and my father's. We had rational agreement that he should remarry if he could find someone worthy, and emotional anguish at the very thought.

My father took up dating as an onerous duty. He kept reiterating that he needed to find someone, that Mom had said to do so, but the process was lugubrious. He would come in from his dates tired and distracted and say, "I hate this; I don't want to be with these women; I only want to be with Carolyn." About six months after my mother died, he started seeing Bobye, whose husband had died at about the same time as my mother. They got along in part because they kept each other company in their mourning, talking about their lost spouses constantly. One of my mother's friends said to me that she was having them to dinner— "just the four of them," she said. "Your father, Bobye, his dead wife, and her dead husband." I was eager to meet this boon companion of my father's, and so we arranged an evening when I sat next to her. I can say now, almost fifteen years later, that Bobye is one of the nicest people in New York, but when I sat next to her that night I took offense at everything she said, and when I got home I wrote my father a letter saying that Bobye was a terrible person. My father called back and we both cried. "The person you're describing isn't Bobye," he said. "Give her another chance." Chastised, I had dinner with them again, and glimpsed some essential goodness in her. By the next month, she and I went out to lunch, just us, and I talked from deep in my heart, and tried to get her to respond the way my mother might have responded. It wasn't easy for anyone. She was both a person in her own right and a stage in my grief, and it was not always possible to reconcile these functions.

By the time my father and Bobye broke up, I no longer hated her and I no longer thought that she was my mother. I thought she was herself and terrific and I was devastated at losing her. It was too soon for both of them, and the shadow of the dead had forestalled their intimacy, but for me it was a grievous loss.

Then there were a few awful people. I was suspicious of my own suspicion, remembering how harshly I had judged Bobye, but some of these ladies were really unacceptable. There was one my brother vetoed, and a few I eliminated. Then there was one we liked a lot, but who couldn't handle full-on domesticity. Then there was one who was a friend of mine, and that ended very badly all around.

And then there was Sarah Billinghurst. She and my father went along happily for a bit, and then they broke up and my father started seeing someone kindhearted but slightly depressing, who I think reminded him of his mother. Then one of the women from pre–Sarah B., whom I will call Lola, came back on the scene. I remembered *Bonjour Tristesse*, the best-selling novel about a girl who is determined to undermine her father's relationship and does so with tragic consequences. My brother and I thought it might be worth the tragic consequences. We recruited my father's friends, who all admitted that they thought Lola was bad news but didn't know quite what to do about it. We told them to speak up now. We mounted a campaign. My father said, "I couldn't marry anyone you boys didn't like," and we said, "Good. Dump Lola," and he said we were being unfair. Lola wasn't really evil, but she was cold, tedious, and humorless to the bone.

When my father mentioned that he had seen Sarah again, we were exultant. Frankly, we would have been exultant if he had started going out with the Wednesday Witch at that point. But Sarah, whom we called Sarah B. to distinguish her from my brother's wife, also named Sarah, we had been fond of all along, and the contrast with Lola showed her many strengths to best advantage. Everyone likes Sarah B. upon meeting her: she's got a cozy, warm quality that makes you feel like you're in a gingerbread house with her, and a dramatic flair and some glamour, and that's an instantly winning combination of qualities. She comes from New Zealand and I lived for a long time in England, and so we had immediately a sort of common vocabulary of the British Empire. She has an ironic, upbeat sense of humor, and there is no better way through a period of mutual cautiousness than to laugh at the funny part of everything. She has both verve and kindness. We felt there was something there with Sarah B., that she was made of the earth and that you could count on her. She was not without issues and ambitions of her own, and she didn't pretend that she was easy; I preferred that honesty to Lola's obsequious simplicity. Sarah B. had riveting stories to tell, and she adored her friends and they adored her and she had extremely nice children. She dealt with my father's existing life by taking it all on. While some women had wanted to wean him from his habits, Sarah B. wanted to practice them with him. She became close to the people to whom he was close; she took an animated interest in his professional life; she came to grips with his schedule. Sarah B. was committed to an exciting career, and that was novel to my father. In fact, one of the best things about Sarah B. was that she was very different from my mother in her style and way of life. My mother was a hard act to follow, and the women who were like her had always seemed like pale imitations. Sarah Billinghurst, at once regal and fun, was very much her own person, and her splendor impressed us all at once. My father, genial as the day is long but also possessed of an alarming lucidity on virtually any topic, tends to frighten people. Sarah B. was not one bit afraid, and though she was lavish in her attentions, she was also lavish in her expectations. She had character. And she was, and is, an extraordinarily sympathetic and generous woman.

The tragedy of my parents' marriage was that my mother's great love was art, and my father is color blind; and my father's great love is music and my mother was tone-deaf. Sarah B. is the assistant general manager of the Metropolitan Opera, and she and my father have an entire relationship organized around music. It is terrific that my father has been able to reclaim this pleasure that he had to some considerable extent abandoned during his first marriage. He and Sarah B. thrive on their music, and over time he has come also to enjoy the large world that lies around it—festivals, friendships with singers and conductors, going to auditions. My father has had a chance to know so many people he had long admired, and his understanding of them and their work constantly deepens. I was as much delighted that he was open to such growth as I was that Sarah B. could provide the engine for it. It had sometimes seemed that he wanted only to be indulged in his old age. Sarah B. flatters him like mad, but she also demands things, stretches him, awakens what is dormant in him. Full of social energy, she always has a hundred interesting people around the house. She keeps him young by keeping him interested, not only in her but also in all that she brings to him.

A life in the opera has rubbed off on Sarah B.—she has a great, big, theatrical personality and a gift for high drama. I tend toward high drama myself, so we share a tendency to escalate, which is rather nice when faced with my father's implacable rationality. She and I have found sympathetic ears when my father is being intransigent, and we often e-mail each other in sleepless hours about particular frustrations with which the other one is likely to sympathize. I used to like taking private credit for the continuation of the relationship because I would calm Sarah B. down when she was upset and tell my father when he was being unreasonable. My brother and I were committed to making this one work; we thought Sarah B. was wonderful for my father and wonderful for us. The very caretaking that we some-times found onerous seemed to give her a sense of fulfillment, but she did not so overindulge his foibles that they became exag-gerated, nor did she ever cast us in a bad light. I like to position myself at the center of everyone else's life, and Sarah B. had a touching vulnerability with me that made me feel enormously important, and I knew that in my interactions with her I was ensuring that all would be good for my beloved father. While I had encouraged my father to find someone, I had also cherished resentment at anyone's coming to fill the particular void in our family, and had devoted considerable energy to noting the faults of the contestants. Then Sarah B. came along, and I found that despite my best efforts, there was no way to dislike or feel superior to her, because she was immediately so overwhelmingly magnanimous and caring. I saw how she softened the anger and frustration that had afflicted my father after his loss; I saw her open up emotions in him that I never expected to see again.

A few months later, we went on a trip to L.A., my brother and his wife, my partner and me, my two nephews, and my father; and Sarah B. wasn't able to join us. My father was in a sort of towering grumpiness that was absolutely horrifying and that we hadn't seen in some years, and there was no one else to cater to it, and we all realized that Sarah B. was a sort of shock absorber, taking all the bumps in the road and giving the rest of us a smooth ride. We realized that we needed her more than we had previously allowed. In the end, she came out to L.A., and when she arrived it was oil upon the churning waters and we all had a terrific time. I love Sarah's ability to take over any situation and bring it to order; she is not a producer for nothing. And I love the fact that she makes no bones about it. She calls up to announce she is organizing Christmas and by the end of an efficient fifteen-minute conversation, twenty-eight decisions that could have kept the rest of us going for a month are settled. She organizes trips in every perfect detail, and she always invites me and my partner along and works things out to suit our taste and needs. Her daughter nicknamed her the General, but it is all done with great good humor, and usually feels more coddling than aggressive. A few hours before a party she organized in the country was to begin, she said to me, "I'm getting very worried about the weather." "Sarah," I replied, "there's no point worrying. It's the weather. You can't do anything about it." "I know," she said. "It's so irritating!"

You would think that after all that, I would have welcomed their getting married as a glorious apotheosis; indeed I would have thought that myself. But we would have been quite wrong. My father had said over and over again, to me and to my brother and indeed to Sarah B. herself, that he would never, ever remarry. I thought this was foolish—it seemed to me that marriage would mean a very great deal to Sarah B. and that it would not cost my father anything. But the status quo served him well and she seemed to accept things as they were. It all changed in 2003, and I heard about the sudden realignment of the stars not from my father but from Sarah B., who asked in an e-mail which of several dates would best suit me for a wedding. Very much to my own surprise, I was apoplectic; it seemed like a complete disruption of a delicate ecosystem and jarred on my inner life and my sense of what rooted me to the earth. My friends and my therapist have all racked up hours pondering the why and wherefore. Much of it was to do with my mother. She had encouraged this result, but I had nonetheless had an underlying feeling that marriage was her province, which no one else would be allowed to enter. The idea that my father could do this again seemed to trivialize the institution he had shared with my mother. Then too, I disliked the fact that my father had reversed himself. My father does not usually reverse himself with me, and the fact that he would do so with someone else made me jealous. I objected to the fact that he hadn't consulted with my brother and me before he made this momentous decision, and that he hadn't called to tell us either what he was going to do, beforehand, or what he had done, afterward. And I objected most to the feeling that I had been deceived, that his protestations of eternal fidelity had been tricks of an unreliable narrator. He told me that he hadn't mentioned it because it was not really significant, because it wouldn't really change anything, and I became irate. It wasn't a bad change per se, but it was a change, and I didn't want to countenance this disingenuousness, which I presumed was the expression of his feelings of unconscious guilt, which I tied to the memory of my mother. The web was getting rather tangled.

The relationship between my father and Sarah B., which had been my pet project, was now taken quite out of my reach and became very much their own. The wedding went ahead on a date that was convenient for all, and I tried to be celebratory. It was a very difficult time and helped propel me into a depression. I felt a fathomless sea of anxieties opening out. If Sarah B. and I differ, then when will he do what I want and when will he do what she wants? With my mother it was never an issue—he did what she wanted, because they were seamless in that way, but what she wanted was generally what was best for me. With Sarah B., we avoid the topic assiduously because we both feel that we stand to lose in any confrontation; I try to support her positions and she to support mine and we move away from conflicts. But it is my underlying fear that my father will be weak and subject to her influence and that I will somehow alienate her and in so doing lose him. This anxiety is not incommensurate with my great affection for her, nor with my experience of her great affection for me; it is not a rational likelihood but a deep paranoia. I didn't grow up reading *Cinderella* for nothing. I can't really imagine what the topic of such difference would be, but she and I are both extremely demanding people and it's hard to believe that my father won't sometime be too tired for all of her demands and all of mine. I claim historical precedence, and she claims current primacy. I sometimes think our greatest difficulty is our similarity.

And then just when I am getting myself into a frenzy of anxiety, Sarah B. will do something else so benevolent that I feel ashamed of having been afraid of her, and I feel foolish. I have a great aunt who recently turned a hundred and five. I love her very much, but I have loved her since I was a little boy. I know that for someone coming along now, there's not so much there to love, because she has faded around the edges and is no longer able to communicate anything of much substance. But Sarah B. has been unstinting with Aunt Bea. I should emphasize that Aunt Bea is not my father's aunt, but my mother's, and that my father is fond of her but not enormously interested in her welfare. So Sarah B. has no motive for taking care of Aunt Bea except altruism. She goes to visit all the time, and whenever she goes, she takes flowers with her. The carpeting at Aunt Bea's house was in horrible condition, but Aunt Bea's vision is not great and I was content to leave things as they were. Sarah B. swept in and ordered new carpet and a man to install it, and arranged for Aunt Bea to spend the day up at my father's apartment, and Aunt Bea's house is in consequence a great deal cleaner and fresher than ever before. Most significantly, Aunt Bea had had a bleeding sore on her finger, which I had tended to think would heal up on its own, but which Sarah B. felt should be seen. It turned out to be a melanoma, and prompt treatment for it saved Aunt Bea from a great deal of fruitless pain. I have seen Sarah B. engage with my nephews and niece in the most loving way. She makes ice cream with Calvin and she plays games with Emmett and she encourages my father to go see them as often as possible. She has embraced the family wholeheartedly.

My father wanted to give me a fantastic surprise party for my fortieth birthday, and Sarah took on the job. Remember that she produces operas for a living—she was well and truly overqualified to stage my birthday party, but she has never gone at a new *Tristan und Isolde* with more gusto than she brought to this production. The theme was great performances, and she got leading singers to come and sing, ballet dancers to come and dance, a brilliant songster to write a song about me and Audra McDonald to sing it. She organized transport for friends from overseas, kept track of the RSVPs, figured out the seating. It was a splendid party and none of the other collaborators—my father, my brother, and my partner—could have begun to stage anything like it without her. When I thanked her for it, she said, "Of course, dear. Your father wanted to give you a wonderful party, and I wanted to make him happy." I realized that there is a transitive property to love, and that quite apart from the fact that we very much enjoy each other, we have to love each other because we both love my father.

I still hate it when people refer to my father and Sarah B. as my parents. I am perfectly happy with "your father and stepmother" or "your father and Sarah" or any of a vast array of other terms, but my parents are my father and mother. If my mother had died younger, if I had grown up with Sarah B., then perhaps it would have been different. But I don't mind it as much as I used to. She is not just my father's moll; she is my stepmother. It was shocking to me the first time I had to introduce myself to someone as Sarah Billinghurst's stepson. It was a new identity, one I had neither contemplated nor wished for. But it turned out that, like most identities, it could come in very handy. I meet the great musicians of our time, opera singers and conductors, and they look at me with artistic vagueness, and then I say that I am Sarah B.'s stepson and suddenly everything turns warm. Those words on which I once half-choked are now customary, and that is simply a part of who I am. Family is not a zero-sum game. Having more of it does not reduce the key connections. It is an addition, a supplement to my love. It has been hard to see Sarah B. take apart what were my mother's houses, but the new things she has spun are extremely wonderful; when I step into the country house she decorated and supervised for my father, I feel tension dropping away from me. It's a house that I associate with elegance and comfort and happiness. I call it the idyll. We had missed the woman's touch, and it is thrilling to have it once more to hand. I have always been fascinated by difficult loves, and stepmothers, as the fairy tales all tell, are inherently a challenge; but our affection for each other is refracted through our mutual love for my father, and through that process takes on a certain brilliance that transcends our situation.

My Father's Chinese Wives*

SANDRA TSING LOH

> It's not Zhou Ping who's the stranger at this table. It's Kaitlin
> and I. They are the same culture. We are not.

My father has decided—ten years after my mother's death, without the benefit of consulting either me or my sister—to take a Chinese wife.

He has written his family in Shanghai, seeking their help in locating likely candidates. He has good confidence in this project. He hopes to be married within six months.

Let us unpeel this news one layer at a time.

Question: Is my father even what one would consider *marriageable* at this point?

At age seventy, my father—a retired Chinese aerospace engineer—is starting to look more and more like somebody's gardener. His feet shuffle along the patio in their broken sandals. He stoops to pull out one or two stray weeds, coughing phlegmatically. Later, he sits in a rattan chair and eats leathery green vegetables in brown sauce, his old eyes slitted wearily.

He is the sort of person one would refer to as "Old Dragon Whiskers." And not just because it's a picturesque Oriental way of speaking.

At times my father seems to be overacting this lizardy old part. "I am old now," he'll say with a certain studied poignance. "I am just your crazy old Chinese father."

If he's that old, why does he still do the same vigorous daily exercise regime he's done for the past twenty-five years—forty-five minutes of pull-ups, something that looks like the twist, and much unfocused bellowing? All this done on the most public beaches possible, in his favorite Speedo—one he found in a Dumpster.

No. "Crazy old Chinese father" is actually a kind of code word for the fact that my father has always had a hard time . . . spending money. Why buy a leather briefcase to take to work, goes the rap, when this empty Frosted Flakes cereal box will do just as well? Papers slip down neatly inside, pens can be clipped conveniently on either side.

Why buy Bounty paper towels when, at work, my father can just walk down the hallway to the men's washroom, open the dispenser, and lift out a stack? They're free—he can bring home as many as we want!

When you've worn a sweater for so long that the elbows have worn right through, just turn it around! Wear it backwards! Clip a bowtie on—no one will notice!

Why drive the car to work when you can take the so-convenient RTD bus? More time to read interesting scientific papers . . . and here they are, in my empty Frosted Flakes box!

"Oh . . . terrific!" is my older sister Kaitlin's response when I phone her with the news. Bear in mind that Kaitlin has not seen my father in ten years, preferring to nurse her bad memories of him independently, via a therapist. She allows herself a laugh, laying aside her customary dull hostility for a moment of more jocular hostility. "And who does he think would want to marry *him*?"

"Someone Chinese," I say.

"Oh, good! That narrows the field to what? Half a billion? No, as always, he's doing this to punish us.

"Think about it," she continues with her usual chilling logic. "He marries a German woman the first time around. It's a disaster. You and I symbolize that. It's a disaster because he's passive-aggressive, he's cheap, and he's angry. But of course he won't see it that way. To him, it will have been that rebellious Aryan strain that's the problem.

"You take an Asian immigrant just off the boat, on the other hand. Here is a woman fleeing a life of oppression under a Communist government and no public sanitation and working in a bicycle factory for ten cents an hour and repeated floggings every hour on the hour, every day of every week of every month of every year. After that, living with our father might seem like just another bizarre incident of some kind."

As usual, Kaitlin scores some compelling points, but I'm bothered for yet a different reason . . .

BECAUSE IN DESCRIBING this potential new wife, my father has used one word: Chinese. He has not said: "I'm looking for a smart wife," or even "a fat wife." He has said "Chinese." That word is meant to stand for so much.

Asian. Asian women. Young Asian *ladies*.

I think back to a writing workshop I once attended. (No credit, and perhaps that was appropriate.) The students consisted of thirteen hysterical women—and one Fred. Fred was a wealthy Caucasian sixtysomething urologist who always insisted on holding the door open for me. Just for me. "Because you're such a lovely lady," he'd say—even as I stood there, literally, in glasses and sweatpants.

We thirteen women, on the other hand, were a wildly mixed group. We were writing anything from wintery Ann Beattie–esque snippets to sci-fi romance/porn novels (aka: "She would be King Zenothar's concubine whether she liked it or not"). We attacked each other's writing accordingly. People were bursting into tears every week, then making up as we emotionally shared stories about mutual eating disorders.

But there was one moment where all thirteen of us were of like minds. It was the moment when Fred would enter the classroom, laden with Xeroxes, blushing shyly as a new bride. We'd look at each other in horror as if to say: "Oh my God. Fred has brought in work again."

As though springing from a murky, bottomless well, each week new chapters would appear from this semi-epistolary novel Fred was penning about a wealthy Caucasian sixtysomething urologist (named Fred) who goes on sabbatical for a year to Japan. There he finds unexpected love in the form of a twenty-three-year-old Japanese medical student named Aku who smells of cherry blossoms.

There were many awkward scenes in which Fred and Aku were exploring each other's bodies as they lay—as far as I could gather—upon the bare floor, only a *tatami* mat for comfort. (Fred would always italicize the Japanese words, as if to separate and somehow protect them from the other, lesser words.) But it was all much more beautiful and much more pure than anything any of us could imagine, totally unlike the urban squalor of America—the rock music, the drugs, the uncouth teenagers!

But there's one line I've never been able to blot from my mind. Nor the way Fred read it, in that hoarse, tremulous voice.

"I put my hand in hers, and her little fingers opened like the petals of a moist flower."

———

IT IS A month later. As if in a dream, I sit with my father at the worn Formica family dining room table, photos and letters spread out before us.

Since my father has written to Shanghai, the mail has come pouring in. I have to face the fact that my father is, well, hot.

"You see?" he says. "Seven women have written! Ha!" He beams, his gold molar glinting. He drinks steaming green tea from a chipped laboratory beaker, which he handles with a "Beauty and the Beast" potholder.

With a sigh, I turn to the matter at hand. And in spite of myself, I am wowed!

Tzau Pa, Ling Ling, Sui Pai . . . the names jump off the pages in both their English and Chinese translations. While totally Asian, these are not retiring Madame Butterfly types.

"Twenty-eight, administrative assistant!" "Forty-nine, owner of a seamstress business!" "Thirty-seven, freelance beautician!" These women are dynamos, with black curly hair, in turtlenecks, jauntily riding bicycles, seated squarely on canons before military museums, beaming proudly with three grown daughters.

One thing unites them: They're all ready to leap off the mainland at the drop of a hat.

And don't think their careers and hobbies are going to keep them from being terrific wives. Quite the opposite. Several have excellent experience, including one who's been married twice already. The seamstress has sent him shorts and several pairs of socks; there is much talk of seven-course meals and ironing and terrific expertise in gardening.

Super achievement, in short, is a major theme that applies to all! But the biggest star of all, of course, will be my father. He gleefully hands me a letter written by one Liu Tzun. It reads:

> *Dr. Loh,*
>
> *Your family has told me of your excellent scientific genius and your many awards. I respect academic scholarship very highly, and would be honored to meet you on your next visit.*

"You see? They have respect for me in China! When I go there, they treat me like President Bush. Free meals, free drinks! I do not pay for anything!"

FORTY-SEVEN-YEAR-OLD Liu Tzun—the writer of the magic letter—is indeed the lucky winner. Within three months, she is flown to Los Angeles. She and my father are married a week later.

I do not get to meet her right away, but my father fills me in on the stats. And I have to confess, I'm surprised at how urban she is, how modern. Liu Tzun is a divorcee with, well, ambitions in the entertainment business. Although she speaks no English, she seems to be an expert on American culture. The fact that Los Angeles is near Hollywood has not escaped her.

This is made clear to me one Sunday evening, via telephone.

"I know you have friends in the entertainment business," my father declares. He has never fully grasped the fact that most of the people I know do, like, hair for "America's Most Wanted."

"So you should know that, aside from having repaired my shoes and being very skilled at Chinese folk dance, Liu Tzun is an excellent singer . . ."

"I'm sure Liu is quite accomplished. It's just that . . ."

"Oh . . . she is terrific!" My father is shocked that I could be calling Liu's musical talent into question. "Do you want to hear her sing? I will put her on the phone right now!"

"Oh my God. Don't humiliate her. Has it ever occurred to you that this singing is something that you want her to do, not that she wants to do? Like with my piano lessons as a kid? When you used to push me to the piano, push me to the piano, push me to the piano, and I'd cry, and you'd push me and I'd cry . . ."

But my father has not heard a word of it. He is too busy hustling new talent. I hear the clunking sound of two extensions being picked up.

"Okay, okay: she will sing for you now."

"Hallooo!" a third voice trills—and I realize that, unlike me, Liu Tzun is not afraid to perform for my father. There is a professional clearing of the throat, and then:

"Nee-ee hoo-oo mau, tieh-hen see bau-hau jioo . . . !"

I have left you, Dr. Loh, and taken the Toyota—so there!

This is the note my father finds on the worn Formica family dining room table five weeks later. Apparently Liu's career was not moving quickly enough, so she left him to marry someone higher up—perhaps Ted Koppel.

My father is in shock. Then again, he is philosophical.

"That Liu—she was bad that one, bah! She says I do not buy her gifts. She says I do not like to go out at night. And it is true, I do not. But I say: 'Go! See your friends in Chinatown. It is okay with me!' I like it better when she leaves the house sometimes, it is more quiet.

"But Liu does not want to take the bus. She wants to drive the car! But you know me, I am your . . . crazy old Chinese father. I don't want to pay for her auto insurance."

And then he actually says, "As with many Asians, Liu Tzun is a very bad driver."

"Ha!" is Kaitlin's only response. "Isn't it interesting how he seems to repel even his own kind."

SUMMER TURNS TO fall in southern California, causing the palm trees to sway a bit. The divorce is soon final, Liu's prizes including $10,000, the microwave and the Toyota.

Never one to dwell, my father has soon picked a new bride: one Zhou Ping, thirty-seven, homemaker from Qang-Zhou province! I groan.

"But no . . . Zhou Ping is very good. She comes very highly recommended, not, I have to say, like that Liu. She was bad, that one, bah! Zhou Ping is very sensible and hardworking. She has had a tough life. Boy! She worked in a coal mine in Manchuria until she was twenty-five years old. The winters there were very, very bitter! She had to make her own shoes and clothing. Then she worked on a farming collective, where she raised cattle and several different kinds of crops—by herself! Corn, rice, beans, lichees . . ."

"I'm sure Zhou Ping is going to fit in really, really well in Los Angeles," I reply.

BUT ZHOU PING is indeed full of surprises. The news comes, to my surprise, from Kaitlin.

"I received . . . a *birthday card*. From Papa . . . and *Zhou Ping*. On the cover there is a clown holding balloons. It's from Hallmark. Inside in gold lettering, cursive, it says, 'Happy Birthday! Love, Zhou Ping and your *daddy*.'"

"Your what?"

"This is obviously Zhou Ping's handiwork. The envelope is not addressed in his handwriting. She clearly doesn't know that he doesn't give birthday cards. Especially not to *me*."

But a week later, Kaitlin receives birthday gifts in the mail: a box of "mooncakes," a bunch of orchids, and a sweater hand knit by Zhou Ping. "Oh no! Now I really have to call her. She clearly has no friends in America. He really picked someone he can walk all over this time. I think it's sad."

KAITLIN FINALLY DOES call, catching Zhou Ping at an hour when my father is on the beach doing his exercises. And in spite of her broken English, Zhou Ping manages to convince Kaitlin to come home with me for a visit!

It will be Kaitlin's first trip home since our mother's death. And my first meeting of either of my father's two Chinese wives.

WE PULL UP the familiar driveway in my Geo. Neither of us says a word. We peer out the windows.

The yard . . . doesn't look too bad. There are new sprinklers, and a kind of intricate irrigation system made of ingeniously placed rain gutters. New saplings have been planted. Enormous bundles of weeds flank the porch as if for some momentous occasion.

We ring the doorbell.

The door opens and a short, somewhat plump Chinese woman, in round glasses and a perfect bowl haircut, beams at us. She is wearing a bright yellow "I hate housework!" apron that my mother was once given as a gag gift—and I think never wore.

"Kat-lin! Sand-wa!" she exclaims in what seems like authentic joy. She is laughing and almost crying with emotion. "Wel-come home!" Then to Kaitlin, a shadow falling over her face: "I am so glad you finally come home to see your daddy. He old now."

As if exhausted by that moment of solemnity, Zhou Ping collapses into giggles. "Hoo-hoo-hoo! My English is no good, no good!"

Kaitlin's expression strains between joy and nausea. I jump in nervously: "Oh, it's nice to finally meet you!" "How do you like L.A.?" "What's that I smell from the kitchen? Is that Szechuan food? Or Mandarin? Or what province is that—?"

My father materializes from behind a potted plant. He is wearing a new handknit sweater and oddly formal dress pants. His gaze is fixed at a point on the floor.

"Long time no see!" he says to the point on the floor.

"Yes!" Kaitlin sings back, defiant, a kind of Winged Vengeance in perfect beige Anne Klein II leisurewear. "It certainly is!"

My father stands stiffly.

Kaitlin blazes.

"Well," he concludes. "It is good to see you."

Feeling, perhaps, that we should leave well enough alone, the Loh family, such as we are, continues on through the house. It is ablaze with color—in those sorts of eye-popping combinations you associate with Thai restaurants and Hindu shrines. There are big purple couches, peach rugs, and shiny brass trellises with creeping charlies everywhere.

All this redecorating came at no great expense, however.

"Do you see this rug?" my father points proudly. "Zhou Ping found it! In a Dumpster! They were going to throw it away!"

"Throw it away! See? It very nice!"

Over their heads, Kaitlin mouths one silent word at me: "Help."

My father trundles off to put music on his . . . brand-new CD player? "That bad Liu made me buy it!" he says. "Bah! But it is very nice."

"Dinner will be ready—in five minute!" Zhou Ping is off in a blaze of yellow.

Kaitlin grabs me by the arm, pulls me into the bathroom, slams the door. "This is so weird!"

We have not stood together in this bathroom in some fifteen

years. It seems somehow different. The wallpaper is faded, the towels are new . . .

"Look," I say, "there in the corner. It's Mama's favorite framed etching of Leonardo da Vinci's *Praying Hands*."

"But look," Kaitlin says, "right next to it. Is that a glossy 'Bank of Canton' calendar from which a zaftig Asian female chortles?

"Look what he's making her do!" Kaitlin begins to pace, veins stand out on her temples. "Look what he's making her do! Can't he give the woman a decorating budget? This is a man who has $300,000 in mutual funds alone! Can't he liberate fifty of it to spend on a throw rug? I mean, I know things were really, really, really difficult in Shanghai but he hasn't lived there now for forty years, has he? Will it never end? Will it never end?"

"We'll eat, and then we'll leave" is my soothing mantra. "We'll eat, and then we'll leave. Twenty minutes. We'll be out on the freeway. Driving. Wind in our hair. Radio on. It'll all be behind us. And I promise, we'll never have to come back again."

DINNER IS AN authentic Chinese meal: chicken, shrimp, and egg dishes twirl before us. Steam is rising. Plates are passing. Rachmaninoff drifts in from the CD player. It almost resembles a meal any normal family would be having at this hour.

To see my father sitting at this familiar table with his new Chinese wife is to see something surprisingly . . . natural. In common rhythm they eat deftly with chopsticks—which Kaitlin and I fumble with—and converse quietly in Mandarin—not a word of which we can understand.

And I realize: it's not Zhou Ping who's the stranger at this table. It's Kaitlin and I. They are the same culture. We are not.

But Zhou Ping will have none of it. Hardy Manchurian builder that she is, she is determined to use the crude two-by-fours of her broken English to forge a rickety rope bridge between us.

"And you, Sand-wa! You play the piano, no? Mo-sart: he very nice. You will show me! And you, Katlin, you are a teacher, no? That is good, Katlin, good! Good. You, Katlin, you are very, very . . . good!"

My father puts his spoon down. He is chewing slowly, a frown growing. "This meat . . . is very, very greasy. Bah! I tell you not to buy this meat, Zhou Ping, I tell you not to buy this meat!"

There is a familiar rhythm to his words, gestures, expressions. And I realize that while one character may be new, this is the same dinner table, the same family, the same drama.

And the only question is, What will she do this time? Will she throw her napkin down, burst into tears, run from the room? Will she knock the table over, sending sauces splattering, crockery breaking? Will we hear the car engine turn over from the garage as she flees into the night, leaving us here, frightened and panicked?

But Zhou Ping does none of these things.

She tilts her head back, her eyes crinkle . . . and laughter pours out of her, peal after peal after peal. It is a big laugh, an enormous laugh, the laugh of a woman who has birthed calves and hoed crops and seen winters decimate entire countrysides.

She points to our father and says words that sound incredible to our ears:

"You papa—he so funny!"

And suddenly my father is laughing! And I am laughing!

But Kaitlin is not laughing.

"Why were you always so angry?"

My father just shrugs his shoulders.

"Oh no no no no no no. Why could you never let the tiniest thing go? How could you do that to our family?"

And I realize that my father doesn't have an answer. It is as though rage were a chemical that reacted on him for twenty years and now, like a spirit, it has left him. And he's just old now. He is old.

DUSK FALLS, THROWING long blue shadows across the worn parquet of the dining room floor. After a moment, my father asks Zhou Ping to sing a song. And she does so, simply. He translates:

From the four corners of the earth
My lover comes to me
Playing the lute
Like the wind over the water

He recites the words without embarrassment. And why shouldn't he? The song has nothing to do with him personally. It is from some old Chinese fable that's been passed down from generation to generation. It has to do with missing something, someone, some place maybe you can't even define anymore.

As Zhou Ping sings, everyone longs for home.

But what home? Zhou Ping, for her bitter winters? My father, for the Shanghai he left forty years ago? And what about Kaitlin and me? We are sitting in our own childhood home, and still we long for it.

Infinite Family

LISA SHEA

Does a grown divorced woman with a teenaged son
need a stepfather?

Recently, I spent a weekend in the southern Adirondacks
at my maternal grandparents' farm. They were married—
to each other!—for fifty-eight years. I remember celebrating their fiftieth wedding anniversary at a swanky, old-style
club in downtown Albany, New York, the city where my grandfather had practiced medicine until he retired at age eighty-four
(he lived to be ninety-eight, three years after announcing with his
black Irish wit still intact that he had "given up hope" of dying).

My grandparents' enduring marriage has been a spiritual, emotional, and moral touchstone throughout my life, a loving example in which husband and wife stayed together, and in my
grandparents' case died together, a mere eighteen days apart.

The person with whom I spent the weekend at the 1853 farmhouse had been my boyfriend when we were in our late teens
and early twenties. We had met in Bermuda the summer we
graduated high school. He had sailed down with schoolmates
from Rhode Island on a beautiful teak wood sloop owned by the
school. Our meeting was the zenith of high romance in my
notional head, effortlessly enhanced by the island's gold-struck
sun, granite pink sand, and crystalline water. We zipped around
on noisy little motor scooters, explored the gorgeous beaches and

coves, and later—reckless, sunburned, besotted—in a wash of lavender dusk, made out under cover of the lush hibiscus shrubs on the grounds of the Princess Hotel.

The weekend in the Addies, by contrast, featured two wary middle-aged former lovers going on hikes, sharing meals, finding conversation and (mostly) comfortable silences while exploring Lake George and Saratoga Springs. Driving back to the farmhouse listening to Cream's "I'm So Glad" on his rented car's CD player, I remember saying that I liked his longish (think Owen Wilson) hair; he mentioned not having seen my legs in, what, twenty-five years. Awkward, intimate laughter ensued. Midweekend, we sat together on the long couch in the family room watching *Saturday Night Live*. He fell asleep before the show ended and then suddenly stood up—was he sleepwalking?—and guided himself into the bedroom.

Later, when I came into the room, I studied his shape under the blankets, familiar and new. Aroused, I headed for the bed, then steered myself away, headed back, steered away. Finally, cold feet vanquished curiosity and I climbed into the bed across the room, visions of Claudette Colbert and Clark Gable in the 1930s classic *It Happened One Night*. That morning, by light of day, we finally mustered the temerity to share a bed. In place of pink sand and hibiscus, there was my little dog, Scarlet, jumping on the bed running interference, protecting me from this shaggy-haired stranger, a man!

Driving home after the weekend, I fancied what it would be like to step into the role of stepparent. Could my long ago ex-boyfriend, now a suburban divorcé with three children ages fourteen to twenty, blend successfully, happily, smoothly (do these adverbs even come close to capturing the complexities?) with me and my thirteen-year-old city kid? What chemistry might emerge from such a union? Fairy tale or Frankenstein?

————

WHEN I THINK of my first stepfather, Alex, a lawyer and real-estate agent who had fled Latvia as a young man, the words "courtly," "mischievous," "serious," and "nostalgic" come to mind. My current stepfather, Jack, a West Point graduate and former aeronautical engineer, is an all-American male—confident, easy-going, disciplined, and forward looking.

Both Alex, who died in 1998, and Jack have shown me first-hand, merely by their presence in my life, that the concept of family in the late twentieth and early twenty-first centuries continues to expand, contract, adapt, mutate, and evolve. Like many families, mine began the shift long ago from strictly nuclear to extranuclear. We are—in the current nomenclature so redolent of cocktail shakers and 1950s families' basement bars—blended. In ways I never could have imagined as a thirteen-year-old girl when my mother and father divorced, I have been powerfully influenced and in surprising ways re-formed by my relationships with Alex and Jack.

Alex was a decade older than my mother and had retained his Latvian accent, impeccable manners, and essential un-Americanness. Together, they enjoyed dining out, seeing his old circle of friends, going to classical music concerts, visiting with his son and daughter on Long Island where he had worked and lived with his first wife and family until her death in the 1970s.

Alex also liked to scare my mother by driving very fast and aggressively on car trips, bringing her to tears; he was argumentative, judgmental, a shouter, a scowler, a snob. Hauntingly in common with my father, he played sadist to my mother's masochistic streak.

For the first decade of their sixteen-year-long relationship, Alex refused to meet my sisters and me and our children. He was still mourning the death of his long-departed wife, my mother explained. She told us that he kept a large oil portrait of his dead wife prominently displayed above the mantelpiece in his living room, which I found creepy and insulting to my mother.

In 1997, fifteen years after they met, my mother and Alex were married in a civil ceremony at a town hall outside Washington, D.C. Only my older sister and Alex's adult son and daughter were asked to attend. His daughter declined the invitation. I felt deeply snubbed by being left out. In a desperate attempt to foster a sense of inclusion, I put together an elegant album of photos I had taken of mom and Alex over the six years that I had actually known him. One year after their wedding, Alex died of a silent heart attack. He left the dentist's office after an appointment, walked to his car in the parking lot, and fell to the ground. Before the ambulance arrived, he was dead.

This was in September of 1998. My mother and Alex had never lived together, even after their marriage, and I found this fascinating and odd. I wondered if it was because at some gut level my mother was afraid of Alex, of his temper and his rigid, Old World ways. Maybe it was her way—at sixty-four—of saving herself not for, but from, the man she loved.

I never really got to know Alex. He was an éminence gris, a tall, pale-faced, big-boned, ever-scrutinizing taskmaster. When he gave a directive, my mother jumped. His smile was tight, no nonsense. In my daughter's battle-scarred, fractured-family mind, I was afraid of him, not so much for his strictness but because he seemed unknowable. I suppose I took his refusal to meet me for all those years as symptomatic of a rejecting or at least an indifferent personality, and my feelings for him sprang from that initial ambivalence.

It surprised me, then, that I cried when Alex died, that I hugged both of his adult children and their children and told at least one humorous story about him at the restaurant after his funeral service. Two years later, at my own troubled father's much smaller service, when asked by the funeral director if any of us in the immediate family, the only people there—ex-wife, three grown daughters—wanted to speak about him, we all fell silent. None of us spoke a word.

Now, when I think about Alex, my feelings for him carry a wary fondness. The fact is, whatever his demons, he provided my mother with companionship, with the life-affirming dynamics of give and take, and with a vital, ongoing sense of engagement. It is strange and astonishing to realize that their relationship lasted longer than my own parents' marriage.

The story of my current stepfather does read—so far—like a page from a fairy tale. He and my mother were college sweethearts; she was pinned to him in what was a popular preengagement rite in the late 1940s. Then my mother met the man who would become my father, while visiting a girlfriend in Washington, D.C., where my father was in law school. They went out on a blind date arranged by a mutual friend. Two years later they were married.

Still, Jack's name was familiar from earliest childhood. He was the West Point soldier-scholar my mother always included in her tales of double-dating, attending football games, and dancing at college socials. I turned the story of Jack into my own story of how my mother made the fatal romantic mistake of leaving disciplined, responsible Jack for my self-destructive, wild-natured dad. There was no other way for me to understand how my mother could have married such a scary, unstable man—my father, whom I feared, and loved.

The dark romance I had constructed stayed with me until the most unexpected thing of all intruded, reasserting itself over my tragic dream of wounded love: reality. In the spring of 2001, after fifty-two years, my mother and Jack, each widowed, remet and fell instantly back in love.

At a dinner party set up surreptitiously and given by cousins on my mother's side, there was no hesitation from the moment my mother was asked to open the door for the evening's surprise guest. Within two months they were married, planning the sale of his house in Connecticut and hers in Washington, D.C., and then heading to southcentral Florida, where they settled in the same gated community as my mother's prescient matchmaker cousins.

Three years on, I would describe my relationship with Jack as friendly if distant. It begs the question: does a grown divorced woman with a teenaged son need a stepfather? The still frightened little girl inside with the dreadful romantic imagination would answer, unequivocally, yes. The fairly efficient if financially challenged head-of-household writer/mom/teacher who is blessed with many friends, a cohesive community, and weekly therapy sessions would likely say no.

But I do hold out hope of having a closer bond with my latest father figure, the soldier-scholar who, at seventy-eight, can be found on the golf course working on his slightly skewed slice, or cruising down the Rhone with his blushing seventy-six-year-old bride, or planting his lush vegetable and flower garden at their summer cottage in upstate New York. It was the stepfamily "what if" exercise on the way home from the Adirondacks that helped me appreciate how both of my stepfathers must have harbored fears, hopes, blind spots, and notions about what kind of daughters they were inheriting when they married my mother. If I were to attempt thumbnail sketches, I would describe my older sister as whip-smart, responsible, and driven; my younger sister as canny and hungry and theatrical; and myself as creative, articulate, and insecure.

———

IT'S TOO LATE ever to know what Alex might have revealed about himself and, in turn, about us as a stepfamily, but it isn't too late with Jack. And if there is something stirring in its quiet, yet to be completely declared way with my new old boyfriend, the stepfamily equation may yet again go into arithmetic overdrive. Since the Addies weekend he and I have adopted an approach-avoidance, albeit pheromone-charged stance, the saving grace of which is that it's mutual. That feels right, for now.

How swiftly the logical and unerring constancy of the times tables, mastered all the way back in grade school, dissolves when applied to the unruly rubric of the blended family, comprising as it does unpredictable, unreliable whole number humans—a numerical species more akin to mysterious fractals than fundamental factors.

My own primitive calculations about recombinant families come strictly from the belly, not the blackboard. They reveal stepfamilies as volatile, evolving, visionary—a revolutionary mix of sets and subsets whose one constant is to invent and reinvent themselves over and over into the future and on into infinity. What private truth could be more romantic, and indivisible, than that?

My Mother's Women

DAVID GOODWILLIE

We never spoke of what had clearly occurred—
my mother had left him, left *us*, for another woman.

This is my first memory of freedom: racing south on I-95, New York to our left, America to our right, a new life somewhere up ahead. My mother is behind the wheel, almost leaning into it, that's how excited she is. In vehicles behind us, a postmodern caravan of lovers and children and furniture, all bearing down on the future, on a new start, someplace that will take us. It's a sunny summer day at the whimpering end of the '80s. I'm fifteen; my brother Douglas, bouncing around in the backseat, is eleven. There is music. There is laughter. And there are games, like this one.

"OK," my mother says. "Where do you boys think we're going? You can each guess two cities. The winner gets first choice of bedrooms when we get there."

That's how things were then; wide open—to ideas, suggestions, everything. I remember Douglas unfolding a map of the East Coast, Maine to Florida, and rattling off every city he saw. I'd like to think I looked in the rearview mirror. That I didn't know where we were going seemed trivial; I was still working out where we'd been.

———

I GREW UP in Paris and then London. My father was an American energy lawyer who traveled the world advising governments on oil pipelines and magnetic levitation trains. My mother—seven years younger—was still fresh from the war protests that consumed her student days at Barnard. But she took quickly to the expat life. London in the '70s was a vibrant place; it was the dawn of punk, the middle of the Cold War, the end of so much innocence. The place was full of colorful people with cloudy backgrounds, all making a last stab at a certain kind of life. And my mother, who was still young enough to turn heads, who with her red hair and freckles bore more than a passing resemblance to a certain princess-to-be, flourished in the soft glow of all that glamour.

My father was called back to the States not long after Reagan took office; New York to be exact, though we settled in the suburbs. Montclair, New Jersey: it was—it is—such a picture-perfect commuter town that network news producers constantly drove the twelve miles west from Manhattan whenever they needed a leafy background shot or a reaction quote from someone normal. And so that's what we became: normal. My father commuted to work and played golf on weekends. Douglas and I went to public school and played Little League. My mother cooked and played . . . actually I can't remember what she did. I know she never fell for the country club scene, never got involved with a church group or the Junior League. She tried her hand at gardening, even played paddle tennis for a while, but these were just things to do. Already she was stuck, but I didn't notice. What child looks up from the pleasures and pastimes of youth for long enough to notice anything?

She applied to law school when I was twelve (she was thirty-four). It was the first indication of what was to come, but at the time it was just another detail. She went to Rutgers at night, then found a job at a good law firm a few towns away. I don't know what behind-the-scenes role my father played in her smooth rise to prominence, but I expect it was substantial. He was like that. By 1986, yellow legal pads covered the available countertops of our house; baseball gloves and hockey sticks covered the floors. The family was firing on all cylinders. That fall my father took us to game six of the World Series between the Mets and Red Sox. It was the Bill Buckner game, the greatest comeback of the decade. How could I have known that night, as we cheered ourselves hoarse, that everything else was coming apart?

THE FIRST TIME I met Sydney, she was sitting with my mother at our kitchen table, papers spread out in front of them. They were friends from the law firm, my mother quickly explained. Sydney had short dark hair and a gap between her front teeth that made her look childlike in spite of a solemn, almost glowering demeanor. She was there again the next night, and the one after. They were starting a small business, my mother proudly told me the following weekend, some kind of Asian-influenced furniture concern.

"Does Dad know about this?" I asked.

"About what?"

"Your furniture idea."

"Of course," she said, quickly.

I don't know why I asked. Maybe it was because my father was hardly ever around.

My mother seemed so cheerfully busy that winter that I just came to accept the kitchen-table enterprise as her long-awaited hobby. Sydney wasn't cold exactly, but she wasn't warm either. When I came in to raid the fridge after school, I could actually see her decide to make an effort to be pleasant. A moment would pass and then a tight wincing smile would appear, only to vanish as soon as I did. Which was quickly.

I should have seen it coming, but these were the heady days of teenage life, days so full of activity that I lived in ignorance of larger circumstances. School, sports, friends, girls. It's a wonder I was even home the night my parents sat us down to say they were separating.

I'D LIKE TO think everything was on the level, that Sydney in those first months represented nothing more to my mother than a new way of looking at life. But as so often happens, the exact timing of events in my mother's escalating "friendship" remains murky. My parents agreed to joint custody of Douglas and me, and my mother rented a small house on the other side of town. It was a mile down the hill, but it could have been a different country. Sydney, sensing opportunity, and no longer operating on enemy turf, stepped up her charm campaign. She took us on trips to Greenwich Village and Hoboken, where she lived in a small walkup near the PATH train. I don't remember the apartment itself, only the girl who was draped across the couch when we walked in. Her name was Pilar, and after a few confusing moments it came out that she was Sydney's daughter. Pilar was a freshman at Smith, home for the weekend to model in a New York fashion show. I'm sure there was more to the story, but this was quite enough for me. Rendered mute by her beauty, her age, her *occupation*, I slunk off to a corner to consider my various deficiencies.

AND WHAT OF my father? My mother probably broke his heart. Or at least some part of it. But he stayed resolute in the face of an unfamiliar world. Work. Travel. Golf. We never spoke of what had clearly occurred—my mother had left him, left *us*, for another woman. He had always kept emotion at arm's length. It was a once admirable practice that now seemed indelibly flawed. But if it was a flaw, it was one of his few. Here was a man who had made his own way in the world. He'd lived his life so well, in so many ways, and this was what he'd gotten for his efforts. Why then, why in God's name, did I side with my mother?

Because it was incredibly exciting. Because she was taking the biggest risk of her life. Because we always root for underdogs. Those are easy answers. The greater truth probably lies in the time and place in which we lived—the monotony of suburban existence, the stifling conservatism of 1980s America. Even as a child I felt these things. The rhythm of our days, of our decade, was synthesized, and my mother had clearly decided to keep her own wobbly beat.

But joining her revolution meant facing the gay question head on. It's come up a lot in the years since. *What did you think when you first found out your mother was gay?* Honestly? I never thought of it in strictly those terms. I saw my two diverging parents not as gay and straight but as liberal and conservative, intriguingly progressive and soberly conventional. When Sydney and Pilar moved in—which they did, about six months after the separation—I remember being oddly intrigued, even if I, like all children, kept the sexual specifics, the actual sharing of beds and bodies, safely out of mind. Sydney unpacked boxes of books by Betty Friedan, Gloria Steinem, Susan Sontag. Dinner discussions shifted from school and sports to politics and causes. And the law firm and Asian-furniture business were abandoned for the loftier work of world saving.

I left for boarding school that fall (sending me away was the one thing my parents agreed on), and lacking any singular talents, I decided my mother's recent history would be my ace in the hole, the special secret that would set me apart at a place where everyone seemed smarter, wealthier, more experienced. Her sexuality became a sort of litmus test, and I chose friends based on who I thought could handle—and be impressed by—it. I took up with an open-minded crowd of troublemakers, the radical fringe of the trust-fund elite, and were it not that I played sports, was still wary of drugs, and had little use for the Dead or The Cure, I probably wouldn't have lasted too long.

IT WAS THAT winter, or the following spring, that my mother mentioned starting over geographically as well. We're going someplace better, she announced, and I could hardly argue. Montclair wasn't the best locale for alternative lifestyles, and to compound matters, my father had taken up with a wealthy widow named Cynthia. She was an attractive minor-league socialite with four children and an inherited fortune that included a sprawling house in Nantucket. She was also conservative (i.e., she didn't work, and hadn't since the '60s, when as a TWA flight attendant she'd met her previous husband in the first-class cabin), and to my father she must have seemed the perfect response to the surreal events of the last two years. His life had been turned upside down, and here now was a woman who cooked and cocktailed and played golf, a woman who was also trying to numb the events of the recent past. He didn't care that she wore her money like a lottery winner. She was a lottery winner. And now so was he. It was the rest of us who lost. When my father moved into her six-bedroom mansion, Douglas, too young for boarding school, accepted his shuttle-bus fate with quiet resignation. I—after hearing Cynthia's drunken take on my mother's sexuality—chose to rebel.

———

AT SOME POINT during that dramatic car ride down I-95, I decided that my mother was extraordinary. And refusing to tell us where we were going just added to the boundless possibilities of the moment, of our lives. In the end, someplace better turned out to be Baltimore. I had guessed cities farther south— Charleston and Savannah (why not?)—and Douglas had eliminated himself by naming every city on the map, so we flipped a coin for the bedroom. I'd never been to Baltimore, and as we got off I-95, followed closely by Sydney, Pilar, and the movers, the sense of starting over, of severing any last thin ties to normality, hit me all at once. My mother turned the music off and we drove through the Inner Harbor in nervous silence. The waterfront was clean and crowded, but as we turned north onto Charles Street, the real city revealed itself. It was a broken place: the blocks were desolate, the buildings sad testaments to some better time. I turned around to make sure Sydney and Pilar hadn't cut and run.

Ten minutes later, we pulled up outside a small brownstone in Bolton Hill. I hadn't yet acquired the real-estate instincts that come with a decade of New York living, but the immediate tension in the air was impossible to miss. Bolton Hill was a neighborhood on the brink, a microcosm of the city itself. It was the home of the Maryland Art Institute, and you didn't need to look any farther than the rusting VW vans and BMW 2002s lining the narrow tree-lined streets to get a sense of our new enclave's Bohemian vibe. But look up past the century-old rooftops, to the low-income projects towering over and around us on three sides, and the bleaker facts of our surroundings took shape. The house itself, purchased by my mother in part from alimony payments (a tricky fact, alimony was, and one brushed aside in those early days in order to keep the rebellion pure), was a narrow three-story affair with a tiny European backyard that never quite saw the sun. That first night—and during many to follow—I woke up with a start to the sound of gunfire, then tossed and turned through the remaining hours, frightened, exhilarated, curious, confused. In the anxious half-light of dawn, I tiptoed down to the kitchen, only to be startled when I found my mother there, quietly organizing shelves.

Life, for me, reveals itself in odd hours and unexpected moments. And so it was, at 6:45 A.M., alone together in an unfamiliar house, that my mother laid out our future. Baltimore, it turns out, wasn't just picked out of a hat. Sydney had taken a Human Resources job at one of the few large corporations still headquartered downtown. And my mother—always good for a surprise—had already accepted a position as a criminal prosecutor for the city. "Baltimore could use the help," she said, "and anyway it's about time we did something good for the world, something just a little bit . . . worthy." Did the sun stream in just then? Did the sound of morning birds replace bullets? Sure, why not. Everything had suddenly become so open and alive, why couldn't the birds chirp on cue?

IT WAS THE summer of reinvention. Pilar dropped out of Smith to model full-time. She'd arrive home complaining, as she unpacked her latest wardrobe, about fashion's utter meaninglessness, and I'd sit on her floor, captivated, nodding like a bobblehead doll. Sydney hung female nudes and spoke fervently of civil disobedience. She began openly disparaging men in front of Doug and me. And my mother? She slid right into her new life, just as she had her old one. She quickly became a hit in the courtroom, and on days when the Orioles weren't playing at home, I started showing up to watch her try cases. One afternoon, she gave me a tour of the holding cells under the courthouse, and I, petrified, practically held on to her as prisoners shot me looks and took my measure. By the end of the summer, my mother and Sydney had fallen in with a radical crowd—bleeding-heart lawyers, liberal judges, Democratic lobbyists, gay rights and environmental activists. Almost all were women. They threw weekly dinner parties, edgy affairs dominated by talk of politics and protest. Occasionally, one of Sydney's friends, spurred on by classic Burgundy grand cru (my mother kept a well-stocked cellar to remind her, she once joked, of former pleasures), would take me to task for the ills of my gender or generation, and my mother would cut her off with a quick look or word. When it got too awkward, I'd sneak upstairs to catch the baseball scores, leaving the dinner guests to argue women's rights, health care, or poverty, until, inevitably, a car alarm went off or gunfire rang out and the real world showed up to crash the party.

BACK AT SCHOOL, my mother's legend grew. I told wild tales of courtroom triumphs—convicting rapists, staring down murderers (in truth, she was still prosecuting lesser crimes)—and hinted at knowledge of an activist underground plotting violence against our fascist government. I spoke of the house in Bolton Hill as some grand experiment in living, a logical progression from my mother's days as a student protester at Barnard.

One weekend my father showed up to watch me play hockey. At dinner, after the game, I suggested he give up his shallow life for something more genuine, something that mattered. He looked me over slowly.

"I hope you never know as much as you know right now," he said, shaking his head.

PERSISTENT IS REALITY. Persistent, but unpredictable. My father married Cynthia a few months after our chat. And then my mother and Sydney broke up. She told me over the phone (I was at school), and for some reason I took the news hard—until Douglas got on the line and reminded me that Sydney had never really liked us anyway.

I tried to imagine the scene, Sydney and Pilar angrily packing up their books and paintings and portfolios and disappearing down the road, only to land like a bomb in the middle of someone else's happy family. My mother told me she was fine, but in the quiet hours I worried about her, all alone in that narrow house, that nerve-racking neighborhood. And I wondered if she ever had second thoughts. No, I decided. She'd made her choices and wouldn't look back. This was just a small bump on the road to revolution.

WHEN SCHOOL LET out for the summer, I took the train to Montclair. Cynthia's house had a half-dozen open bedrooms (her kids were variously at cheerleading camp, posing for *Playboy*, or following the Dead), and still Doug and I were told to share one. Within days, a layer of ice developed between my new stepmother and me. Within a week I fell through. It started when I asked her to get rid of a cast-iron doorstop featuring a black man dressed as a jockey (my roommate at school was black, a fact I believed gave me moral standing in issues of race) and ended when she threw an empty vodka bottle at my head while my father entertained clients in the living room. The bottle smashed against the wall behind me, and in spite of his rapidly developing see-no-evil/hear-no-evil approach to family matters, my father came running.

I think he threatened to leave her that night. But in the end, it was Doug and I who left, via Amtrak, early the following morning.

———

"DO YOU THINK Mom will start dating men now?" Doug asked.

I had been dozing in the seat next to him as the train made its way south, but the question jolted me awake. I'd just assumed, I guess, that once you switched sexes that was it. But why not men? Again. After all, they were always expressing interest in her. My mother was still thin, attractive, successful, and God knows, interesting. Suddenly, a host of new possibilities began to emerge. What, for instance, if gender didn't really matter to her at all? What if she was attracted only to the individual, absent traditional boundaries such as sex or race?

"I . . . I don't know," I said, finally.

"Well, I think she's dating someone new," Douglas said, "because she's all excited again on the phone."

Her name was Beth. She came over that first night for dinner. Having spent the day running through dozens of possible scenarios—men, women, black, white—I realized I'd left this one out. Beth was shockingly normal. She wore makeup and earrings and sensible clothes. Her salt-and-pepper hair was short but in no way severe. It was a real-estate broker's bob, which made sense because that's what she was. She smiled warmly as she asked Douglas and me about school, and as we mumbled answers (we were out of practice; Sydney had never asked us anything), I found myself missing the tense talk of upheaval. Beth had no obvious agenda. She had no apparent causes. And she didn't wear her sexuality on her sleeve. She could have been the mother of any one of my friends, if she weren't casually holding my mother's hand across the table.

They seemed, on a basic level, to enjoy each other's company, and that was enough for Douglas but not for me. I was confused. Beth drove a Volvo and lived in the rolling horse country north of the city. It was Baltimore's equivalent of Montclair, which is exactly what my mother had been running from. Wasn't it?

Clearly, the grassroots insurgency we'd started—whatever it was exactly—was now on hiatus, and the next morning I told my mother as much.

"It must be fun living in that head of yours," she said.

FINE, I MAY have had an active imagination, but I wasn't completely oblivious. My mother's life was changing. Because Baltimore was changing. You could tell by the cars on the street, the noises invading our nights. Gentrification was losing, and nowhere was that more obvious than in our small urban enclave. Neighbors spoke of muggings. Car theft became part of life. My mother started parking in a private garage a few blocks from the house, then, if it was dark out, calling neighbors to escort her home.

Her job compounded the problem. She was good at what she did, and had quickly worked her way up the legal ranks. Now she *was* prosecuting major crimes, but with success came a certain lack of privacy, and worse, safety. The city couldn't keep up with its criminal elements. The jails were overrun, and violent felons were often back on the street within weeks of their sentencing. A few, here and there, remembered the prosecutor who had con-victed them.

If there was an upside, it was my mother's relationship with the Baltimore Police Department. Police officers were often her star witnesses, and in due course, friendships evolved. Soon a small group of cops was driving past my mother's house at regu-lar intervals. When they parked outside, I could only guess that my mother had received another threat.

This, then, became her new life. In two years she'd moved

from the offensive to the defensive. Dinners now consisted of long laments on government corruption, cronyism, incompetence. It was a new kind of talk, infused with unfamiliar bleakness. Beth would nod as my mother described some lazy judge or crooked politician, and then quickly change the subject to something cheerier, more banal. She was mothering my mother.

I LEFT FOR college the following year. By now I'd gotten used to being a part-time son, showing up only now and then—a long weekend in Montclair, a holiday in Baltimore. Kenyon was a liberal arts refuge in the cornfields of Ohio, and it offered a veritable petri dish of identities to those seeking one. I gradually gave up trying to mold my parents into best-case scenarios of themselves—not that anyone was listening to me anyway—and focused instead on finding my own way through life's increasingly complex equations.

BETH DIDN'T LAST a semester. I came home for Christmas to find my mother single again. A year ago I would have assumed that Beth wasn't radical enough, but now I figured it just didn't work out. My mother had started running in different circles. Her new friends were still advocates for one cause or another, but they were insiders too, more powerful, more plugged in, than the motley crew of local organizers that Sydney had championed. Most worked and lived in nearby Washington, D.C., and I recognized a few from Sunday morning talk shows. There was a polish to these people, a kind of self-assurance I'd later identify with the word "establishment." Instead of attacking the system from the outside, they were trying to change it from within. Or at least they said they were.

It took me a few years to realize my mother had become one

of them. I'd like to think I wasn't paying attention, but in truth, I just didn't want to admit it. She never had a problem with the establishment; she just wanted to join it on her own terms.

I FIRST HEARD of Susan during my junior year. My mother had been dating here and there, but no one seriously enough to mention or bring out for a visit (I know it all sounds backward, but back then my mother's love life *was* more interesting than mine). Suddenly, though, it was Susan this and Susan that, and then I was shaking her hand in the lounge at the Kenyon Inn while my mother stood there beaming. Supposedly, they'd flown in to watch me play baseball, but the real reason was evident enough.

Susan was a political reporter for one of the major networks. I'd seen her on TV—interviewing world leaders and reporting from convention floors—and in person she didn't disappoint. I must have asked her a hundred starry-eyed questions about newly elected President Clinton, and she patiently answered them all. But what I remembered most was my mother. With Sydney and Beth, she had always called the shots, but now she happily ceded ground. This was a union of equals, two women who knew exactly what they wanted, and against all odds, had found it in each other.

WITHIN A YEAR my mother had quit her job, sold the house in Bolton Hill, and moved in with Susan in Washington. No more threats from robbers and rapists. No more mace-gripping midnight walks home. And yet I can't help feeling those years in Baltimore were exactly what we needed. The place was flawed but real, and in those early years of reinvention that was all we could hope for.

People who live outside Washington wonder, with politics becoming so vitriolic, how the capital exists at all. It's a question of compromise, of course, but I think there's something else at work too. Working within the system—any system, really—tends to soften stances, temper indignation. Susan was like that. I just assumed that being an intelligent gay woman would make her an outspoken liberal, but that wasn't the case. I slowly came to realize that she might not even be a Democrat. Some of it was her job. She didn't vote because she didn't want to seem biased. She didn't like Clinton because he had lied to her during an interview. And she made enough money to care about taxes. Worse, she seemed to be affecting my mother.

"But you two are *gay*," I'd stammer halfway through dinner.

"And look at what Clinton did with gays in the military," Susan would answer.

"But it's the principle of the thing. I mean . . . the Democrats are still a lot better than the Republicans."

"Are they?" my mother asked. "Tell me one thing Clinton has actually followed through on. Health care? Gay rights? Gun control?"

"You've lost your mind."

Perhaps, but my mother had also found peace. As their relationship deepened, they bought a new, bigger house just north of Georgetown. They joined a country club and started playing golf on weekends. And they started traveling the world. Life had come neatly full circle.

I MOVED TO New York City after college, and my relationship with my father and his wife steadily improved. It was clear by now that Cynthia was here for the duration, and so I took a page out of my father's book and took the high road. And for the most part, it's worked. I go out to family dinners in Montclair and smile politely as she tells me about her day on the golf course or how nice the weather was on her latest trip to Europe.

And what of my father? He still goes to the office every day and plays golf all weekend long. It's funny, how we change. The consistency I once saw as monotonous, I now see as heartwarmingly reliable. We meet up for dinner in the city when we can— just the two of us—and though his politics are still questionable, I sit there enthralled as he speaks of all he's seen. Turns out he knows a thing or two.

ANOTHER HIGHWAY, FIFTEEN years later. My mother has come up to visit me and my girlfriend Jules at a cabin we rent in Woodstock, New York. It's still early spring and most of the shops and restaurants are still closed, so late last night Jules suggested we take her down to see the same-sex wedding ceremonies taking place a few towns away. It was an intriguing idea, but I wasn't so sure.

Every Sunday morning for the last month, the young mayor of New Paltz has been presiding over the nuptials of any same-sex couple that shows up. The same thing is happening in San Francisco and a few other progressive towns across America, but New Paltz is getting most of the press because it's so close to New York.

It's ironic that Jules thought of it and not me. I know it sounds strange, but Susan and my mother live such normal lives these days that I tend to forget they're even gay. Does my mother even care about this stuff anymore? At breakfast I casually threw the idea out there, and to my surprise she said she'd love to go. Now, an hour later, here we are in the car, my mother in the backseat chatting about golf school in Florida.

"If you'd only liked golf this much the first time around," I say.

"You think you're so clever."

Governor Pataki has declared the New Paltz ceremonies unconstitutional and has threatened arrests if they go on. But I'm more worried about the whole thing being some big media-created freak show. I guess I just want this to be real, the kind of historical moment we dared imagine all those years ago.

The ceremonies are to take place two at a time, in a field at the edge of town. We're a bit early so we wander around, watching the various parties—brides, grooms, friends, relatives, cops, reporters, protesters, clergy—prepare for whatever the day may hold. A *New York Times* reporter approaches my mother, and I'm surprised when she agrees to be interviewed. And then it starts. The first two couples appear: two older men in tuxedos, and on the other side of the field, two young women nervously holding hands. My mother gravitates toward the latter. People start taking pictures, protesters wave signs. And then the minister begins the vows. When the women exchange rings, the crowd erupts in applause. I glance over at my mother. She's crying.

A Package Deal

KATE CHRISTENSEN

Ben and I are truly each other's family.

From the get-go, Ben La Farge was my literary mentor as much as he was my stepfather. He and my mother fell in love in the summer of 1982—I was twenty, on my way to college, an aspiring writer and English major. Throughout my four years there, Ben, an English professor and poet, took the time to read all my papers and stories and talk to me about them. When I was getting an MFA in fiction, he carefully critiqued all my stories and the abortive beginnings of a novel. I'm still grateful for and amazed by the respect he accorded my most imitative, puerile ideas and writing.

Ben and my mother separated in 1989, when I was twenty-seven, the year I finished school and moved to New York. They divorced when I was thirty. In the years following their divorce, Ben and I kept in touch intermittently at first, then fell into a long silence necessitated by my loyalty to my mother and his loyalty to his new girlfriend. I continued to miss him even though I felt the gulf between us widening, possibly beyond repair.

Then, in 1996, around the time of my marriage, Ben and I managed slowly to forge a new bond, on a new footing: we chose to be each other's family again independently of our link through my mother. Things were different now: Ben had separated from the woman he'd been with after his divorce from my mother. My new husband, Jon Lewis, encouraged the reconciliation—I had told him all about Ben, how much I loved and missed him, what a father he'd always been to me. Two years later, when my sister Susan married Ben's nephew, Alan Nicolas, Ben and I became, literally, part of the same family. My two nephews are Ben's great-nephews; we now share descendants.

Ben is a poet and professor of English who comes from an American aristocratic family—he's descended from Benjamin Franklin, John Jacob Astor, and the painter John La Farge, and seems to be related in one way or another to the entire vast network of East Coast Ivy League blue bloods. He went to Harvard and Oxford and served a stint in the army before he married First Wife Susan (as he's always called her). He worked as a book editor in New York in the heyday of the three-martini lunch and spent hours at Elaine's, bending his elbow over vodka on the rocks and late-night scotch. He got out to save his liver and lights about thirty years ago and went to teach English at Bard College, where he's still going strong at seventy-three.

As for me, I come from a small, splintered, far-flung family made up of eccentrics, fanatics, and artists on my mother's side and Minnesota Norwegians on my father's, most of whom I've never met. My own father has been totally absent from my life since I was nine. I grew up out West, in California and Arizona. When I was a kid, we moved every two or three years. Next to Ben, I feel like a desert rat, a mutt, an outsider. But as divergent as our backgrounds and histories may be, these circumstantial differences feel largely superficial. As Ben put it in a recent e-mail to me, "A good part of my attraction to your mother was the underlying similarity between her family and my mother's family—especially between Ruth and Hester [their mothers] as eccentrics."

To show some of the many ways in which Ben and I are truly

each other's family, I went through the nearly nine hundred e-mails we've written to each other since the spring of 2000, when Ben got his first computer, and chose the following (edited) handful of e-mails, exchanged during the winter of 2002–2003.

Katie,

How are you two? I'm wondering if you have yet found time to listen to the Johnny Hodges CDs I lent you. You said you would copy them. I'd like to know if you like them, or are they too classical—too controlled, like Mozart or Jane Austen?

Love,

Ben

Dear Ben,

I never said Mozart and Jane Austen were too controlled. Anyway, Jon and I have rifled through our CD collection. We know they're here somewhere because where else would they be? But in the interest of getting them back to you as soon as possible, I'm going to order them on Amazon, have them sent here first so we can copy them for ourselves and send them on to you. What are they called? I checked out Johnny Hodges CDs on Amazon.com and there are 37, so I hope you remember which one it was . . . I'm so sorry. We've been disorganized lately, haven't listened to CDs in a while—

Love,

Katie

Dear Katie,

It crossed my mind after I handed you those CDs (in one plastic packet) that I might never see them again.

Like your mother, I've noticed, you're rather careless about material things. Could that be a perverse vestige of your family's high-minded anthropop [short for anthroposophist/-ical, follower/philosophy of Rudolf Steiner, referring to my maternal grandparents] culture (i.e., material goods don't count)? I'm not entirely kidding: the older I get the more convinced I am that family culture is our principal formative influence. I remember handing you the packet (which includes 2 CDs) just before we got up from the table in the Museum. You put it in your handbag. On the cover of the packet is a black-and-white photo of Hodges, facing us, playing his sax.

Sorry I am sounding so crotchety, but I thought I made it clear when I handed you the case that I wanted it back; you even said you would copy them so that you could give them back next time we met.

Love,

Ben

Dear Ben,

I don't blame you for being upset, but at this point I can't really do anything but apologize and offer to replace them. And the following strikes me as unnecessary lashing out, not kidding at all and extremely annoying: "Like your mother, I've noticed, you're rather careless about material things. Could that be a perverse vestige of your family's high-minded anthropop culture (i.e., material goods don't count)?" You've noticed from when, half my life ago? "Like your mother"?! Since when is she careless?

Of course I'll buy you a new set. And I know the ones you loaned us will turn up. I offered to replace the other ones because I could tell you wanted them back in a hurry. If they were part of a precious set and you had a feeling you would never see them again, why then did you loan them out? We didn't ask you for them.

Actually, I am careful about material things, and I'm not a fucking anthropop.

More when I cool down.

Katie

Dearest Katie,

You're right. The remark in my letter that you quote IS unfair. I know you're not an anthropop, and I'm glad to be told you are in fact quite careful about material things. So please accept my apology for being so irascibly unfair. But please do NOT try to buy me a new set. I am sure it will turn up, as you say. If you can't find it, I don't want you to buy me a new one. It's easier for me to buy it than for you, since they know me and may be willing to sell me one packet out of the whole boxed set, which comes in a large book-like package, doubtless designed that way to make one feel he's getting his money's worth. The ultimate irony will be if you don't like it when you finally get to hear it.

Maybe the real problem is that I've become a crotchety old misfit.

Love,

Ben

Dear Ben,

I just logged on to say that I've cooled down, and found your e-mail. Thank you so much for writing back

so conciliatorily . . . I've been upset about not being able
to find the CD(s) (now it's not clear whether it was 1 or
2) you loaned us . . . I've been poking around byways of
our loft all evening thinking it's lodged in one of them
but no luck so far. Maybe I took it to my studio and stuck
it in with all the other CDs I have there—I'll check
tomorrow—I haven't been there in a while and didn't
make it there today. In the meantime, I apologize again
for making you crotchety.

I know you think we're all products of our upbringing
and families, and I disagree, I think we are whoever we
are at birth no matter where we land. I picture you over
there in the nurture camp, a sort of day-care therapy spa
with wet nurses for counselors; my nature camp has
counselors in Birkenstocks in hempen tents, sylvan
meadow and mountain lake. If you tell me I'm in the
nature camp because my mother is and I learned this
attitude from her, I might have to sock you as the only
possible rejoinder.

Much, much love,
Katie

Dear Katie,

I knew that line would stick in your craw even while I
was punching the "Send Now" button, but I was in a
rush and I figured I could justify the remark if you took
offense. Just so you know, my seemingly nasty remark
about your family culture was not intended as an insult
but as praise: yes, I think Ruth's high-minded idealism
gave your family an admirable culture (even though your
mother had to suffer for it).

I love your picture of a day-care camp for grown-ups like me. Very insulting, but I laughed, so you don't have to sock me.

Love,

Ben

Dear Ben,

I still might have to sock you.

I checked my studio: not there. I am going to keep looking . . . I want nothing more than to restore Johnny's missing parts to him.

Last night Jon and I went to a Dawn Powell play with three friends, and of course the actors swilled stage-booze for the whole play, making us so thirsty and jeal-ous we had to rush to the Russian Vodka Room the minute it ended. We toasted Dawn a few times . . . It was worth it, because the intimidating, scowling (why are they all like that?) Russian waitress told us that we knew how to drink. Now I have nothing more to prove. All righty then, I'm off to do my wonderful chores . . .

Love,

Katie

Dear Katie,

I don't know where the Russian Vodka Room is, but I take it you don't mean the Russian Tea Room, next door to Carnegie Hall. I'm surprised you find the Russian waitresses intimidating, scowling. On my cruise through the inland waterways of Russia three years ago, I was in love with at least three of the waitresses, all of them smiling. On the night when members of the crew, according to an old custom, entertained the passengers with music, dancing, etc, the sexiest of those girls dragged me from my seat, where I was cowering in the back of the top-deck bar, and made me dance while she, dressed as an Arab, pretended to seduce me (in front of my fellow American tourists) with a belly-dance. I got my revenge by pretending to be a matador and holding my jacket like a red cloth in front of her as the bull while she writhed her way down to the floor.

Love,
Ben

Dear Ben,
NEWS FLASH!!! Jon found the Johnny Hodges CDs right where we've both been looking all along: the front row of our CD collection . . . right under our noses.

Who killed whom, you or the waitress?

All right, it's almost time to run off to therapy, the safety valve for all us (naively) optimistic self-improving self-determining self-defining self-centric Americans.

Much love,
Katie

Dear Katie,
Hooray for Jon! But now you will be getting an album full of Hodges CDs which will probably bore you. It might have been different, of course, if I had been there to nurture you in your childhood: then you would have grown up whistling Hodges on your way to school.

And a thousand Amens. We live in a Culture of Therapy which has had the unhappy effect of convincing the last two generations of college students that they are Victims. Last year a student got permission to address the whole faculty (forty five full minutes) on the problem of students "afflicted" with one ailment or another (starting of course with dyslexia, which he claimed to be his own problem). He appealed to us to show more sensitivity, etc. The irony was that he spoke, in fact he read, without any difficulty from a text he had written, which was grammatically impeccable. He had us all cowed. Not one of us dared suggest, even after he had departed, that maybe he was putting us on.

Love,

Ben

Dear Ben,

I'm laughing out loud about that student. God, academia sounds awful. How can you stand it?

We finally listened to the Johnny Hodges; you'll be shocked to learn that we liked it. And I get to return the Johnny Hodges I ordered, because Mosaic sent me the wrong boxed set—they sent some dude I'd never heard of who's probably great, but I plan to send it back and request a refund and that'll be the end of that.

Do you want to see the marriage essay I wrote for my friend Cathi's book? (Remember how you were so amused that after 4—well, now 5—years of marriage I think I have anything to say about it . . . ? well, maybe I don't, but I managed to eke out a few pages on the subject anyway.)

Love,

Katie

Dear Katie,

I have to take back my condescending amusement at the thought of you making pronouncements on this subject after only four years of being married. Not only are you now in your fifth year, but I myself was only married to Liz (I mean living with her) for five years. And it's pretty clear that you guys are better at it than she and I were. Your marriage essay is very beautiful. I ended it with a big lump in my throat. But now that you tell us you're both still wrestling with the issue, I find myself almost wishing you would agree to have a child. At the same time two obnoxious voices keep nagging. One says, Yes, but don't forget the Pusch gene for deafness. The other says, Yes, but none of the greatest women writers in English (Austen, Eliot, Woolf, Wharton, Cather, and Powell) had children. Eine probleme.

I just saw *A Beautiful Mind*, swallowed a bucket of tears at the end, wishing I were a genius and had a wife like that, but walked out realizing I'd been had.

Love,

Ben

Dear Katie,

I'm feeling guilty about the remarks I made in my last e-mail—my take on your beautiful marriage essay. It's another example of my not knowing how to respect the boundary lines of what is or is not appropriate. Your essay had triggered memories of a comparable (though not similar) struggle that First Wife Susan and I had in the last year or so of our marriage. As I think you know, a case of the mumps when I was 17 had rendered me infertile, and after several sperm tests confirmed that I really was, Susan and I began to discuss the possibility of adopting a child.

At first she took the position that it was all right with

her if we couldn't have children—after all, a childless marriage without competing love-ties may have a better chance of lasting happily. But her physician had planted the notion in my head that most women wanted children, and probably out of guilt (because I couldn't give her one) I insisted we think about it. But then, as she began to warm up to the idea, I began to back off from it. Actually, I remember being frightened. What if the child turned out to be stupid? Or neurotic, etc.? To each of my objections, Susan had a convincing reply: the chances of a child turning out to be stupid or neurotic were no greater with an adopted than with a biological child, etc. Yet deep down in my insecure soul, which had been nurtured by my parents' unacknowledged snobbery, I didn't believe that I could love or even respect a child who did not carry the Emmet-La Farge genes, although this was a fear that I was not able to admit to myself at the time.

All of these memories were buzzing around my head when I wrote you that note on Monday. If I had had First-Wife Susan's wits about me, I would have realized that even if you stick with your decision not to have children, your childlessness will be no guarantee that either you or Jon will turn out to be great artists. The risk of being sorry you did not have kids is probably greater than the risk that neither one of you may turn out to have brilliant careers. One reason I married your mother even though I knew I was taking an enormous risk, was that the marriage was a package deal—with three extraordinary daughters. It was my last and only chance to have a family of my own.

I realize of course that this letter only compounds the

boundary-breaching previous letter, but perhaps the little narrative about my own struggle with the question
will explain, if not justify, the breach.

Love,

Ben

Dear Ben,

I'm glad you got us, three fatherless girls, and we got
you, a teenage mumps victim who couldn't have his own
kids. Susan [my sister] and I were just saying to each other
that you are the father we never had—from the start you
always bolstered us, made us feel like what we had to say
was worthwhile, gave us the confidence to argue with you,
express our opinions. You took us seriously even as you
guided us, like a father . . . and you still do.

And put your paranoia to rest—nothing you can say
on the subject of children is anything Jon and I haven't
thought and said and rehashed ourselves a zillion
times—of course any and all advice is appreciated, from
both sides of the issue, you can't possibly offend me. As
for what you're assuming is a gamble on two brilliant
careers . . . of course we hope our own work and each
other's will be good—but even if we die obscure, we still
will have had the freedom to do our (mediocre) work. I
don't want to regret not having had the chance to write
enough books because of sleepless nights of fevers,
school meetings and all those endless fucking birthday
parties and playdates and all the constant chatter and
noise of kids—even now, I feel panicked and pressed for
time, and I have all the time in the world. It's a choice
we've made with eyes open as possible. It's not as if we're
making it a trade-off with kids—as in, I think we're both

going to be famous so let's not have them—plenty of people do both, of course, but we see that as a compromise of sorts that we don't want to have to make.

Love,

Katie

p.s. Dawn Powell actually had an autistic, emotionally disturbed son who once beat her up and generally made her life hell although she was devoted to him. Very instructive.

Katie,

Thanks for reassuring me that my letter was not offensive. From "If we die obscure . . ." down to "but we see that as a compromise of sorts that we don't want to have to make" should be engraved on some space age metal like the exterior of the Bilbao Guggenheim. All I can say is Right on, I'm with you all the way.

Today is Friday, if I'm not mistaken. So tomorrow we meet for dinner at 8:00 p.m. chez Jules, joined by First Wife Susan. I can hardly wait.

Love,

Ben

Dear Katie,

That was a lot of fun. It even pleased me at the end that you and First Wife Susan were bonding at my expense—I mean, when you joked about my putative addiction to knee-jerk Freudian ways of explaining things ("He's that way because his mother . . . etc."). I still maintain that Tolstoy has an agenda in *Anna Karenina*: for all his impressive empathy (his ability to imagine himself as a woman), he was out to punish Anna for leaving her son and her husband. In Tolstoy's view, women should be content with their role as wives and mothers. One doesn't have to know that he felt threatened by the new feminism that was sweeping over Europe in the 1870s (and that he encountered in George Sand's novels, etc.) to see this, but given the famous ending it cannot be denied that he condemned Anna's behavior even while he understood it perfectly. On the other hand, I would certainly agree that his extraordinary empathy for Anna (like his empathy for the other major female characters in his fiction: Natasha and Princess Mary in *War and Peace*, the female narrator in *Family Happiness*, Pozdnyshev's wife in *The Kreutzer Sonata*) is so beautifully and convincingly rendered that one finds it hard to believe that he wanted to keep women in "their place."

Love,
Ben

Dear Ben,

What a fun night! It was such a treat to see you. I hope the restaurant choice was okay. I think Jon's filet mignon was the best thing, although I didn't taste First Wife Susan's duck . . . About the *Anna Karenina* argument—unlike F.W.S., I completely agreed with what you were saying . . . I think it's interesting that Tolstoy was able to force himself to overcome his original revulsion for Anna enough to make her so real and sympathetic, but I can't stand that she has to die because he apparently could envision no other ending for her; the plot feels to me like the train that eventually kills her, inex-

orable and on a narrow track, but it's still one of the
greatest novels I've ever read.
    Love,
    Katie

    Dear Katie,
    Your metaphor about the plot—that "it feels to you
like the train that eventually kills her, inexorable and on
a narrow track"—is deft but also of great interest to me
for another reason: that you, like most writers and readers of your generation, seem to be repelled by the very
idea of plot. Is it because the artificiality is so contrary to
the unpredictable flow of real life, or for some other reason I'm too dense (and hot) to see? I suspect your feelings are analogous to the way so many contemporaries
(yours and mine) feel about rhyme and meter in poetry.
The formal restrictions seem to curtail the natural
expression of feeling in poetry and the possibilities of different solutions, different resolutions in fiction.
    I don't share those feelings; I still love meter and
rhyme, and I still love a well-made plot (as in Jane
Austen's ironic use of sentimental comedy, with its de
rigueur happy ending), but I know they seem false to
nearly everyone else nowadays. Well, except that more
and more students are coming to me to learn how to
write metrical verse; in fact, I'm giving a course called
Writing Metrical Verse this fall. The plots of your first
two novels seem true to life—i.e., NOT governed by
some predetermined scheme—and yet they are almost
identical to each other: the protagonist starts out in a
state of low-self-esteem or dependency and gradually
pulls out of it, rising to a state of feeling more in control

of her/his own life. You succeed in making this seem very plausible, but I wish to point out (he said, mischievously) that the identity of plot in both novels suggests that their author was compelled by some pre-existing narrative of self-liberation she wants to believe and wants us to believe, however unconsciously!

Ian McEwen's new novel, *Atonement*, which is the most brilliant work of fiction I've read this year, starts out in the Austen mode, then switches to something very different, then switches again, all of these switches giving the impression of breaking away (or trying to break away) from PLOT but simultaneously drawing the reader on with the same kind of expectation that highly plotted novels engender—only to pull the rug out from underneath that expectation at the end. McEwen is notorious for being too much in control, but this time I think he has succeeded in writing a great or near-great work of art. So plot is still alive and well!

Speaking of which, did you read the review of the two new biographies of Edna St. Vincent Millay in the July issue of *Harper's* that I mentioned in one of my e-mails several weeks ago? The reviewer made a very strong case for taking Millay seriously again, and in re-reading her I find, much to my surprise, that her best poems (mostly sonnets but some others too) are by no means as sentimental or girlish as I had thought. Her values and her attitude about sexual love are quintessential Nineteen Twenties, like Cavalier poetry of the 17th century: carpe diem!

Love,

Ben

Dear Ben,

About plot, it never bothered me at all that, for example, Wharton knew Lily Bart's fate from the outset in *The House of Mirth*. It does bother me in *Anna Karenina*, but even so, the fact that Anna is so real is somehow a testament to Tolstoy's brilliance—her realness transcends the limitations of his dogmatic social ideas, and that's why I think she deserved a better ending. Not Lily though, for some reason. She's as real as Anna, but maybe her death feels more justified by what comes before.

The plot of my first novel was inspired by an English novel (*Lucky Jim*). So take that, professor. My second one is all you say, mea culpa, but this new one I'm working on is a whole new tamale—not autobiographical at all.

I agree that *Atonement* is brilliant—until the horrible ending, when I see his hand moving the characters around like puppets. If there's any revulsion I feel for plot, it's when the author shows his hand—it literally makes me want to throw the book out the window. But as long as the characters appear to have wills of their own, I'm happy as a little kid with a bedtime story. That, I think, is the essential difference for me between Anna's death and Lily's . . . Lily's feels inevitable and tragic, Anna's feels like Tolstoy is punishing her.

As far as Millay goes, I've read and loved her since high school. She never struck me as sentimental. Her combination of detachment and passion always seemed sophisticated, brave, raw to me . . . the constraints of the sonnet enhance the wide swath cut by her content, gird it up, bolster it in a way . . . maybe not dissimilarly to the way Austen's well-made plots enhance her depth of character and refreshingly ironic take on humanity. You seem to forget that I've always been extremely old-fashioned and conservative when it comes to books and poetry, like you.

Love,
Katie

Katie,

I like what you're saying about "the constraints of form" in Millay, how they "enhance the wide swath cut by her content, gird it up . . . maybe not dissimilarly to the way Austen's well-made plots enhance her depth of character . . . etc." But I don't think those constraints just enhance; I think they actually make possible what both writers are able to achieve. Both Millay and Austen work within literary conventions, but what they do with them is what makes them unique. Millay kept re-writing the 16th century sonnet, which is why the academic modernists dismissed her for the past fifty years, but many of her sonnets are as great as the ones she was imitating. (Imitation is not the same as copying.) Austen's plots are very similar to the great plots of 18th century comedy (Congreve's *Way of the World*, Sheridan's *School for Scandal*, etc.), but she ironizes them, subverts them with her sly unheroic view of her characters.

Austen came back into favor ten years ago because she spoke to our need for a more "civil" society, a society in which "good manners" governed the relation between the sexes and within families—this at a time when New York City seemed to be coming apart at the seams and divorce was raging through the suburbs. But Austen was also fighting against those formal constraints, resisting them even while being dutifully faithful to the shibboleths of literary convention, and this I think is the source of her wit. Wit is something foreign to American sensibilities. We like our fictions and our poems to be "earnest" and "natural," true to life as we think we know it. Wit puts us off, because it seems aloof; and indeed it comes out of a view of life that is contrary to our American earnestness. The English McEwen has it, the American Russo does not. (I cannot say that one is better than the other, only that their ways of looking at life are different.) Wit is not possible without formal constraints: Dickinson, Frost, and Eliot all have it, Stevens at times; it's harder to achieve in free verse, although Billy Collins, our new Poet Laureate (but a light-weight) has it. (By wit I don't mean ha-ha funny; I mean the discovery of some resemblance in things apparently dissimilar.) Millay's language is seldom witty, but her view of life, which you aptly call a "combination of detachment and passion," is. I think the greatest novelists are able to reach beyond autobiography, even while drawing from it, as Tolstoy does in Anna K., and as Jane Austen wrote about the people and the society she knew, drawing upon her autobiographical experience but simultaneously converting it into something different.

Love,
Ben

Dear Ben,
The conversion of raw life experience into a totally new thing reminds me of Rumpelstiltskin turning straw into gold—interesting about Austen's coming back into favor, the way long-dead writers can have second, third, fourth lives depending on who's around at the time.

What I took away from last night, most of all, was gratitude that you and I talked about the years we lost touch and both agreed we regretted them. I'm SO glad you came into our family, or vice versa, even though your inability to have kids of your own was a large part of what ended your marriage to F.W.S. We were so lucky to get you.

Love,

Katie

Dear Katie

I love your remark that what you took away from the evening was "gratitude" that you and I had talked about the "years we lost touch and both agreed we regretted them." You have no idea how much it has meant to me that you and I were able to pick up where we had left off when Liz and I were divorced. You have brought a great deal of sheer joy—the joy of life—into my life.

Love,

Ben

Wicked*

ROXANA ROBINSON

> I ask her the question, trying to sound calm and
> objective. I ask her what it was like, being a stepchild.
> Being my stepchild.

It is 1996. My stepdaughter and I are at Starbucks, on First Avenue, where I have asked her to meet me. We are standing side by side at the counter, waiting to order. We're almost the same height, and we both have straight dark hair and blue eyes, but we don't look at all alike. She looks exactly like her mother, and always has.

I was perfectly happy to become a stepmother, though I was troubled by the reputation. In all the stories, the stepmother is always wicked, always cruel to children. Wolves are cruel, too, but not wicked. Wolves are the natural enemies of children, and they're meant to be savage. Widowed kings and poor woodcutters don't marry wolves and ask them to raise their children. They marry women, the natural protectors of children, who are meant to be warm and maternal. So why was it that women who became stepmothers acted like wolves?

I was mystified by this, but not alarmed. I was already a mother, and I knew that being a stepmother was like being a mother, amplified. I knew who I was. I was a woman. I knew what my nature was. I wouldn't act like a wolf.

* Portions of this essay appeared under a different title and in a different form in *Vogue*, February 1997.

SHE WAS FIVE when I first met her, a skinny restless little girl with fierce eyebrows. She was angry, and why not? Her world had just been blown to bits by the people most responsible for keeping it safe. I understood that, and sympathized. Her anger didn't worry me.

Becoming a stepmother isn't something you do deliberately. You aren't driven to it by love and longing; you're driven to something else by love and longing, and you slip sideways into stepmothering. At the time, this sideways slip seems secondary, manageable.

IT'S TWO O'CLOCK in the afternoon. It was I who suggested Starbucks, where I've never been. I thought it would be a good place for us to talk. But I think it only sells coffee, and now, since I've missed lunch, I wish I'd suggested a restaurant.

"I wish they had food here," I say to my stepdaughter. "I'm *famished*." I say this theatrically, trying to be amusing.

My stepdaughter raises her eyebrows. Her face is remote and expressionless, except for the raised eyebrows, as though she is too polite to show anything but this small part of her response: faint and languid surprise.

"They have food here," she says without inflection.

"Oh, they do?" I repeat stupidly.

She does not bother to speak again. She nods, her face now completely blank, and looks away.

My stepdaughter is highly urban; of course she has been to Starbucks many times. This exchange—my ignorance, her cool response—makes me feel gauche and elderly, an incompetent visitor to her world.

She is now twenty-seven, still lean, still with fierce eyebrows. She is forceful and beautiful, with high cheekbones and a broad intelligent face. Her hair is very short, parted on one side and combed to the other, like James Dean. Just now her hair is black, and stiffened, so that it looks wet, and holds the strokes of her comb. She wears only black: short little black skirts, thin droopy black sweaters, clunky black shoes. This also makes me feel gauche and elderly.

After I became her stepmother she went on being angry; my sympathy had no effect. She stayed angry for nearly two decades, slamming doors, breaking rules, leaving schools. She rebelled against everything, but, it seemed to me, particularly us, particularly me. I stopped wondering why stepmothers were always so wicked.

YOU'RE A WIDOW, with two daughters in their late teens. You have remarried, which is fortunate, because, at this moment in history, marriage is the only career available. It's especially fortunate that you have married a wealthy nobleman, but your story doesn't end here, happily ever after, because you are not only a wife but a mother. Your own happy ending depends on your daughters' happy beginnings. You love your daughters very much, especially since their father is dead. A part of their life is missing, and you are particularly tender and protective toward them.

Your husband has a daughter too. She's younger than yours and, you have to admit, more beautiful. You could not love your daughters more, but you know that a girl's face is her fortune, and in your heart you know that your daughters are not rich. They are, rather charmingly, plump, and it's true that the older one's chin juts forward rather, and the younger one's mouth is perhaps too small for her nose. But they are wonderful young women, so lively and funny.

In the evenings, when the fire is lit, they come in and sit with you in your little room next to the Bedchamber. The three of you sit by the fire, doing needlework and telling stories. Sometimes you tell them about their father. Sometimes the older one tickles the younger one, and the younger one shrieks, and falls over backward on the fur hearthrug. She laughs helplessly, and, kicking, she tangles up your skeins of wool. You tell her to stop shrieking, and you tell her sister to leave her alone, but you are not angry: you love them. The firelight flickers on the tapestries against the thick stone walls of your house. It flickers on the silk damask that covers the divan, and on the two girls laughing and wrestling on the fur hearthrug.

In the doorway appears Cinderella. The firelight flickers on her, too: her shawl of blond hair, her radiant skin. The grave blue eyes, the gentle sweep of her mouth. She is so beautiful that you cannot take your eyes from her, which infuriates you.

Irritably, you ask her what she wants. She has no good answer, and you send her off somewhere, out of your sight. You want her gone: if she is there when your husband arrives, he will sit down on the divan and pull her down next to him. He will put his arm around her and kiss her forehead. A row of small kisses that should go to you will go to her, tiny ones, along her hairline. He will hold her close, thinking of her beautiful mother, who died and whom he loved; whom he may have loved more than he loves you, whom he may still love more than he loves you, you will never know.

Every time you see Cinderella she reminds you of all this, and of the terrible inequality between her and your daughters, which nothing you can do can alter. Even if you were to make her wash the dishes every night, and sleep in the kitchen, even if you locked her in the dungeon (which you would never dream of doing: you are, after all, a good person), no matter what, she will still be heartrendingly beautiful.

Every time you see her, you fear again that your daughters, who are not the daughters of a nobleman, will not find husbands.

They will not bear children, and in the eyes of the world they will be failures. You will have no grandchildren, your family will die with your daughters. They will stay in the castle with you for the rest of their lives. They will turn quieter and sadder, and in the evenings they will no longer wrestle on the hearthrug but sit silently beside you on the silk sofa, and the needlework you do will pile up around you.

But a handsome prince arrives, a ball planned. Your daughters are invited, of course. Cinderella, who is younger, is not invited. Obviously, it would not be appropriate for her to go, but since she is an adolescent, she doesn't care what is appropriate, and wants to go anyway. Of course you tell her she may not, and when her father asks, you tell him with some asperity that it is out of the question.

At home there is a flurry of preparations: lace, ribbons, sweeping skirts. Your girls are tremulous with excitement. They arrive at the ball in high spirits. The floor is smooth and polished, the huge chandeliers gleam in flickering tiers. Your gallant girls look wonderful, in cascades of silk and velvet. Their hair is sleek and glossy, their eyes are shining. Why would a prince not love them?

But there is treachery afoot. Cinderella, who stops at nothing, has flatly disobeyed you. The moment your back was turned she produced a fairy godmother, who cast a magic spell. Of course, anyone would look beautiful under a magic spell. Your own beloved girls could have had their eyes taken care of, the chin, the mouth! They wouldn't have bothered with such absurd things—footmen in livery!

So it is that you see your daughters, standing, mute and partnerless, in the shadows by the door. Their eyes are on the Prince. He is dancing with a beautiful young woman, who gazes up at him. You cannot believe your eyes: it is her, it is your worst enemy, with her magic spells and her long eyelashes. It will be she who wins the great prize—a woman's happiness in the world. Your own darling girls, who are so funny, so worthwhile, will not achieve this, and you are helpless to help them. It is back to the small chamber in the evenings, and the needlework. Of course it's too late now, but you think of the dungeon.

BEFOREHAND, OF COURSE, we all plan to act like women. We know what we are: warm, kind. We're women. But there are powerful forces, driving us to act like wolves.

IT SEEMS THAT your stepdaughter is not a whole, separate person to you, as anyone else's child would be. Your stepdaughter is a transparent form, an outline in space through which you can see Her Mother. Everything your stepdaughter does, her clothes, her haircut, her habits, her speech, all speak threateningly to you of that rival organization, The First Marriage. They are all messages from Her Mother, that dread and monstrous Other. She is the woman to whom your own husband, your own private continent (across whom you now stretch and roam so freely) was once joined.

In another time, another universe, before this normal, real universe began, no matter what he tells you now, your husband loved her. Her body embraced his, received it. They said things to each other, alone, in bed, in the car, at breakfast, that you will never know about. It is inconceivable to you, outrageous, but it is true. You can't erase it, you can't make it not true. You'd like to go back and expunge that piece of history, erase it from the sky, and make your husband deny that marriage as he now denies his love, but he can't. Every time you see that child, the issue again arises: he loved someone else, she loved him.

And here is the issue herself, coming in through the door and letting it slam. Here she is, tattooed, messy, chewing gum and dropping her jacket on the floor, despite the fact you have told her that in this marriage, in this epoch, all these things are forbidden. She disregards your rules because they are not her mother's; she flouts your authority because you are not important to her, or anyway this is what you believe.

Even if these are not her motives, she is, merely by her presence, establishing an outpost, a small piece of alien territory deep within the borders of your life. Worse, your husband, who should be your ally against this subtle and insidious invasion, is not. In this matter he is your enemy too. He encourages the invasion, he protects the intruder. You have no ally here, you have no choice. You are alone on this rocky slope. Your mountain fastness, in fact your entire domain, perhaps even your life as a wife, is under attack. You have no choice. Deep in your throat, you growl. You lift your black lip. You show your savage teeth.

STARBUCKS IS NEARLY empty, and we carry our things to a table in the window. The room is large and open, with a high ceiling and big windows onto First Avenue. I talk too much, chattering; she is silent and unresponsive. This is normal behavior for us, but today we have a reason to be particularly anxious: I've told her that I want to talk about our past. I want to know her version of it, I want to know how it felt to be my stepdaughter.

At the table, I unwrap my sandwich and ask her about her work. She is in the movie business, the production side. I can't even imagine what this is like: impossible hours, overpowering egos, advanced technology. She is good at it: after years of rebellion, she is now disciplined and immensely hard-working.

She tells me a cool and funny anecdote about the current movie. I laugh hard, because she never does. She is always cool. As a child, she was never enthusiastic, she shrugged her shoulders at our newborn puppies. She is still deeply reserved, but of course I only see her when I'm around.

She lives downtown, in the East Village. I've only seen her apartment once, when her father asked if we could come. She has never invited me. It's a fifth-floor walk-up, little rooms that open into each other, no halls. The style is austere nineteen fifties: everything is metal, everything is black or white or gray. It's spare and immaculate; I've never seen such a clean apartment. One thing we used to fight over was the state of her room.

I finish my sandwich, crumple the plastic wrap and clear my throat. The moment has arrived. I ask her the question, trying to sound calm and objective. I ask her what it was like, being a stepchild. Being my stepchild. I take a drink of lemonade and cross my legs under the table, wrapping them tightly around each other, for protection.

My stepdaughter looks out the big plate glass window, at the traffic rumbling up First Avenue. She leans her elbow on the table, and puts her chin on her fist. She frowns, concentrating, and begins to talk, without looking at me. A woman in a red coat stops outside, with a Shi-Tzu on a leash. The woman is large, with a cloud of frizzy hair. The dog has a barrette on its forehead, holding the hair out of its eyes. My stepdaughter talks steadily. She has thought about this, she is candid and articulate. She isn't angry, which makes what she says more powerful. The woman outside twitches at the leash. Her mouth goes straight down at the corners, and she looks impatient and disagreeable. I cannot take my eyes off her. I listen to my stepdaughter: everything she says makes my heart sink further.

I don't explain myself to her, I don't justify my behavior. I know what it was like for me, I have my excuses, I've repeated them to myself for years. Now it's her turn. I let her talk, and she does.

We stare at the woman on the sidewalk, tugging crossly at the leash. I hear about those awful weekends, the terrible vacations, from her side.

I hear what it was like to appear in the doorway as an enemy; to stay in a place where all you said and did was counted against you; to be the child in the alien household, where all the rules were different, where there was no mother to comfort and protect you.

PAINFUL, SO MUCH later, to hear about the chances you missed. Painful to hear all the ways in which you fitted so neatly, so perfectly into the long savage snarl of that lupine profile. Painful to realize now, that that transparent outline held inside it a little girl, toward whom you had a chance to be the kind of person you thought you were.

My Papa Married Your Mama

TED ROSE

*What happens when the marriage that forged the
alliance no longer exists?*

The introductions at Jonah's wedding proved particularly
thorny: "How do you know each other?" his friends pre-
dictably asked me. I fumbled for a reply. Our relationship
didn't fit into predictable categories. We weren't old college bud-
dies or former business colleagues. By name, by law, and by
blood, we shared no familial connection. We were not even distant cousins. Yet there I was, at an inn in the middle of the Colorado Rockies, a guest at his wedding. And I had traveled halfway
across the country to attend.

When Jonah and I met, he was eight and I was seven. In my
first memory of him, he is squatting behind the side of a bed in
a hotel room; I am squatting behind the other. His mother and
my father have taken us to Disneyland. We are both only children, both dedicated loners, and our parents' decision to introduce us over the course of a weekend at the theme park has
proved brilliant. Inside the gates of the Magic Kingdom, we
quickly bond. Of course, it only goes so far. The time has come
to change into our swim trunks, and we eye each other warily.
Neither of us wants the other to see him naked.

In my second memory, we are drinking Shirley Temples. We
are being jostled by adults at a wedding reception for our parents.

We wear matching red T-shirts with black lettering. Mine says *My Papa Married Your Mama*. His says *My Mama Married Your Papa*. We both have bowl haircuts, rosy fat cheeks, and funny looking teeth. Jonah's hair is a little darker than mine, but the resemblance is uncanny. We look like brothers.

AFTER THE WEDDING, Jonah and his mama move in with my papa in southern California. I head back east to Connecticut, where I live with my own mama. I visit during the summers, but often that's when Jonah visits his papa in the Bay Area. We share a few experiences: we divide up the backseat of the car on a trip across the desert; we peek over the rim of the Grand Canyon together and toss softballs into milk urns at Circus Circus in Las Vegas. When seventh grade begins, I fly out to southern California to spend the year. For the first and only time, Jonah and I will live together. I arrive in California the garden-variety mama's boy. I am confident that true happiness lies in convincing the adults of my world that I am infallible.

Jonah is everything I am not. He is a rebel. He smokes clove cigarettes, rides a skateboard, and listens to the Clash. The school calls regularly to invite our parents to meetings discussing Jonah's absenteeism and disruptive behavior. My father frets about Jonah. My stepmother frets too, but she finds another way to cope. She grows scornful of me. When I ace a test or a paper, she calls me a "good boy" and she does not mean it as a compliment. She suggests that my successes are efforts to make Jonah look bad. This argument is preposterous—I worship Jonah—and yet I become worried that it nonetheless is true. She has appealed to my preternatural guilt. I'm terrified that my stepmother will turn my father against me, that I'll be kicked out of the family, and that my new worst fear will be realized: I won't get to be Jonah's brother anymore.

Meanwhile, I buy a skateboard and grow a rat tail. Jonah plays his part. When I ask to hang out with his friends, he laughs derisively. When I pester him to let me smoke marijuana, he rolls me oregano. I call things "gnarly" and declare myself "stoked," and Jonah pretends not to hear. Then one day he asks me if I've got plans. I shake my head. Of course I don't have plans. You do now, he says, and tells me that tonight we are going shoplifting at Thrifty's.

I still don't know what compelled Jonah to invite me. Maybe his friends were busy that day, maybe they didn't want to participate in a criminal conspiracy. It certainly wasn't my ideal opportunity. I would have vastly preferred a Howard Jones concert or an afternoon at the skate park. But I didn't give the matter much more thought at the time: Jonah had invited me to do something. It was an offer that I would not refuse.

We ride our skateboards downtown and Jonah lays out the plan. We will walk through the store, holding our skateboards by our sides. We will stuff small items in our pockets and use our skateboards as shields, hiding the incriminating bulges from view. It is not exactly a million-dollar plan, but we aren't going for a million dollars. It works flawlessly. We are in and out in ten minutes. We paw over our loot in a nearby parking lot. We've netted a few pieces of candy for ourselves and some cheap necklaces for our girlfriends. I am relieved: I played the accomplice and succeeded. Maybe now Jonah will take me out skating with his friends. But that's not what he's thinking. He wants to go stealing at Thrifty's tomorrow night.

I don't want to go. But I *really* don't want Jonah to call me a chicken shit, so I agree to go. I don't remember what we take. Jonah insists on returning again the third night. We do. When Jonah announces we'll go the fourth night, however, I refuse. I try to act as if I've had enough, like I've proven myself and I have better things to do, but really I've lost my nerve. I don't want to get caught.

"Can't we just stay home and watch the Dodgers game?" I ask. Jonah snorts dismissively.

"*Chicken shit*," he says. He grabs his skateboard and heads out.

THE DODGERS ARE in the seventh inning when the phone rings. My father answers in the other room: "He's *what*?"

Jonah is under arrest. He is at the police station. He has been caught shoplifting. His mother and my father are shaken by the news. They both pace around the house. I stay in the other room watching baseball. Suddenly, my stepmother comes into the television room, stands facing me and puts her hands on her hips.

"Did you know anything about this?" she asks. I shake my head.

I understand this is only a short-term solution. I know that at this very moment my small world is crumbling down. I see it all quite clearly. Jonah will implicate me, and this denial to my stepmother will prove crucial. It will be the ammunition she needs to kick me out of the family.

"You see? He's *not* a good boy," she'll tell my father. "He's a thief *and* a liar." They'll turn me over directly to the police. Within days, I'll be doing hard labor in a dirty iron mine somewhere, a juvenile prison glibly nicknamed Magic Mountain.

JONAH AND THE parents return an hour later. All three are silent. It is the kind of silence that only occurs after lots of shouting. Jonah trudges into the house like a stubborn horse. When a horse sees his barn, he takes off in a gallop toward it, and Jonah does the same thing when he spots our bedroom. I try to catch his eye, but Jonah doesn't look at me.

"Fuck you!" he shouts and slams the door.

This is the first moment when I realize that Jonah wanted to be caught. Only two kinds of kids go shoplifting in the same store night after night: the kid who wants to be noticed by other kids and the kid who wants to be noticed by adults.

The rebel may have achieved some success, but for the mama's boy, things have gone terribly awry. I am convinced that my denial to my stepmother has infuriated Jonah. He has responded by unmasking my role to our parents in our sordid exploits. Now my father is on his way over to me to deliver the news: the cops are ready to take custody of me. I will be off to Magic Mountain in the morning.

My father stares. I swallow hard.

"Your stepbrother . . ." he says, ". . . is very troubled. I don't understand. I'm so glad to know that you would never do a thing like this."

I nod. I feel like a chicken shit.

I go into the bedroom and close the door. Jonah is sitting on his mattress playing with his toes. He looks up at me and grins weakly. He looks exhausted. He tells me how the manager grabbed him on his way out of the store. He'd seen Jonah and "his friend" coming in before, but he hadn't had the time to bust him—until tonight.

I clear my throat. "So," I ask nervously, "you didn't tell them about me?"

He looks up at me and I can tell he is surprised.

"Of course not," he says. "Why would I do *that*?" That's when I realize that Jonah might tease me and call me names, but he would never, ever, try to hurt me.

FAMILIES PERFORM MANY functions, but above all else they are designed to provide safety and security. If I become paralyzed, I will turn to my family. If America is invaded, I will attempt to protect my family. Stepfamilies are another form of alliance. For Jonah and me, our parents' marriage provided an ideal opportunity for a natural coalition. We both lacked siblings, and by virtue of the nuptials we each gained a brother. It was a relationship, I realized the day Jonah was arrested, that meant a lot to each of us. But every alliance carries its own potential challenges, and within a few years ours would face some big ones. What happens when your mama abandons my papa? What happens when my papa divorces your mama? What happens when the marriage that forged the alliance no longer exists?

Jonah and I didn't talk for a long time. Naturally, there was some awkwardness. The married couple had gone through a messy breakup, and we each only heard our respective parent's version. But that wasn't the whole story. We had one phone conversation during this time—I was twenty years old—and neither of us seemed constrained by our parents' positions. Beneath everything, it had always been us against them anyway, and we felt that dynamic again. We took turns sharing the recent twists and turns of our lives easily; each listened to the other attentively and affectionately. Then we hung up and dropped into silence again.

Neither of us harbored a secret grudge against the other. We just didn't have any *need* to connect. We didn't have family events to arrange or gossip to share or obligations to fulfill. If his mother got sick, he wouldn't call me to help. If my father got sick, I wouldn't call him. Obligations are the silk that forms the web of familial relations. We didn't have any. I continued to describe Jonah to friends as my stepbrother, for a while, but it was confusing to explain and after a while I stopped bothering to try.

WHEN THE INVITATION arrived for Jonah's wedding, I would have skipped most events to be there. Both my father and my former stepmother seemed genuinely pleased that I had chosen to attend, especially since it was obvious that I did so under no particular obligation. While snubbing the nuptials of a close friend would bring serious consequences, everyone agreed that I could have easily dropped a polite regretful response in the mail to my ex-stepbrother, and returned to my life, guilt-free. But I knew that in order to do that, I would have had to acknowledge a painful truth. I would have to accept that I had spent my teenage years viewing this person as my older brother and now he had simply become another distant acquaintance. I would have had to acknowledge a level of uncertainty in the world that was simply too depressing to accept. So I didn't give myself the opportunity. Instead, I nurtured some natural curiosity, invented my own sense of an obligation, and booked my ticket.

AFTER THE CEREMONY, Jonah and I made a lot of promises. We hoped to stay in better touch. We'd call each other regularly. I talked about visiting him soon in his new home. That was two years ago. We haven't talked once since. That's not important. If I get married, I believe that Jonah will be there, no matter what. We've never talked about this, but I just have a hunch. I suspect that I am not the only survivor of our parents' broken partnership who takes some comfort in knowing that somewhere out there, a couple of ex-stepbrothers can still add up to something more.

My Wedding Presents

STEPHANIE STOKES OLIVER

What was I doing with a man with three children?
What had I gotten myself into?

Does starting out on the wrong foot have to mean that you can't end up dancing?

Reggie and I had just moved in together in an apartment on the Upper West Side of Manhattan. It was his weekend of joint custody, and we were headed up to a state park called Bear Mountain. We loaded up our compact Toyota Corolla with his three little girls in the backseat, squished in with the stray tabby cat Reggie had found and named Ethiopia.

During weekdays, I got Reggie's full attention, and I enjoyed it. He listened to my every word about my job, and seemed to care when I talked about my living three thousand miles away from my family in Seattle. We laughed at each other's jokes and spent all our nonwork time together. That is, until the weekend. Then it was like the hot water ran cold. His daughters got his undivided attention. I was invited along, but the indulgence to which I was accustomed became totally directed to the children. I was not always contemplative enough or sensitive to Reggie's pain about not being a full-time, everyday dad to his beloved girls. He had grown up with both his parents, and divorce was not what he had expected when the children were born one after the other. But never having dated a man with children before, I didn't take the turn of attention easily. He seemed like a different person when the children were around.

WHEN I FIRST met Reggie, I was a twenty-four-year-old fashion magazine editor who knew more about the latest maternity wear than how to change a diaper. At age thirty, he was already the devoted father of three little girls from an early marriage, now ending in divorce. In the bachelor pad he shared with his two brothers, the walls were adorned not with the expected sexy girlie posters but with sepia photographs of his own beautiful babies. As I fell in love with him, I also fell for the soft-focused eight-by-ten picture of the sleeping curly-haired toddler with the long, lush eyelashes. "That's my Aleeyah," he told me adoringly, "the daddy's girl."

I kept asking when I could meet his girls, Amena, age eight, Aleeyah, three, and the baby born just eleven months after her, Ahmondyllah.

"When we've been together for a year, I'll introduce you," Reggie told me not unkindly.

Sure enough, one day after we had been dating for about a year, he showed up at my door to take me to the airport for a business trip holding a little girl. I was on the phone when they arrived, and as I let him in and smiled at his then-two-year-old with the café au lait complexion, she just stared back at me. When I hung up the phone and gave her my fawning attention, she didn't change expression. The only thing that seemed to interest her was the bottle full of apple juice she was hanging on to.

In the car on the way from my Brooklyn apartment to LaGuardia Airport, she sat in the backseat babbling, "Leeleelee-leeleeleelee . . ."

"What's she saying?" I asked Reg.

"Oh, she's talking about her sister, Aleeyah. We call her LeeLee."

"You're a pretty little girl," I cooed. "You know that?"

She seemed to look right through me.

When we arrived at the curbside check-in for my flight, Reggie came around the car to give me a kiss good-bye with one arm around me and his daughter in the other. Then as I turned to grab my bag, he said to Ahmondyllah, "Do you like Daddy's girlfriend?"

"No!" she replied firmly.

I was mortified. What had I done to deserve that?

"Oh, I bet you really like her, don't you?" Reggie prodded.

"No!" she said louder.

"Oh, well," I said, trying to muster a smile. "I like you. You are just adorable."

She turned her head and buried it in her father's shoulder.

It wasn't until I returned and was able to spend another afternoon with her when Reggie brought her along for a picnic à trois in Central Park that I learned that she was at the stage of child development when saying "No!" was just plain easier and more fun than forming the word "yes." Children at that age say no with authority and assertiveness to *everyone*, but the affirmative comes out more like "Yeth." Even the baby knows it doesn't have the same power. And indeed, in my ignorance, as the youngest of my family and not even having been much of a baby-sitter as a teenager, I had definitely taken her answer to mean the worst: *No, I don't like your girlfriend who is not Mommy.*

AT THE EXPANSIVE recreational park in upstate New York, as Reg and the kids played in the pool, I watched from the sidelines in a lounge chair. Observing the joy and comfort the four of them had with each other, I wondered when and how I would ever become a part of it. In addition to the one-year rule before introducing me to the kids, Reggie had other relationship guidelines. Fresh from divorce court, he didn't want to talk about getting married again.

"I wouldn't marry anyone I hadn't known for at least three years," he lovingly explained.

What was there to know? I wondered. I knew he was gainfully employed as a manager of a furniture store in the heart of Manhattan, and that his kisses took my breath away. I knew that at six-foot-four, with the build of an athlete and the face of a celebrity, he was "fine" according to all my girlfriends. Most of all, I felt that he cared for me and that he was what my Aunt Katie referred to in letters from home as "Mr. Right." All this single girl from Seattle needed to make my life complete in the Big Apple was to get married.

"That's forever," I said. Looking back three years to my college days seemed a lifetime ago. *I'm going to get you long before that!* I said to myself.

But as the years passed quickly, I began to realize that one thing he needed to know about me was how I got along with his children. We all got to know each other through weekends spent with one, two, or all of them, or holidays spent with the girls at his mother's house or at his hilarious Aunt Pat's. But sometimes during these outings in which the children seemed to get all his attention, I felt like an outsider.

AFTER A WHILE of watching Reg and the girls splashing happily, oblivious to me, I decided to drift away to walk around the lake at the foot of the mountain that was now full of hikers and campers. Picnic areas shaded by groves of tall trees provided pockets of privacy for young couples with children. In the heat of the summer day, parents in paddle boats taught offspring how to glide around calm, cool Hessian Lake. As in most places in New York, I was surrounded by people. Yet I felt alone.

At the water's edge, I came across several large, flat rocks that extended out from the end of the lake where wading was prohibited. I jumped from boulder to boulder, trying hard not to fall in the water. When I reached the stone farthest out into the lake, I sat down on it, put my head in my hands, and scolded myself for even thinking about allowing tears to fall—I didn't want to look pathetic in public. Feeling sorry for myself, I thought back to another day of similar, displaced feelings.

One Fourth of July, Reggie took the children with us to a barbecue at his Aunt Pat's house in Queens. We spent the day amused with Aunt Pat's tales of her childhood in Mississippi and adulthood in New York—the kind of stories that are so preposterous you have to laugh to keep from crying.

Then as the sun was beginning to set, I heard someone say that the kids' mother was outside, that she had come to pick them up. I had never met Reggie's first wife. I just knew she was the attractive woman who had given birth to the beautiful babies. She and her mother came into the house, and I was introduced. Everyone was kind and courteous. As she led the girls out to the car, I watched from the living-room window and saw Reggie join them. The girls climbed inside and Reggie and the mother of his three children stood talking, exchanging anecdotes about the children between his teasing with the children through the lowered car window.

There is a family, I thought to myself. *There is a father, a mother, and their children—a good-looking family of five.* I was confused by my feelings about the scene in front of me, although I tried to tell myself that my thoughts didn't add up. The divorce was final; by societal standards, that made them a "broken" family. But what I saw was "not broke" at all. Instead I observed two parents who put their children first, and a car full of kids who basked in the love. I couldn't help thinking that because I didn't fit into the picture, I must be doing something wrong.

Reggie closed the car door, waved good-bye to the children, and turned back toward the house to speak to his younger brother as the car pulled out. I walked to the back of the house and took off through the backyard. I had to get away to think. *What was I doing with a man with three children? What had I gotten myself into?* These were the questions I asked myself as I walked around the unfamiliar neighborhood without telling anyone where I was going. Seeing Reggie, his daughters, and his ex-wife had totally thrown me for a loop. Returning to the house unnoticed, I gathered myself together and didn't share my feelings with Reggie. Even though I knew I was stepping into a long, strong tradition of African-American women raising other people's children, it was the first time I had considered that maybe it didn't always come naturally.

But that didn't mean it didn't come, I told myself on the rock in the lake. Now that we were engaged after the prerequisite three years, I knew it was time for a change in the situation. I had to admit that there was really nothing that Reggie and the girls were doing to make me feel uncomfortable. The girls seemed to like and accept me; it was me who had the problem. So, I decided to solve it right there and then—before we all got together again.

What did I want my relationship to be with Reggie and the children? I asked myself. In the solitude, I recalled how he often had to work on the weekends, leaving me with the children on Saturdays after he commuted over an hour to pick them up on Friday night—all so that he could have Saturday evenings and Sunday mornings with them. I thought about how sweet the girls were, now that they were all beyond the "terrible twos."

They always did as I asked and never gave me a word of back talk or disrespect.

Sitting cross-legged, sunbathing on that rock in the lake, I considered how much I appreciated Reg's dedication to the girls, and that it meant that if we were to have our own child, he would be the kind of good father that I had had myself. Then it came to me: what I needed to do was to forge my own personal relationship with the girls. I realized that I was not just "Daddy's girlfriend," but someone who would soon be related to them.

I began to think of the girlie things we could do together, like going for frozen hot chocolate at the ice-cream parlor in Manhattan, or taking them one at a time to my kid-friendly job. Didn't I already love buying fancy dresses and lacy undies for them while their parents made sure they had the basics? It was such fun to comb their thick and healthy hair into the long, black braids that I adorned with ribbons I kept at my house just for them.

As I was daydreaming, I heard my name being called in the distance by a trio of little girls. The family was looking for me. "Here I am!" I yelled, and jumped up to greet Reggie, Amena, Aleeyah, Ahmondyllah—and the kitty, Ethiopia, who was being carted around in my straw Kikuyu bag. Laughing and talking with wet towels wrapped around their swimsuits, Reggie and the girls told me about their adventures in the swimming pool and all the fun I had missed. Amidst their chatter, I heard someone say that it was Ahmondyllah who had first noticed my absence.

LATER THAT YEAR at Christmastime, we were married. On our first family weekend away during spring break, I took advantage of a quiet moment to ask Ahmondyllah if she knew what relationship I was to her now that Daddy and I had married. She took a moment to think, but was a bit distracted watching her sisters running out to play. With respect, she looked up at me and gave a hasty answer: "My godmother?" I laughed, and satisfied with her response, I let her go outside.

DURING THE TWENTY-FIVE years that Reggie and I now have been married, each of the girls has lived with us at some time or other. We've been a big family in a tiny New York apartment, we've transplanted our tribe to a brand-new house in Seattle, and now we've been settled for many happy years in suburban New Jersey. Moments of trepidation at taking on three girls have been replaced by joyful memories of family travel, Thanksgiving dinners at our house, never-missed Father's Days, and teasing about the numerous boyfriends that gather the nerve to endure the scrutiny of a fond father. On occasion—at graduations, Sweet Sixteens, and more recently, engagement parties—I have thanked their mom (who has also remarried) for having birthed "our babies."

I love Mother's Day, when the flowery Hallmark cards arrive to articulate the feelings of my girls. "You've never tried to replace my mother," expressed the script in my favorite color, purple, on Amena's greeting this year, "yet you've been there for me in your own special and important way." The girls tell us that their friends marvel at how well their four parents get along. "That's because they have something in common," they reply. "They all love *us*!"

I have tried to make "step" a positive four-letter word at my house. When people ask how many children I have, I say, "I was blessed with three that I got for wedding presents, and then I gave birth to one more girl." We called her Anique—a name that starts with A, like her sisters'.

Admittedly, I had role models in how to live and love within a blended family. My father and mother had both been previously married and each brought to their joint union one child, and then they had me. The family philosophy was often summed up and passed down by my father, who was known to say with relish, "I had one, she had one, we had one—and they're all *ours*."

A Good Man Is Hard to Find

SASHA TROYAN

She told me that her worst fear was getting married.
I told her my worst fear was getting divorced.

I grew up surrounded by women. Every summer, my grandmother and great-aunt traveled all the way from South Africa to France to stay with us for the months of July and August. There was the English nanny, Janet. Often, Paola, a dear friend of the family's, who came from Italy. Not surprisingly perhaps, my father felt outnumbered and chose to absent himself, spending time with his mistress, as it turns out, but we learned about that only later as teenagers.

By the time my sisters and I were born, both our grandfathers were dead. My paternal grandfather had married three times. Our grandmother was his third wife, whom he divorced when my father was three. My mother was also born to an older father; it was his second marriage, and he died when Mother was only seven years old. My mother told us that she had few memories of him.

I give this background information about my family only to shed light on my feelings about men at the time of my meeting Bill, my future stepfather. I believed that men on the whole were unimportant, superfluous even. They were not to be depended on. They had mistresses. At best, they made brief appearances only to disappear again. My maternal grandmother appeared to do wonderfully without a husband. She had her knitting, and her closest companion was her sister Pie.

I met Bill in 1982. I was twenty years old, a junior at Barnard College, studying music. I'd come to my mother's apartment in order to practice the piano. I remember distinctly the apartment building my mother was living in at the time, an anonymous brick building between Seventy-third and Seventy-fourth Streets on Riverside Drive with long dark corridors imbued with the smells of breakfast-lunch-dinner. I'd completely forgotten that she planned to introduce me to her new boyfriend, Bill, whom she had been dating for a few months. It was only as I rang the bell that I remembered.

"Shoot," I muttered, not liking the thought of meeting someone new. I have never been good at meeting new people, particularly men.

But he was not there yet, so I went to play the piano in my younger sister, Brett's, bedroom, leaving the door ajar.

When Bill did arrive, he slipped into my mother's apartment unobtrusively, almost stealthily. He was dressed in a gray suit. I noticed a narrow face, gray eyes, and a shock of white hair. He was very soft-spoken. I shook hands with him hurriedly before returning to work on my Chopin étude.

Several hours later, after Bill had gone, I heard a knock on the door, and my mother peeked in. "Dinner's ready," she said. Brett and I perched ourselves on stools in the narrow kitchen and listened to my mother extolling Bill's qualities. "He's just like me, girls. He loves children. Imagine, he was the one who used to get up in the night for his boys. He would drive them through the streets of New York until they fell asleep. He would carry them up the stairs, carefully, one step at a time."

I pictured Bill holding his son in his arms, walking slowly, ever so carefully up the stairs, then gently lowering his son into his crib.

"Yes," we said, a little weary of hearing about his virtues for the hundredth time.

I felt old and cynical compared with my mother. (My mother is exactly twenty years older than me. She was close to the age I am today.) But also jealous—what would it be like to have a father like Bill rather than my own father who is the very opposite of maternal—and insists to this day that my sisters and I are responsible for the dissolution of his marriage with my mother? If I'd been a few years younger, these feelings would have been stronger, but I was already twenty years old, supposedly grown up and not in need of a father or a stepfather. I was determined to live my own tortured relationships; drawn to men who were as depressed as I was at the time, men who had trouble getting out of bed, men who were complex, difficult, or irate.

Following this brief encounter with Bill, my sister and I observed what we thought of as a peculiar, hilarious, phenomenon: my mother now spent hours preparing dishes for this new love of hers. We listened with amusement to my mother's obsession with Bill. Rather pubescent, we thought. Weren't we supposed to behave like this? Not our staid mother of forty.

"He's a psychiatrist, but he loves literature," our mother told us. "He quotes poetry, Wordsworth, Shelley." "I just loved——" she said, referring to a movie with Christopher Reeve, who is passionately in love.

My sister and I stared at each other in disbelief.

I recall one night, lying in bed, the blind pulled down so that the streetlight did not fill our room, the sound of buses and cars audible, saying to Brett, "He sounds too good to be true," and she agreed, "Oh dear, yes." She told me that her worst fear was getting married. I told her my worst fear was getting divorced. We laughed, then concluded that the only solution was for us to stay single for the rest of our lives.

A few weeks later, my sister and I felt somewhat vindicated, but also disappointed, when we learned that Bill was not just dating our mother. We pretended not to notice the change in our mother's behavior—the way she jumped every time the telephone rang, her distraction when we talked with her. The apartment was no longer filled with the delicious aroma of bread-crumb pudding and beef stew. Now she went for long runs along Riverside Park and suggested we all diet.

We were somewhat reassured when she told us a few months later that Bill was seeing only her, though we held on to our skepticism a little longer. "Let's just hope he's telling the truth," I remember saying. "That's what he says," my sister remarked. At the end of that year, our mother moved into Bill's apartment and Brett returned to France to live with my father. I decided I was not talented enough to become a pianist and had to give up that dream.

My interactions with Bill were limited. He was a very busy man, working as a psychiatrist and for the Bureau of Mental Health. He was also caught up with his boys, who are ten years younger than I am. He took them to their soccer meetings on the weekends. He helped them with their homework. My mother complained that she hardly got to see Bill. Through her, I learned that Bill does not like to drink. In fact, he cannot tolerate wine at all. He likes to watch sports on television. He is a pragmatist. She told me that one of his patients confided that he saw the devil on a regular basis and that Bill responded, "That's fine, just don't tell anyone!"

I caught glimpses of Bill. I learned that the only place he does not get along with my mother is in the kitchen. When he cooks, he likes to make a loud clatter of dishes. It sounds as if he's playing cymbals with the pots. He likes to go grocery shopping. He does not like eating in restaurants. In fact, he does not like to sit down to eat. If it were up to him, he would stand. Frequently, he skips lunch.

When Bill asked my mother to marry him, I was relieved; still, as I knew, marriage did not preclude infidelity. On the contrary, it sometimes provided the impetus. By then my mother and Bill had moved into an apartment that was composed of two apartments put together. The apartments were on different levels so that one side of the apartment was higher than the other. A few days before their wedding, I recall the apartment filled with my grandmother's furniture. There was so much old furniture you could barely make your way into the apartment. I admired Bill's equanimity faced with this deluge of furniture. He spent all night fitting it into the giant closet in the hallway.

I recall helping my mother pick out her wedding dress: silk with a white background, flecked with orange, green, and black. It fit my mother's body tightly. Bill liked her to dress in tight clothes. Bill also liked his clothes to fit snugly.

A few months after their wedding, Bill insisted on taking me shopping at Bloomingdale's for my birthday. For the first time, we went on an outing, like father and daughter. He insisted on buying me a short black miniskirt. He also wanted to buy a shirt to go with the skirt but did not see anything he liked in the store. At last, he stopped a salesperson wearing a tight-fitting silk shirt and asked her where she had bought hers. The woman blushed and muttered something like "not here." He wanted to buy one just like it for me. I suppose Bill and my mother thought that if I wore just the right outfit I would meet the right man.

It was really the summer after their marriage that I got to know my stepfather. We were vacationing in Sardinia. It was one of our last summers at the villa. From the table we could see the ocean in the distance, bougainvillea fluttered outside one window. We were discussing the famous story by Camus, called "The Adulterous Woman." The discussion became heated; my mother and I were in complete agreement; ironically, given our histories, we identified with the poor bored wife, who has her epiphany at the end, while Bill identified with the husband who is, after all, a good man. "I believe that a man who is unfaithful should have his balls cut off!" he told us. End of story. We laughed. "What about women then?" we asked. During that summer, Bill had embarked on a project to write a book that focused on literature, examining great short stories, but specifically in the context of how each character changes. He planned to use these stories with his students studying psychiatry. They would examine these characters as case studies.

We discussed Moravia's "Bitter Honeymoon," "The Rocking-Horse Winner" by D. H. Lawrence, "Araby" by Joyce, Thomas Mann's *Mario the Magician*, and many others. Through these stories, I learned to know my stepfather. I discovered that he was an optimist. He believed in the possibility of change, a position you might have expected, coming from a psychiatrist, but not one I took for granted. My mother, who also has a degree in psychology, was rather dubious about people's ability to change.

Despite my mother's opinion, I observed that she was different. With my father, she'd often been sad and anxious. She had tried very hard to please him by wearing the right clothes and keeping the house in order, but my father always found something wrong: dust on top of the television, meat overcooked. She was careful about expressing an opinion contrary to my father's. Now, with Bill, she asserted categorically that the man in "The Adulterous Woman" was a bore. His wife deserved to find happiness. "What a beautiful ending," she said, referring to the wife's orgiastic response to the sky and the desert. At night, my mother and Bill's voices would drift into my room. As I slipped in and out of sleep, I heard them talking and talking. I wondered what it would be like to have a relationship like theirs. I envisioned the possibility of a different kind of relationship for myself. Remembering my father's attempts to explain himself, I wondered if there were nuances I had missed. That night I started to question beliefs I had held for a long time.

The next morning, before leaving to visit a friend who was ill, my mother confided to me that Bill did not like her to be away. "Not even for a night," she said. One evening, while she was gone, Bill opened his wallet and showed me a photograph of our mother. At the time she had long hair that was pulled back and she looked like a schoolgirl, wearing a navy blue cardigan. Over the following days, I observed him open his wallet from time to time. The expression on his face reminded me of my mother's expression when she talked about Bill, and I felt confident, at last, that my mother had found a good man.

On the Uses of Animals

SHEILA KOHLER

I was more than ready to take on what I had never had: two
adorable boys. The boys, naturally, who had a mother of their
own, were not so eager to be taken on.

My second marriage, unlike my first—where I fell pregnant at nineteen and married the man—was a love
match from the start. I was introduced to my second
husband by friends—a couple who took us both out to dinner in
a Japanese restaurant. At the end of the meal, my husband-to-be,
a psychiatrist, who sat opposite me, turned green and asked,
"Would you like to have a coffee with me?"

I stared back at him. There was a hushed and expectant
silence at the table, all eyes on me.

You have to understand that my husband-to-be was, as I was,
pushing forty, and we had each been married for more than fifteen years to someone else whom we had loved, and I had not
dated anyone else in between.

"But how will I get home?" I asked, as though New York City
had suddenly been transformed into the wild African veld of my
childhood.

"I could, perhaps, drive you there," he said softly, his voice rising slightly at the end of the sentence.

Anyway, we did have coffee and then some, and I fell in love
or perhaps into passion would be a better word. I came to him

whenever he summoned me, arriving too early at night when his patients had not yet left, obliged to wander around the block in the snow with a basket of food for him, like Little Red Riding Hood: soups, stews, and compotes, the food from my colonial childhood, which he later confessed he disliked. Despite the English food, he eventually consented to have me move into his apartment in the Village.

There was now only a small problem: my husband's two boys, whom he adored—both dark eyed and dark haired and beautiful. They spent half their time with their father and half with their mother, and now looked up at me, a stranger, with eyes full of suspicion.

No problem, I thought, in my ignorance. My own three girls were at the teenager stage when all they wanted was to be off on their own. My husband, the busy doctor, was often obliged to work long hours. I was more than ready to take on what I had never had: two adorable boys. The boys, naturally, who had a mother of their own, were not so eager to be taken on.

I tried everything that had worked so well with my own children: I cooked up all that colonial food, told stories, climbed dangerous fences into illicit places, taught them how to cheat at Monopoly, swam in cold water, dived off rocks, did handstands, helped with homework and the chicken pox. But when I served the boys the food that I had bought so lavishly at Balducci's—thick steaks, chips, double chocolate cake—or made them soups that I had stirred and strained for hours, the younger one looked up at his father and said, "Do I have to eat this, Dad?"

This is where the dog comes in. I'm not now, or wasn't then, a dog person. In my previous marriage we had had cats whom we loved. The first thing my first husband and I did when we were married was to rush out and buy two silver-gray Siamese cats. I liked their independence, their warmth in my lap, their decorative, quiet company.

But desperate at this stage, I considered that what might work with these boys was a *dog*. Besides, my husband had told me some vague and rather disturbing story about a foundling dog who had misbehaved and afterward been sold or given away, to the boys' chagrin.

So one afternoon, when I was left at home to care for the younger boy, in one of the frequent lulls in our conversation, I said to him hopefully, "What if we were to get a dog?"

He deigned to look up at me directly, his dark eyes lit up with a flicker of interest I had not yet seen there.

"Who would walk him, when we are not here?" he asked me suspiciously, with his nine-year-old wisdom.

"Well, I would," I said. "It would be good exercise for me. Get me away from my computer."

I REMEMBER THE visit to the pound clearly: my husband sitting slumped in total dejection on a steel chair, his handsome head in his hands, thinking of the many rainy nights of dog walking up ahead, no doubt, and the two boys, for the first time hanging eagerly onto my hands as I walked exultantly down the aisle of yapping dogs in cages.

I had been planning something fairly small in order to go from the cat to the dog stage, something I would be able to put in a bag when traveling, but as we passed one of the cages, two ominously large, golden brown paws were thrust together toward us, imploringly.

"This one! I want this one!" the younger boy exclaimed immediately, jumping up and down.

"What about this one?" I tried, attempting to steer him to the next cage where a little ball of fluff lay curled sweetly on one side.

"No, no! We want this one," the older boy proclaimed firmly. At twelve, he was already the sort of boy who would protect his younger brother against outside opposition.

And so this was the one we got, a large light brown puppy with amber eyes, half-wolf and half-husky with something mysterious mixed in besides. We were given a box and various instructions about vaccinations, and repaired to a restaurant nearby where we all ate a meal together with unusually good appetite and humor.

After that, of course, the boys quickly reverted to being who they were: my stepsons, with lives and a mother of their own. My own sixteen-year-old daughter, whose father had also remarried, explained things to me.

"There is absolutely nothing you can do, so don't even try, Mummy," she said, shaking her head at my stupidity. So I stopped trying so hard, and the boys and I gradually established a polite and not unfriendly relationship.

And it was I, of course, who walked and cared for the dog obtained to ingratiate myself into the boys' good graces. He was not a particularly good dog. He was big and rambunctious and a barker. He could even be vicious at times, and once bit the oculist who dared to lean over me and touch my face to adjust a new pair of glasses.

But ultimately he and I, walking and talking together through our solitary days, fell in love, as humans tend to do with their dogs, if they are given the chance, and we were the ones who became inseparable. The dog sat patiently by my side as I worked the long solitary hours of a writer. We took endless walks together through the New York streets in the evenings, the dog following without a leash. He came with us to Italy every summer, traveling half-drugged in the hold and swimming for miles with us in the calm waters of the Mediterranean Sea. In the water, his herding instincts emerged and he swam in big circles around the family, keeping us all together and safe.

My husband and I acquired a new apartment near the park so that the dog would have a place to run, and the three of us took up running, my husband charging ahead and the dog running after him with me tied with his leash at my waist, dragging along in his wake.

TEN YEARS AFTER he had been adopted, the dog was diagnosed with cancer and had to be operated on. After the operation, I was told I could come and visit and sit with the dog for a while. My younger stepson, now a tall teenager, offered, to my surprise, to accompany me on this visit.

The two of us sat cross-legged on the floor of the animal hospital with the dog between us for a long while, the tears falling silently down my cheeks. All we could hear was the soft whimpering of the animal in pain.

I said, "I have never heard him cry before."

The boy held him and stroked him gently. He looked up at me.

"I've never seen you cry before either," he said, looking at me with a half smile and something like a glimmer of admiration in his dark eyes. I nodded and reached out and took his hand.

My Room

ALICE ELLIOTT DARK

I thought I knew what to expect.

On April 4, 1964, my mother married Mr. Christopher Price. After a brief celebration, the couple left for a honeymoon weekend, and at my insistence, my brother Ian and I moved into his house while they were away. I was two days from turning eleven, and full of hope about our new life. I couldn't wait.

I wanted my own room, a real room. When my parents separated, my mother moved us out of our house over to her parents', where we'd lived for three years. I'd bounced between rooms, usually sharing with someone. Until recently I'd still had my old room at my father's house, but I was only there one night a week. The room hadn't changed with me either. It was a shrine to who I'd been at seven, when our lives broke. We hadn't taken anything with us when we left, and Daddy insisted we keep everything as it had been. He always expected us to come back someday. Whenever Daddy walked in my room to talk to me, I saw him look around searchingly, as if my jewelry box with the spinning ballerina and my Petunia and life-size Chatty Cathy dolls were stars by which he might find his direction. I wished I could redecorate, but I was afraid that would hurt his feelings too much.

That room was gone now, anyway. Daddy had died that January, and his house was immediately sealed and later sold by the bank. My parents were divorced, so my mother wasn't allowed to go inside to retrieve any of her belongings. Her piano, wedding presents, personal items, and all of our things were permanently gone. I have nothing from my early childhood; not one toy, school paper, piece of clothing. Years later, a psychiatrist would tell me it was as if I was a refugee, leaving home with only what was on my back. I felt that, although I couldn't have put it into words. Instead I closely observed the details of my friends' rooms and pretended that certain window seats and canopy beds were my own. I was a gypsy girl rebelling against my rootlessness. I wanted to settle down.

I hadn't yet seen the room that would be mine in the new house. I hadn't been upstairs at all. Mr. Price was quite formal. His courtship of my mother was largely invisible. They'd been seeing each other for a while before we even heard about it. After she told us, he'd occasionally come and sit in a correct, regal posture on the hardest chair in my grandparents' living room. He wore suits, and silk ascots at his neck. We'd never met him before, but he knew my best friend because she lived across the street from him, and we knew where he lived, because there was a pond on the property that he opened to the public for skating in winter. You could go there in summer too, to fish, as long as you stayed on the far bank, out of view of the house, and didn't even consider venturing onto the narrow blade of land where the Canada geese nested every spring. It was thrilling to ignore the NO TRESPASSING signs, to feel like an insider. How much better to actually live there! We'd be able to go anywhere—up on the lava rocks at the end of the driveway, and into the pool on the terrace. We knew there was a pool because you could see people up there in bathing suits. They raised their arms, tucked their heads, sailed through the air, then—splash. Ian and I imagined doing that. After we visited the inside of the house, Ian bet you could jump into the pool from the roof; it was that close. No one we knew had a pool on the terrace. Would my room overlook it?

On the afternoon that Ian and I were set to move, I packed a small suitcase to get me through the next couple of days, carefully choosing what I thought I'd need.

"Did you remember your toothbrush?" my grandmother asked. I nodded.

"Do you have everything else?"

I knew what she meant. She washed out her lingerie every night in the sink in her bathroom. If you peeked in there in the early morning you saw her bra and underpants hanging draped across the faucets of the tub. I'd tried to do this myself, but my cotton underpants and shirts dried too slowly to wear them again the next day, and they were stiff as cardboard when they were finally ready. I'd have to wait until I was old enough for nylon to practice that habit. Who would do the laundry at the new house? My father did his own after we left, but I couldn't picture Mr. Price running a washing machine. He had servants too, who lived in the house. Would my mother still do it? I'd seen her fold hundreds of loads in her efficient, energetic way. She poured a basket out on the sofa in our old den and on the bench in the den in my grandparents' house and used her hands to press out the jerseys and pants against the front of her body. I had trouble picturing her doing that in the new house. Mr. Price's den wasn't behind a door but completely open onto the central hall. I began to get nervous.

"You can always call if you forget anything," my grandmother told me.

I said good-bye to her and to my little brother and sister casually, as if the move were nothing—which, in a way, was true. My grandparents' house was really only up the hill from Mr. Price's if you bushwacked through the woods, but officially it was a large hairpin away on old curbless roads, so we got in the car for the trip. Mr. Price lived across the street from my best friend. I looked for her as we approached his driveway, but she wasn't outside.

My grandfather pointed his Thunderbird down Mr. Price's long driveway. I memorized the address on the mailbox: 792 March Road. It sounded dignified, solid, and safe. I would like giving out that address to my camp friends. I craned to see the tennis court and the lake. There they were, on my left, a new vantage point. Until now I'd been like everyone else in town who entered the property from Dove Lake Road. My father parked on the shoulder in a line of cars, and we walked down the hill in our skates, digging the back tips into the sod if the ground was bare, or attempting to skate down if it had already snowed. Willow trees surrounded the cloudy lake, and I always paused beneath their tendrils to remember how I used to hide in my mother's closet, my head inside her skirts. It was a happy memory in a childhood that had been long already and divided into several eras, some far better than others. Through it all, Mr. Price's lake—Dove Lake—was a constant. There were other places to skate nearby, but this was where you were likely to run into friends. At Christmas, a tree shone through the living-room window, even in the daytime. Now I'd be the girl decorating that tree with my new father. I'd look back up at the house from the pond, knowing that I didn't have to stop skating for the whole day if I were cold, but could go in for a little while to warm up and then come back out.

We reached the bottom of the driveway and stepped out of the car.

"Well, well, well," Grandad said.

Even though we'd been there before, we all stared. Mr. Price lived in a house unlike any other around. He'd commissioned an architect to help him design a modern structure of glass and stone. From the outside it looked low and flat, more like how I pictured a Japanese house than the Colonials I was used to.

There was a hedge on top of a low wall that created a cloistered walkway, but we went up the front steps and rang the bell.

"Come on, come on."

Catharine, the cook, opened the turquoise door and flapped her arthritic hand at us. My grandfather touched my back, and in we went.

I thought I knew what to expect, but I realized I hadn't been there very often. Knowing I'd live there from then on thickened the air.

The living room stretched dozens of feet toward the lip of a small hill. A long glass wall of windows framed a view of the lake. There was a large copper fireplace at one end and a raised built-in bookshelf on the other that marked off the hall. In front of the built-in sofa—it seated at least ten—stood a cunning coffee table the exact shape of Dove Lake.

The table amazed me when I first saw it; it seemed a coincidence on the level of magic. It was beyond me then to imagine a person who had the wherewithal to dream up his own house and to ask a carpenter to build a table in a shape that matched his pond. This was a different way to live in the world than anything I'd ever known. Mr. Price believed he could shape his life the way he wanted it rather than adapting to circumstances, the way most people do. The prospect both excited and frightened me.

The master bedroom lay beyond the living and dining rooms. Later, but not just yet—we didn't presume to go look at it yet—

I learned that to get to it you had to walk through a large bath-room that contained a wall of built-in drawers and closets, and a pink tub set on a diagonal between two walls of mirrors. That was where my mother would live. I'd never slept as far from her as I would now. Just after my father died I'd followed her everywhere, even to the bathroom, where I'd lurk outside the door, pretend-ing I had a reason for being there. This practice got on her nerves. One day she snapped. "Can't I be alone for one minute?" But if I can't see you, I thought, you might disappear completely. I was already ten, though, and realized this made no sense. I began to leave her alone, which caused in me a desolate fear. I hoped to start over in this new house. I hoped it would be all right now, with a new father to take care of us, for her to sleep far away.

Ian and I stood in the hall, unsure what to do. "Go on up," Catharine said, shooing us again. "Unpack your cases. Dinner at eight."

I glanced at my grandfather.

"The children usually eat at six," he said.

Not to mention that my little brother and sister went to bed at eight. They'd move in after my mother got back. Would they not get any dinner?

Catharine's face puckered. "Mr. Price eats at eight."

"He's not here, though, is he?"

Catharine shook her head.

"So will you feed them early tonight?"

"I cook for eight."

I tugged on his sleeve. I didn't want to make any trouble. Any-way, the last thing I was worried about was food.

"I'll put out some cheese and crackers," she offered. "William will take your cases upstairs."

I spoke up at last. "No! We'll do it."

William was an ancient man who'd long been a servant in the house. Mr. Price told me he still lived there because he had nowhere else to go. The story made me terribly sad. I planned to be kind to him, and didn't want him to do a thing for me.

"You should go now," I said to Grandad, but I couldn't look as he went out through the door. This was it. I suppose I was frozen, because Ian nudged me. I picked up my bag.

The stairs were wide and shallow, lit from above by a picture window on the upper landing. We walked up; I tiptoed. When we reached the top, we realized we didn't know what to do. The hall stretched in front of us, a blank tube except for more built-in drawers on the left. How would we know which room was ours? It hadn't occurred to either of us to even think of such a question. People had always told us what to do, and we'd learned that we had no choice about much. Were we supposed to pick? Or what?

"Ask her," Ian said, meaning Catharine.

"You," I said.

He called down the steps. "How do we know which one?"

His voice was excruciatingly loud to me in that grown-up, modern space.

She waddled to the bottom of the steps. "Nobody told me anything."

He shrugged and opened the first door to our right. We entered a small hallway, where there were three doors. The one at the end was a bathroom. He turned the knob on the first one. It was very tiny, and filled with belongings. I saw a drawing of Jesus on the chest of drawers. We shut that door.

Behind the next one William lay stretched out on the bed, fully dressed in a dark suit of clothing, sound asleep. We got out of there as quickly as we could.

There was no choice but to continue down the hall. Beyond

the drawers were built-in closets. Ian opened the next door, but that room was clearly already inhabited too. I assumed it belonged to my stepsister, who still partly lived there, although she was an adult and mostly stayed in New York. It was a nice-sized room made feminine by her strewn clothes and other belongings. There was a picture window across the back, and a private bathroom off the far end. I hadn't considered that I'd be sleeping near her. When was she coming back? Would she come while my mother was away? I'd barely met her.

We continued down to the very end of the hall, where two doors stood partially open. This was it—my new room.

Gingerly, we pushed open the doors. My heart dropped.

The rooms were small and dark, with no furniture at all except a bed and a lamp in each. A desk, drawers, and closet were all built in, unmovable. The walls were painted a depressing color, a gray-green that I might like now but didn't understand as a child. Rather than facing the lake and the meadows, these bedrooms looked at the back hill that climbed quickly and steeply into a wood that ran through all the properties along the ridge.

How would we decide whose room was whose? Somehow we did. I had the last one, nearest the bathroom. It had the view over the lake.

I sat on my new bed and looked around. I don't know what I expected, but more than nothing. I searched the drawers and under the bed, but if one of Mr. Price's children had once occu-pied it, he or she had been out of there for years. I pulled out the built-in drawers and found scraps of paper behind them, but they told me nothing. The floor was gritty, as if it hadn't been cleaned. At least the beds were made up. Where would our brother and sister sleep when they moved in? There wasn't enough room for us in this house.

Ian came to my door. "It's cool," he said. He hadn't noticed all the drawbacks I did. He wasn't a worrier.

It was hard to fall asleep that night. The light from the moon poked through the slats of the wooden blinds to make unfamiliar patterns on the ceiling. I listened to my brother shifting in the unfamiliar bed next door, taming the experience by making his own sounds, mostly of war planes flying and crashing into things. I was homesick. Our old house was only a few minutes away, but other people lived there now, and I'd never even see that room again. My father had died in that house. He'd managed to find me at my grandparents', but would he dare come here? I thought I'd put all that behind me, though. Why was it bothering me now, when I was supposed to be so thrilled?

I buried my face in the pillow. When were Mummy and Mr. Price coming back? I noticed myself thinking of him that way again. When he and my mother became engaged, I suggested that we call him Dad, and we'd already started. I said it eagerly, with emphasis. We'd called our real father Daddy, so it was different—not disloyal. Now I wondered about that, but didn't think I could take it back without hurting Mr. Price's feelings. I'd been too eager to move in here too. This little cubicle wasn't my room, not the one I longed for. That room would come complete with whatever it would take to fill up the chasm of loss inside me. I haven't found it, even yet.

A Trickle of Talk

LINDA PHILLIPS ASHOUR

Nick was just beginning to understand the intricacies of
relationships. He didn't need the nuance and uncertainty of
his mother's budding romance.

W hen we finally got down to the nitty-gritty of planning, my fiancé, a long-term bachelor who lived in
Manhattan, suggested eloping. Tom said he would
prop a ladder next to my bedroom window (though I lived in a
one-story house in Los Angeles), and off we would go into the
dead of night. Instead, we got married before a justice of the
peace in the Hamptons, with my two grown children as witnesses. It had taken us twelve years, including a serious three-
year sabbatical, to get here. We spent our honeymoon in a hotel
in Sag Harbor. Cassie and Nick were tucked away one floor
below our cozy room at the top of the stairs. From our bedroom,
we could smell their cigarette smoke and hear their laughter.

We were finally married, and there was a legal document to
prove it. But how would the relationship Tom had established
with my children expand or contract now that he was officially a
stepfather? Matters of diapers and discipline, even the rowdy teen
years, were securely behind us. The question seemed almost
quaint as we lay under our thick down comforter on that drizzly,
cold weekend. We'd gotten here, hadn't we? I burrowed back into
honeymoon mode and pushed the thought out of my mind.

BEFORE HE WAS my boyfriend or husband, Tom was my editor. My son's confusion about roles set in right from the start. "Is he your boss?" Nick asked after I hung up from an especially long conversation. I didn't have a ready answer. I had jumped into a second novel, and a flurry of correspondence with Tom had begun. In those early days, I was confused by the flowers he sent on my birthday and the increasingly frequent visits he made from New York to Los Angeles. I wasn't the only one who was struggling. Nick was just beginning to understand the intricacies of relationships. He didn't need the nuance and uncertainty of his mother's budding romance.

I had returned to Los Angeles from France when my first novel, *Speaking in Tongues*, was published. What might have been a celebration was instead a ragged homecoming; I had also left my marriage and uprooted two young children for a country that had become largely hearsay.

I had come by the title of my novel honestly. After living most of her eleven years on the Côte d'Azur, Cassie talked like a book, holding forth in either the teen speak of the Sweet Valley High series she studied to learn about American girls or the cadenced literary phrasing of books she pulled down from my shelves. Nick, born in France, was an eight-year-old bundle of raw energy and nerves who spoke halting English only on demand. Their dad, born in Egypt but an American citizen for many years, spoke a serviceable if idiosyncratic Franco-American blend. "Vous êtes asshole!" he once shouted with some justification when violently cut off in traffic near the airport in Nice. On the first day of elementary school in West Los Angeles, Cassie and Nick clung bravely to lunchboxes filled with sandwiches and chips. It was a far cry from the semolina and cheese puree my daughter used to spit into a napkin at her école maternelle.

After we moved back, their dad never missed a birthday or

holiday. He had always been a good provider, but his job meant that he was perpetually on the road. Now when he visited, his focus on stocking the larder intensified. He was in a panic to buy for his family. They shopped frenetically and the children were returned home detailed as carefully as the luxury cars he adored. Shortly after one of these excursions my son's Little League coach incredulously asked Nick if he was wearing nail polish. That night we removed every trace of the clear gloss left over from his manicure. Heavy doses of MTV and other forms of applied anthropology helped turn Cassie into a popular girl by the end of sixth grade. Missteps aside, my children were on their way to becoming Americans.

Tom approached Cassie and Nick with appropriate hesitation. They were barely fluent in American culture. How would he ever get to know them, unused as he was to being around children, let alone children three thousand miles away? He invited us all to Universal Studios and we stood on interminable lines on a brutally hot day. Later he settled in at the kitchen table for an in-depth discussion of *Cider House Rules* with my daughter while my son headed out back to the driveway with a basketball tucked under his arm. Nick wedged a rock under the kitchen door to keep it open, and the sound of the basketball slamming against the backboard punctuated that first discussion. A clear dynamic was established that day between Tom and my children. Chatting with Cassie was effortless. It was like talking to a miniature adult. Finding the same common ground with Nick was far less evident. There was Horse, a basketball game two could play together. But the games were over when they were over. They were not conversations that could be extended.

I didn't know what to do with Tom when he came to town. An almost courtly Asian-American man, he had impeccable manners. He was slightly buttoned-up, even in jeans and sneakers, and neither my children nor I were used to such careful formality. During the day we scrambled up and down the backside of the Santa Monica Mountains until my children finally staged a sit-down strike. We rode bikes, huffing and puffing our way down the crowded path at Venice Beach. Too terrified to stop moving, I was always leading the charge and was almost relieved when Tom retreated to his hotel room at night.

When the guest-host dynamic began to wear thin, I decided to put Tom to work. While I ferried Nick to his sport du jour, he began driving Cassie to sleep-over dates and ballet lessons. Tom had once moonlighted as a dance critic, and they talked shop on the way to her dreary little dance studio on Pico Boulevard. The two of them were almost automatically in sync from the beginning. Although the future was the furthest thing from Tom's mind, those early conversations held the shape of what was to come. Exchanging ideas would be Tom's way of becoming a stepfather to Cassie. This was something concrete he could provide for her, especially since her father so ably looked after her material needs.

But what work could he do with Nick? I was afraid if I left them alone together the trickle of small talk they managed to keep going would dry up altogether. Nick during those years was still movement and nervous, angry yearning. He cried convulsively each time his father returned to France and had begun sleeping with an old bathrobe his dad left in an empty closet.

The answer began to come one afternoon as we all sat hunched over the Sunday paper and the remains of buttermilk pancakes. Nick and a friend wanted to see *Terminator 2: Judgment Day*, but they were too young to purchase tickets themselves. Tom offered to buy them and I squawked a bit, pointing to the R rating, upholding the unfortunate, priggish position I understood was exactly that. So we struck our first deal. I was to park at the curb while Tom and the boys went inside to get the tickets. It was a key guy moment, I realized, as Tom sauntered back to the car after he had escorted the boys inside the theater. My son needed Tom to slide him and his friend past the box office more than he needed a literary discussion or even a basketball game. That afternoon wasn't the beginning of a mentorship in crime. It was just an afternoon when a mother's rules were momentarily relaxed.

Tom and I scheduled visits as regularly as we could manage; his downtown life of editor and carefree bachelor got a severe jolt roughly every six weeks. We must have been a tough call for a man who had never lived with anyone else, someone who prized silence and solitude. Becoming a stepfather wasn't daunting—it was impossible. Around that time he reported a revealing dream about riding a giant white horse around his apartment and not knowing how to steer the thing left or right.

While I loved the idea of a gallant but baffled Prince Charming, by the end of three years I had run out of patience. The word "boyfriend" stuck to the roof of my mouth. I thought the term and the situation lacked dignity. I was tired of time zones and airport good-byes and living in spurts. Long distance was lonely, and my jokes about frequent cryer miles were getting stale. My editor, my bachelor boyfriend, and I went on an extended hiatus.

WHEN TOM REENTERED our lives three years later, he discovered a sweet, slowed-down boy dressed in pants that could have accommodated two kids his size. Nick was in high school by then and Cassie was off to college on the East Coast. Nick had dropped out of team sports and locked himself in his room to work on his music. Rap flowed from his turntables night and day, where he was constantly spinning and scratching. My son's identification with urban music was all-consuming. His heroes were rappers, and any self-respecting rapper looked out for his single mom. Especially when she was calling collect from New York City.

It was my first trip since Tom and I had gotten back together, and I expected a passionate reception at JFK. Neither of us had a cell phone in those days, so when he didn't turn up at the airport baggage claim after a long wait or answer my calls to his home or office, I took a taxi into the city, expecting to find him waiting for me at his apartment. But no one answered the buzzer, so I trudged to a coffee shop near his apartment, trying to keep an eye on my bulging suitcase as customers squeezed past. I called home to see if there was a message about our scrambled connection.

"Mom, this isn't starting out well." Nick's voice on the other end of the line echoed as if he stood at the bottom of a deep well. His fears didn't sound assuaged when we called later, happily reunited and babbling about the goofy mix-up. His acceptance of the man in his mother's life would be gradual and often grudging. Nick needed concrete evidence that Tom was someone we could both count on. The two of them needed time together, without me nervously trying to stitch their relationship together. But how could this happen when we were still living in separate cities?

Tom's bachelor pad, which we referred to as the "bunker," came under serious siege when I brought Nick and one of his friends along on visits. A remnant from the '80s, Tom's disco bed with lights that glowed from underneath the wooden platform, was now occupied by one teenaged boy, while another lay on an inflatable mattress on the floor. Pipes in the rarely used guest bathroom hummed night and day, and tiles fell off the wall inside the shower because of all the activity following years of disuse. A neighbor below called in hysterics. Her closet was inundated, but then so was Tom. He made map after hand-drawn map for

Nick and his friend and worried as they set off for Staten Island in search of the Wu-Tang Clan's clothing store. He came home from work, and the elevator opened to the sight of the two boys exchanging punches. Nick and his buddy were perfectly content to use the wet towels they dropped in a pile on the floor.

Tom kept his puzzlement to himself. If his impulse was to correct my son's housekeeping style, he kept it in check. He was tentatively exploring a new role with Nick. He wanted to know what my son saw when he walked the streets of his city, and though the exchanges were hardly lengthy, they became more relaxed. Good-natured neutrality set the tone for what would eventually mark his style of stepparenting. He distributed keys to his home and directions for the subway and shook his head as forgotten half-empty bottles of Peach Snapple began to crop up in every room of the bunker.

We discussed marriage and toured schools in Manhattan or real-estate offices in charming little towns along the Hudson, and this time I was the one who blanched. I couldn't pull Nick out of a life in Los Angeles that clearly lacked a man on the premises but that was secure in every other sense. He still had a year of high school before heading off to college in Boston. Cassie would be moving to New York after graduation from college. We had waited this long, we could wait a little longer.

AT FORTY-NINE, Tom acquired his first car and his first wife. He became the blissful owner of a ten-year-old Camry his parents were planning to scrap, but the honeymoon (that one) was short-lived. Tom offered the car to Nick so that he could haul his turntables and records to the college radio station he now hosted in Boston. An uncomplicated life was officially over the day my husband signed over the title to the car in a "family transfer" at the DMV. It was the first time Tom had ever formally used the term "stepson." The word seemed to surprise him as much as it did the first time he introduced me as his wife. The role he had unwittingly been rehearsing for these past twelve years was finally his.

Almost immediately after my move to New York, we embarked on a construction project. Painting and plastering, replacing grim industrial windows too heavy to open and close, would mean months of chaos. We hunkered down to prepare ourselves for the onslaught. Tom's airy, austere apartment grew more spartan still when he decided to give away most of his living-room furniture to my children. Cassie's roommate, six feet tall with spiky platinum blond hair, arrived one night to wrap her long arms around a couple of parachute chairs and a trestle table. Nick's roommate and his uncle pulled their pickup to the curb and, flip-flops slapping the bottoms of their feet, set off for Boston with a Parsons table and the black modular chairs that had defined Tom's decor for twenty-five years. A downtown dowry was distributed in a single night.

A fastidious bachelor never dreamed that his table would wind up covered with empty pizza boxes and dirty, wadded-up napkins. Or that a retired physician would put his car into reverse and roll over his stepson's foot while standing in a crosswalk waiting for the light to change. In Boston on business, Tom's visit to check on Nick's postoperative recovery surprised us all. His report on the two-foot-high stack of *Maxim* magazines in the bathroom and Nick's hobbling progress was more comforting to me than if I had been there myself to tend to my son.

"I think he was happy to see me," Tom said later, when he called from Boston. "Poor kid."

They were finding their way without my direction. Even though I was used to running the show as a single parent, I was delighted to remain offstage.

Tom and I had been married for about three years when Cassie accidentally referred to my husband as her StepTom. The term stuck. We have two telephone lines in our house, one in my name and one in my husband's, and nine times out of ten when the phone rings now, it's Cassie calling for her StepTom on line two with a delicious piece of gossip or an urgent question. Much of the best stuff goes to him first, though she labors to mete out stories fairly. Some jokes never make it to me at all, for I am told there is much that would simply go over my head. Tom and Cassie attend dance concerts they consider too postmodern for the likes of me and jabber about them afterward in coffee shops. Most of the time their collusion delights me, and when it doesn't, I remind them of how they met in the first place.

Nick doesn't have a StepTom yet, but he does have a very engaged stepfather, one who is helping him put together a business plan for a school for DJs. Tom clips endless newspaper pieces on the music business and makes the occasional desultory remark about the arrivistes who are flooding the market. He worries that hucksters will undercut his talented stepson now that hip-hop is so mainstream.

"Hi, honey." Tom fiddles with my computer nearby as I chat on the phone with my son. Nick has graduated from college and is now back in Los Angeles. I understand that our family destiny is distance. Discussions to have it any other way give everybody a stomachache.

"Uh, I DJ'ed this weekend."

"That's fantastic! Who for?"

Nick goes into reverse, telling me to forget it. He wishes he had never brought it up, and I try not to lose consciousness. Something is wrong and I leap to the worst conclusions: stabbings, shooting—the bloody stuff of nightclubs everywhere. Tom drops all pretext of fixing my computer and watches me as I sputter.

"Just *tell* me. Who were you playing for?"

"The guy's kind of a film distributor."

"But that's wonderful. Do I know the films?"

"Probably not. They're adult films."

Bedlam. I almost drop the phone. But not before I hear about the partygoer who borrowed my son's fan, her hair billowing out behind her as she danced in the wind. Somebody else seized the spotlight by leaping on top of the table that held his equipment. I'm shouting, but I'm not the only one making noise.

"Go, Nick!" Tom has turned red with laughter. He is pumping me for details of the party while I try to keep talking to my son.

"Tell him the main guy was Asian," Nick says.

I wring various promises from my son. He will think twice before advertising again on Craig's List. He will never date any of the actresses he met that night—he expresses an appropriate level of disgust when I make him swear this. He owes me one Sunday in church.

"Ask him if he bartered services." My husband is enjoying the exchange mightily.

"Here." I wave the telephone in Tom's direction. "Why don't you get on the phone yourself?"

I realize, somewhere in the frantic middle of this three-way conversation that is full of banter and bluff and all the guy noises so antithetical to a single-mom universe, that I have gotten exactly what I wanted. My husband and his stepson are finally talking.

Stepmother*

SUSAN CHEEVER

Good stepparenting was impossible until
I had a child of my own.

My first experiences as a stepmother were disastrous. At twenty-three I married a man seven years older than I was. He may not have been Mr. Right, I used to say, but he was certainly Mr. Willing. He had already been married, and he was the father of two rambunctious, beautiful daughters aged three and five. In those days—it was 1967—women were expected to get married as soon as possible and to be literally handed at the altar from father to husband. Women weren't supposed to grow up and get jobs and take responsibility—they were supposed to get men to do that. Trying to deal with my own expectations—that my husband would take care of me; the children's expectations—that when he got over me, my husband would go back to their mother; his expectations—that I would somehow morph into a version of their mother who loved him—was the emotional equivalent of a double root canal. The only people who got hurt worse than I did were the two little girls.

I had no idea how to be a mother anyway. My own mother was a beautiful, talented woman. Her mother had died—a painful death from a long illness—when my mother was a girl, leaving a dreadful wound which was passed down through generations. In my mother's world, women had their children young. Then they got on with the business of being glamorous and witty accoutrements to their husbands' talents—the main business of their lives. In that world, children really were supposed to be seen and not heard, but that wasn't all. When children were seen, they were expected to say please and thank you, to call all adults Mister and Missus in a particularly obsequious tone of voice, to behave impeccably, and—as my father used to say—to "look like something."

I had no desire to be a mother myself, certainly not when I married at twenty-three. My mother used to tell me a story about the day I was born, a day when she was twenty-three. She was walking along Eighth Street in Greenwich Village, a few hours before she went to the hospital. My father was away in the army. It was the end of July. It was hot. It was hotter than hot. The pavements were steaming. She saw a woman pulling a young child into a movie theater. The child was dressed in a cotton shift and she was barefoot. She didn't want to go. The woman pulled. The child resisted. Finally the woman's superior strength prevailed and the child was pulled into the darkness. Even as a child I could figure out what that story meant about my mother's reluctance to have a child.

During our courtship, there had been no children in evidence. We dated for a summer and then corresponded. He said not a word about his children. Sometime that fall, he asked me to come back to New York and move in with him. This was a very bohemian request in those days. My parents disapproved; his parents disapproved. I still hadn't met his two little girls. I said yes. Before we married, I met them once or twice. They seemed noisy and destructive. They broke my husband's most precious things, jumped up and down in his lap, ate all the ice cream in the freezer, and made reasonable conversation impossible. Their demands seemed incessant. Nothing was safe from them.

I assumed that, after their visits, when they finally left to go back to their mother, my husband was as relieved as I was. When they were with us, I counted the hours. I imagined that when he came from taking them back to their mother, he felt as if he could walk on air. He was angry sometimes when he got home, and who could blame him? His ex-wife was impossible. That's why he had divorced her. I assumed he was irritated because of the way she dumped the kids on us. Who in their right mind would want to have their very pleasant life regularly shattered by crying, whining, demanding, expensive little people who were, after all, the unfair and huge result of an early mistake? He often said he should never have married his first wife. I assumed this meant that he felt they should never have had children. I was terribly wrong.

It didn't seem fair that in marrying the man I loved I also seemed to have married his children and even his ex-wife and, on some days, her new boyfriend. I didn't understand why his children should be my problem. "I didn't marry your children," became my mantra. Didn't they already have a mother? When the girls were with us—on the classic Wednesday night and alternate weekend schedule mandated by divorce—I tried to assume parental authority. I got them haircuts. I washed their clothes, and threw out the ones that looked worn-out. I made them go to bed at set times so that we could have a quiet dinner—this was my idea of what constituted parental authority. I had virtually no experience of parental authority.

As our marriage lasted and moved forward, we moved from

the city to the country, then we moved from the country to another country. My husband was eager for children of our own. I could hardly suppress my scorn at this idea. Didn't we have enough trouble with the children he already had? Even living abroad, we had to send a monthly check back to New York to support them. We would never be free. The last thing we needed was more children. His children made me painfully uncomfortable, and my only respite was their absence. If I was stupid enough to have a child of my own, there would be no respite— that's what I thought.

MY SECOND SET of stepchildren were older when I met their father. My first marriage had slowly faded until it became nothing but an inconvenience as far as I was concerned. In those days divorce was just another rite of passage, and I was eager to experience it. I had friends who threw themselves divorce parties—on the theory that there was more to celebrate in a divorce (mutual freedom) than there ever was in a marriage (mutual bondage). It was the 1970s, and having children was what people did in the suburbs. In New York we were slick and cool and we had discovered the joys of sex, the joys of drugs, the joys of working, the joys of living alone, the joys of not being like our parents' tied-down, hidebound generation. Age didn't matter, money didn't matter, the old rules didn't matter.

Still, my new husband had children—he had them back in the dark ages when everyone did—and our rare times with his children often ended with bitter fights. He was older than I was and his children were in their twenties, but that didn't make them want to be close to me. They had been through a divorce already. They were the children of his first wife; I was his third wife. I was amazed and offended by their loyalty to his ex-wife, a woman who wasn't even their mother. She had been their stepmother for fifteen years. I heard that they hadn't liked her much then. Now they visited her and talked about her and worried about her. My husband had left her for me, and they seemed to hold this against me. This seemed very unfair. They were adults, after all. This was the way of the world. I hadn't exactly invented adultery all by myself.

Furthermore, I didn't see why I couldn't be honest about their failings; was I supposed to lie? I criticized them as freely as I criticized any adults whom I found wanting—and that was many adults. They were actually estimable men and women, but at times they dressed strangely, and they lived in out-of-the-way places. I was always amazed that when I criticized one of his children, my husband acted as if I was speaking about *his* failings.

"When you criticize them, it goes through me like a knife," he said.

I just didn't get it. Before I had a child, I had no idea what all the fuss was about. Children were so noisy, and they were such a lot of trouble. When children were around, everyone seemed to change, to go a little crazy or to get very angry. When it came to understanding the human family—the human condition—I was in the dark. I remember being in my gynecologist's office one morning with three impressively beautiful professional women. They wore gleaming low heels and carried authoritative briefcases. They had thick hair cut short or pulled back in buns. I was in sweat pants and a T-shirt. Then a baby appeared, crawling ahead of its mother on the carpet. The three women dropped their poses and hit the floor cooing and goo-gooing and chuckling over the baby. I thought they were ridiculous.

NOW MY CHILDREN have stepmothers. As a mother who watched her precious child be driven away in a young woman's sports car for her weekend with her father, I began to see what kind of stepmother I had been. I knew that the driver of that sports car had no idea of the preciousness of her cargo. Not only did I compete with my stepchildren—after all, I was a child myself—but I completely failed to understand the feelings of their real mother. The children's importance to her was beyond my comprehension. For me, good stepparenting was impossible until I had a child of my own. I didn't know what a family was. The idea of putting aside my own welfare for a common good was completely alien.

The feelings which are at the basis of any love—the acceptance, the unselfishness—were not on my screen. We live in a country where the individual is in the ascendant, and we seem to believe that our individual destinies are more important than anything else. It's a high romantic ideal, this American way, an ideal of the value of each person's freedom. I had embraced that ideal in order to rationalize my own self-absorption. The birth of my daughter ended that.

Liley was a perfect child, and her perfection seemed like an enormous gift. I knew that I had done nothing to deserve such a gift. That was part of what blew away the straitjacket of self-absorption in which I had been living. Watching my baby girl, as I did for hours, I would pinch myself in disbelief. How had I come to possess, to be in the company of such a beautiful child? I was in love with her, and I was also in awe of her—or of whoever had created her. She was everything I was not. She was perfect evidence of God's grace. In coming to love her, I learned to love the world.

Advice to New Stepmothers

On Undertaking the Stepfamily Vacation

LUCIA NEVAI

Time-honored tips developed long ago in the
Dawn of Joint Custody.

There are realists who would advise you new stepmothers that when the time comes to plan your well-earned vacation, you should seek the pleasure and frivolity of an adventure with your fun-loving girlfriends—embark on a Caribbean cruise, tour London, hike the Grand Canyon—go anywhere and do anything, in short, except undertake a stepfamily vacation. Their reasoning is simple: the stepfamily vacation is this generation's most sobering oxymoron, your new second husband being the ox and you being the moron. Nonsense. The stepfamily vacation is a unique opportunity to get to know yourself and the folly of your ways, to practice unwanted sexual abstinence, and to endow both your children and his with the greatest gift of all—and the only one they are emotionally capable of accepting from you—the ever-satisfying reassurance that the glory of the original nuclear family is undimmed, that it has not only endured, it will prevail. To ensure this result, simply follow these time-honored tips, developed long ago in the Dawn of Joint Custody, when my new second husband and his two daughters were forced to endure a week's vacation in a seaside cottage with my two sons and me.

Tip Number One. Throughout the planning of the stepfamily

vacation, flatter your new second husband profusely. No matter how absurd your claims may seem to you, he will find the experience delightful. His features will soften by stages, growing so round and docile as to approach the foolish. Do not crack a smile. He will readily forgive you for appearing either deficient as a student of human nature or slow compared with Wife One. His faults as a man and a husband he knows all too well; the sound of them is still ringing in his ears from the hour they were so clearly articulated by Wife One as she implored him for a divorce. He is grateful that these faults, so recently deemed terminal to romantic relationships, have escaped your notice, and that in place of them, you recognize traits he wishes he possessed and, indeed, one day hopes to acquire. Some examples:

Praise him for his Generosity in deferring to your choice of a seaside town known for the tediousness of its amusement park, the tackiness of its souvenirs, and the ptomaine of its boardwalk menus; for his Bravery in choosing an antiquated three-bedroom cottage on a remote stretch of beach where the primal destructive urges of all four children may gather momentum, in lieu of a harborside condo where the presence of other vacationers in the spa and around the pool guarantees a civilizing influence which will foster only the mildly negative emotion of boredom; for his Wisdom in chartering the deep-sea fishing boat which he knows will thrill and captivate the boys at the expense of the girls, who hate worms, hooks, eyeballs, scales, fins, and blood and will turn green with dry heaves for eight hours in high seas; for his Fortitude in rejigging the arrangements numerous times in the months leading up to the getaway to accommodate sudden interesting offers accepted by both ex-spouses. Even though the final booking lands the stepfamily vacation solidly in hurricane season, don't give up. The consoling effect of your flattery serves two purposes: it will differentiate you in your new second hus-

band's mind from Wife One, thus reducing the number of opportunities in which he refers to you by her name; and it will consti-
tute his only happy memory of the stepfamily vacation.

Tip Number Two. Immediately terminate the above flattery
when his daughters or your sons enter the room. At least one of
each pair of siblings will have developed a supernatural sensitivity to the synaptic scent of happiness being laid down in the
brain of a biological parent in a second marriage. It is common
knowledge that children of divorce become obsessive guardians
of that nostalgically illustrated memorial primer they were the
subject of, returning emotionally again and again to the sweet,
original pages where they first learned to read relationships and
place themselves in our world. Children mistake the above practice of flattery for love. This kind of love was not observed
between their father and mother, so it will not be tolerated
between their father and you. If you two refuse to stop acting
happy, stepchildren feel the compulsion to get to the root of your
pretense and hypocrisy, to flush you out as the parent they know
best: an out-of-control lunatic. You are not to be forgiven for crav-
ing a second chance at marital bliss.

Children seek consistency and uniformity. This motivates
them to reproduce between their father and you all of the tension, antagonism, ridicule, deceit, sarcasm, and rage they grew
up with. If indeed these qualities are not present on the stepfamily vacation, then there are effective, never-fail ways and
means of introducing them.

Tip Number Three. Concede all luxury. Assuming your second
marriage survives the car trip out to the ocean, allow the
stepchildren to storm the cottage and compete for lairs. Resist
the urge to pull rank as the authority figure and cosponsor. Stake
your claim to the hall. You will end up there anyway. This will
eliminate a time-consuming and humiliating sequence of transi-

tions as, first, you abandon the master bedroom to the girls who spy a bug on the wall in their room and evacuate, and second, relinquish the living-room sofa bed to the boys, who have developed the capacity to extract entertainment value from late-night television movies which only last week were bitterly declaimed unfit to rent. Both transactions occur without your gaining sleeping quarters. The girls have already dedicated the floor of their room to the storage of clothing. In the boys' room, an unsavory denuding of the environment has occurred.

Everyone knows that boys are stimulated at the sight of neatly made twin beds to jump up and down until the bed linens twist themselves into separate Gordian knots and slide down the respective walls. In addition, because the spectacle of a clean expanse of bare mattress recommends itself to any boy as a potential tabletop, there quickly follows the hilarious spilling of soda cans, the thorough smashing of potato chips, and the jealousy-induced overturning of the biggest slices of Pizza with Everything. The result is a moldy blight of such proportions as to threaten the return of your security deposit.

Examining the remaining sleeping options, you and your husband settle for separate booby prizes. He takes the reclining lounge chair, and you resort to the above-mentioned hall.

Tip Number Four. Give no advice, no matter how grave and obvious the errors made by your husband. Remember, this is the new, fragile, second Him, a Him postulated and feigned by the first. Never suggest his personality could be improved with an adjustment in attitude or a shift in behavior, especially regarding the chosen means of disciplining his daughters. If, for example, his younger daughter is playing with scissors and cuts a hole in the favorite white shorts of his older daughter, spurring a melee, which he hopes to quell by getting on the phone with Wife One for an hour, remain mum. If, while they are on the phone, the older girl retaliates by stabbing the younger with the scissors, spurring a mortal wound, which he hopes to staunch by staying on the phone with Wife One for another hour, mum is still the word. Advice from you of any kind on parenting, no matter how slight, oblique, or lighthearted, is severely resented by your second husband, because it is an unforgivable reminder of his own powerlessness to effect the actions of either of his daughters or Wife One. Should you be unable to resist, expect him to counter with a viciously voiced litany of examples of your powerlessness with your ex, which you will hardly recognize as such, because you have misfiled these incidents under the heading of Trying to Get Along.

Tip Number Five. As things begin to go wrong, repeat over and over to yourself, *Stepchildren are not really people.* Forget the bountiful array of winning traits you admire in your stepdaughters. Perhaps the older is queenly, beautiful, and competent, possessing a gift for friendship, an infectious sense of humor, a strong sense of family responsibility. Perhaps the younger, though also beautiful, is more notable for her emotional depth, her searing intelligence, her forthrightness. Forget all this. Pray that your new second husband, in turn, can temporarily discard his keen appreciation of your older son, whose artistic precocity dictates that he spend most of his waking hours drawing costumes for the historically accurate epic films he will make as soon as he is able. Let your new husband also forget, if he can, how charming he finds the mischievousness of your younger son, and how completely he forgives that fellow for risking unmanliness by bawling his head off loud and long, thus ending the festive aspect of any stepfamily occasion long before the labor of it is complete.

While as individuals the units of the reconstituted stepfamily are unquestionably interesting, diverse, and talented, when thrown together any four stepchildren begin to operate like an eight-eyed, eight-eared, sixteen-limbed monster whose sole survival depends on maiming your marital harmony.

Tip Number Six. Accept the inevitable—there will be a Big Fight that almost ruins the Second Marriage. As the stepfamily vacation throws people together in smaller quarters with fewer escapes, the opportunities for bringing you two to the edge of homicide are exponentially increased. Boys tend to take the gross-motor approach, applying their skill at running, jumping, knocking, hitting, tossing, and breaking to disfigure or disable objects known to be precious to the girls, as well as to daze, disorient, and divide you two. Often, special creativity is shown in the appropriation of decor items for missiles. Girls, by contrast, prefer to isolate and slander, taking their biological parent aside to whisper accusations, disguising the transaction as the intimacy the said parent is hoping for, vacations being quality time. Don't resist. Enjoy your fight. Remember that the family therapist coached you to use confrontations to let off steam, as you throw yourselves into the roles of hating each other's guts. You'll know you're on the right track when, from all four children, there finally issues the sound of silence.

Tip Number Seven. Don't let confrontations between you and your new second husband occur in parallel universes. Be aware of crucial differences in gender-based and regional adversarial models. Practice gamesmanship. Everyone knows that men are better at competition and women are better at cooperation. Train yourself to update any archaic female adversarial models. If, for example, your models were learned in Des Moines, Iowa, in the '50s, as mine were, instantly discard both tenets meant to cover the full range of severity of confrontation you were to encounter in your lifetime. Opponents who went to your church were confronted with minimum severity—you smiled, understood, and forgave. Opponents who didn't go to your church were confronted with maximum severity—you prayed for their very souls.

Be flexible. To play along with the adversarial model favored by your husband, first teach yourself to ignore all apparent content in his speech. Practice watching his lips flap while humming in your mind his silliest favorite song. With any luck, this will be on a par with "I'm Henry the Eighth, I Am," by Herman's Hermits. His arguments will contain scathing denouncements of your character, contempt for your behavior, disgust for your capacity to survive, let alone evolve. Don't assume this means he doesn't love you. To him, it proves he does. Who else would he allow to become the subject of his greatest win-or-die fantasy than the one woman whose sexual favors mean more to him than anything else in the world? Relax, tune him out, and concentrate on the quality of the psychic blows you sustain. This will allow you to respond in kind.

Here, as a guide, are three of the more common adversarial models in current use.

Labor Versus Management. In this scenario, your husband categorically refuses any reasonable request for change. No increase in hourly wages. No decrease in weekly hours. No improvement in benefits. Instead of crying and pointing out how unappreciated this makes you feel, come to the negotiating table with a number. Explain if your needs aren't met, you'll go on strike. He'll challenge your citing of comparable labor/wage situations in other marriages. He'll promise to outlast you as you walk back and forth in front of him bearing your UNFAIR placard. But he already has in the back of his bean-counting mind exactly the number you will accept. Inch your way toward it, never making the emotionally fatal link with your own worth.

Last Out of the World Series. If your husband prefers this model, you will initiate a specific innocuous complaint only to experience instant general escalation. You've plummeted yourself into the gut-wrenching tension and high-stakes intensity of baseball's ultimate duel. It's the bottom of the ninth with two outs. The score is tied. You're stepping up to home plate. The manager of the opposing team sends to the mound the greatest relief pitcher in the league—your new second husband. He stretches, winds up, and wham! The fastball is over the plate for a called strike one. You didn't even see it. You take a deep breath, adjust your hat, your crotch, your two shoulder seams. Again, you step up to the plate. He stretches and winds up. Whoosh. A slider. You swing and miss for strike two. You're onto him now. It's a full count. The crowd's going wild. Your husband's need to win is overcome by a momentary sadism. His next pitch catches you on the elbow. You walk to first. Three pitches later, you steal home.

Mafia Versus the FBI. This is the thorniest of adversarial scenarios. As head of the FBI, your second husband hires you to end underworld crime. You find yourself cast in the role of naïve greenhorn recruit as you zealously collar your first thug. Instead of winning accolades from your superior, he lets the thug go on a false technicality. You complain to your husband. He encourages you to fight the good fight, to trace corruption within the agency. Following his direction, you encounter only roadblocks and dead ends—until a lucky break allows you to discover complicity at the most unwanted level. Your husband himself is in business with The Godfather, who is none other than Wife One.

Tip Number Eight. Once you've had the Big Fight, don't hold a grudge. The stepchildren will express their guilt and relief by going outside to play in the ocean for the first time all week. Quick, take advantage of their lack of vigilance to have sex. Try to stay angry and don't bring love into it, or your overconfidence might provoke the early return of the children. Remember that

acute sensitivity of theirs will be able to detect in a biological parent even the remotest hint of synaptic happiness. Postpone yours
until it's time to plan your next well-deserved vacation. Remember those fun-loving girlfriends? Embark on a Caribbean cruise,
tour London, hike the glorious Grand Canyon.

Infidelities

ELIZABETH POWELL

> Throughout the whole ordeal of my father's death, one essen-
> tial question about my stepmother rolled through my mind:
> how could our relationship resolve?

I first saw my father's mistress at his funeral. As I stood at the lectern reading a poem called "My Father in a White Space Suit," by Yehuda Amichai, trying to ignore my stepmother's nephew who was mocking me, I had no idea that Dad had had a mistress, let alone that she was in the church, redheaded, pregnant, my age.

In a different pew, not far away, my stepmother sat regally—and none the wiser—in her large black Marianne Moore hat, her cloisonné locket full of my dead father's hair around her neck, a kind of talisman. When I was a child she recounted stories of how she had learned Brazilian witchcraft during her first, unhappy and cruel, marriage and life in South America. "I took some of your father's hair," she said. "Then I tied it together with a ribbon that I had worn around my neck. Then I buried it in the ground. Three weeks later, after two years of living together, he finally proposed," she told me one night long ago. Forever in my mind, then, she was the Delilah, my father the Samson. I waited in earnest for him to regain his strength and leave her. Instead, at sixty-one years old, he keeled over on the side of the road, a cardiac arrest in his car.

My stepmother's power seemed to electrify the plain white

church. She glared at me up at the lectern, as if my father's death had been my fault. I had seen this kind of look on my step-mother's face frequently growing up: one part expectation, two parts contempt. I wasn't sure what I was supposed to prove to her with my elegy for my father; I already felt beaten by her hom-age, a perfect "Letter to Lewis," in which she recapped in lovely, unsentimental prose their experiences in Provence, Paris, and New York.

It was an odd funeral. The crosses had been covered in black cloth as per the instruction of a rabbi who had traveled to the small New England town to perform the ceremony. It looked like Good Friday. Everything had happened so suddenly.

My father peered out from the photograph on top of his cas-ket. It was a portrait taken by a *New York Times* photographer twenty years earlier. The picture had appeared in the business section: in it, he still had his handsome, baby face offset by salt-and-pepper hair. He looked happy; it was before he had left Manhattan with his young, sexy blond second wife and a bundle of money from having sold the Madison Avenue building and business that had been in our family since the 1930s. He looked like the kind of guy other men might be envious of: trips on the Concorde, retired at forty-five.

"Always the bon vivant, pays for the party but never sends us a check," my mother used to say of Dad. My mother, with her unmade-up classic good looks, was a combination of athlete and duty-honor-dinner-party WASP who had converted when she married my father, and who had lost family money and comforts first in her own parents' divorce, and then again in her own divorce. My mother had been forced into affordable housing; often we had no food. When my stepmother appeared for one of our birthday parties, my mother marveled at her replacement. I listened by the hallway to her recounting my stepmother's visit: "It's sad really; I wanted to be jealous."

Many of my friends press me for positive qualities about my stepmother, and I will say she is an excellent cook, cares deeply for all animals in a Saint Francis kind of way, and is very knowledgeable about Estée Lauder products. When I was a teenager I would ask her for beauty secrets because I perceived her as a wealth of man-enticing information. About my bushy eyebrows she advised me to pluck them very thin. When my eyebrows grew back, I sported two eyebrows over each eye. I never asked her for advice again, except for once, when we were drinking and I felt a closeness that perhaps really wasn't there. I'd told her about an especially hard breakup. Later, when I was plagued with anxiety about it, she said, "What's the matter? Can't control your mind?"

Enraged, I said, "Well, we all know what you're all about." To which my stepmother replied, "I did not marry your father for his money!"

Of course, I didn't believe her. In her quiet way she controlled our family by feigning a sort of helplessness my father found irresistible. Watching my stepmother manipulate him in this way, I developed her brand of helplessness that I have worked hard to destroy. Even when she was awful, I still wanted to fit in.

Once she found a nearly dead bird on the sidewalk, brought it up to the apartment to nurture until animal control came. Watching her tend to the bird, I understood she had love, but it was a love she would not let me access; I did not have the code. Later, how I yearned for her to show me that kind of affection as I held my newborn out to her and she refused to hold the baby, so deep was her own sadness in not having children of her own.

We had always been two women at war, beginning when I, a

child of twelve, found her asleep on our sofa looking quite mag-
nificent, a bit like Sleeping Beauty. I had thought to warn my
father to not, under any circumstances, kiss her.

At the funeral home before the service, I was spooked when
she kissed my rigor mortis father on the lips. It was unnerving the
way she stood guard over the casket. I wanted to touch his solar
plexus, the place where I used to rest my head when I was
younger and my stepmother wasn't around. Her possessiveness
scared me as she stood watch over me as I looked at him for the
last time. She looked as if she thought I'd steal his soul.

Later, at the church, I held my hand out to touch the casket
when it passed, as one who holds her hand over the side of a boat
lets her fingers feel the force of water. I took comfort that I would
be the last to touch it since my stepmother wasn't sitting at the
end of a pew. It was my last laying on of hands, proclaiming my
rights of kinship. My normal desire to love my father became
tainted by my fear of being pushed out, and by my stepmother's
wish for her husband to be her father as well. Her own father had
been so stingy, so withholding of love and money, that she sought
comfort in having my father take care of her, exclusively.

Now, in death, he belonged to no one. I could sense my stepmother's challenge, her duel for who would be the keeper of his
memory. In his death, I felt oddly closer to him. In my stepmother's kitchen before the funeral, I felt eerily sure that his
spirit was nowhere in their home. It was a tangible, real feeling.
He had literally and spiritually fled. My stepmother sat at the
center island saying odd things and looking at the window, stirring her tea. "I think there was a whole lot he wasn't telling me,"
she admitted.

At the cemetery, in a group of a hundred people, we waited for
my stepmother to lead the procession up the hill to the graveside.
I could see my father's coffin in the hearse as it waited for the

procession to gather; even in death my father was waiting for my stepmother to get ready. Earlier, I saw the bottle of Bordeaux that she had put in the casket, along with his favorite corkscrew, as if he was an ancient Egyptian who would need a good belt once he reached the other side. He had always been the inveterate traveler. Every six weeks he went to Paris on his huge fiefdom of frequent flyer miles, and my sister and I joked that we must have French half-siblings.

The rabbi said some prayers over the open grave lined with Astroturf. My stepmother sent out a wattage that said "I burn" as we watched the lowering of the casket into the ground. The sun reflected off the brass. I could hear the town dump rumbling off in the distance.

We threw dirt in the grave, headed somberly for the party at the local inn where bowls of Halloween candy were still on the porch tables. My stepmother, drowning in her big hat and Pashmina shawl, disappeared in an instant that ticked shut. My husband, in his gray overcoat, waited for me to catch up.

"Who's that by Dad's grave?" he asked.

As I turned, I saw an attractive woman, the redhead from the funeral service, but gave it no thought then. I surveyed the grave, felt perversely victorious to be the last one standing there, just me and Dad's ghost on a raw November afternoon. Standing there, I felt that my father was mine more than I had since I was a small child.

My stepmother was mysteriously uncommunicative after the funeral, until finally, three months later, she called me with a battery of weird questions about my father.

"Did he gamble?"

"You're kidding, right? He had bad luck with cards," I said.

"Yes, but did he tell you anything?"

"Like what?' I said.

"Like had he been sick?"

"No."

Then one Sunday, I got a conference call from my mother with my siblings on the other end.

"Your stepmother is too ashamed to call you, so she asked me to. Apparently, your father had a pregnant mistress half his age. She lost the child two weeks after he died."

The pretty woman at the funeral, I thought.

My mother continued. "And his millions are missing—not that they ever helped us—but your stepmother is in a fit. Not to mention, she found medical documents that said your father had had a heart attack two years ago and told no one. He had been with this young gal for eight years."

I wondered why he never left for the younger woman if his millions were missing. I wondered about what kind of hold my stepmother had on him.

THROUGHOUT THE WHOLE ordeal of my father's death, one essential question about my stepmother rolled through my mind: how could our relationship resolve? I wondered what I owed her, or if I owed her anything. She had no children of her own. In some ways I felt very sorry for her, but she wanted nothing from me.

Until the day came when she announced she was going to exhume my father from the plot in New Hampshire and move him to New York to rest next to his own parents. The trouble was, in the end, there was no money left to do so. The life insurance had paid the outstanding bills that were left. What happened to his millions remains unresolved, even by private detectives. All the property would be left to my stepmother. I felt the money cursed and, oddly, didn't care. I had always been poor among the wealthy, only to watch my rich relations behave badly, greedily.

But now my stepmother got to know how it felt to be left out by my father, however ironic and sad. She would have to sell the house they had built on the hill. Her favorite thing to say to me when I was a bratty teenager had been, "What goes around comes around." She got it back double, and so did I.

In the end, fear, as they say, was our master, and our fears about each other and my father came to pass. Her hoarding of money, goods, my father, couldn't keep her safe. My fears of losing my father to my stepmother had come to pass as well. In many ways, money, and all it came to mean, was the basting thread that held us together. Now the seam was being ripped out. In death, my Houdini-like father had wiggled out of both of our stronghold clutches. Through it all I tried to bite my tongue when she'd slander my father for cheating on her. In some ways my baser side relished the fact that his heart had drifted.

To this day, my stepmother refuses a headstone on my father's grave. I have been fighting her on this, and for my efforts she has instructed me never to make contact with her again. It is this fact that keeps us bound together now, with an irritating, uncomfortable glue, leaving our stepmother-stepdaughter relationship as unresolved as it is painful. We both wanted desperately to be close to my father; we each wanted to own him in our own way. In his death, his infidelities to us both remain the only bond we share.

Dogs and Daughter

D. S. SULAITIS

I met her when she was big. Older. Why did I have
to pay for medical school?

I met him in Washington Square Park. We both had dogs—
rescued mutts. We both had to stick to secluded park corners, and only during dark early morning hours. The dogs
—nasty, growling, barking, still in trauma over their past junkyard lives.

That wasn't enough. Our dogs fought. I hated this guy. He was
much older than me, bearded like a mountain man, and didn't
seem too alarmed over the teeth and neck clenches. We met,
parted, and I hoped never to see him or his beast again.

But then there's always the next morning, and when you try to
avoid someone there he was again. This is what he told me. In
this order: I live on Eighth Street. I have a daughter.

I remember pulling my dog away from this guy. He seemed too
cocky, artsy, and who lives on Eighth Street, land of shoes? And
a daughter? Who needs it?

Me. I was thirty-five, single, and living in the West Village in
a tiny studio with a hundred-pound pit bull mix. I'd had a row of
long-term boyfriends: stockbroker, history teacher, dog walker. I
was now dating a biker who worked as a caterer.

———

IT WAS A few months after we met, January, and I had the flu. I was at the secluded spot of the park, coughing, leaning against the metal bars of the fence. I was skinny, and at the time my hair was bleached white and I wore several braids and, over that, a mad-bomber hat and I heard a muffled "Hey kid." There he was. He was concerned for me. He buttoned the top bottom of my faux fur coat. Then he took my dog leash.

"Let me help you," he said, and invited me to his loft for chili.

"I'm a vegetarian," I said.

"Me too," he said.

"Is your daughter home?" I asked. I didn't want to meet a daughter.

"She's in college," he said.

Relief.

He lived above one of the countless shoe stores on Eighth Street, an entire floor of a building. He was a photographer. The loft was as large as a hotel lobby and filled with floor-to-ceiling shelves crammed with books, boxes, dead plants, tools, and rocks. A black cat sat up on the top shelf and peered down at me. "You have a cat," I said stupidly. "My daughter's. She found him on the street," he said, then went to make chili.

I snooped.

Where were the daughter's photographs? The smiling child hugging the cat? Posing with a ball in the swimming pool? Classroom pictures? I looked everywhere. I opened a closet. Nothing.

"This is her teddy bear," he told me later, after we ate.

I took it and looked it over. Teddy bear? How horrible could she be?

"She hates everyone I go out with. She's a bitch," he kept telling me. It was a warning, one of those reflecting caution

blinkers on the road, the kind that tell you to slow down. Stop. A
ditch. A fall ahead.

But I didn't realize how fast I was going. I couldn't believe that
any daughter was a bitch. Maybe there was something wrong
with *him* to call her that. I held the teddy bear. Then he took it
from me. He put it back on her bed with the other stuffed animals—most of them, I noticed, snakes.

Soon after that, we had a dog date, which means walking the
dogs to the Hudson River with cups of coffee. I'd never hung out
with a man who had a daughter. He told me she was eighteen.
"A bitch," he said again.

I was glad I wasn't all that interested in him. He was close to
sixty. Old, in my book. And the prospect of meeting a bitch (what
kind of father calls his daughter that?) sickened me. I was sure
to keep walking, slightly ahead of him, my dog pulled close to
my side.

I BROKE UP with the biker and started dating this guy. After
we'd been seeing each other for a month, he asked me to marry
him. I said, "Sure." I knew I wasn't marrying *him*. It was his
washer and dryer. Yes, I was attached to the luxury of a washer
and dryer in his loft, large as coffins, sitting against the wall of
the living room. I couldn't stop doing laundry. I couldn't imagine
not living in this loft, complete with two darkrooms, doghouses,
and twelve windows facing a courtyard garden—and of course
the washing machine and dryer. I washed and washed—sheets,
bedding, towels, clothes, dog leashes, sneakers, dog beds. I
couldn't stop. "Kid," he'd say. "What's with all the laundry?"

It was March and his daughter was coming home for spring
break. She had a bitch mother, and since they didn't get along
she would be staying with her father. Rosemary. She'd been
named for the herb. An herb I really liked. He warned me: she

hated all my girlfriends. She can outtalk, outwit anyone. She was on the debate team.

"But she's vegetarian and loves dogs," I said. My two criteria.

"Yeah," he said. "Did I tell you she got into a fight at an animal rights march?"

I WAS AN administrative assistant in an arts organization and wrote short stories, and didn't have friends, didn't have confidence, and did needlepoint for fun. I preferred quiet, not getting into confrontations, mostly daydreaming and writing.

I was at work the day Rosemary arrived, and I dreaded stepping into the loft of open jaws. Rosemary had grown up there. She'd hate my stuff scattered about—my crosses and amber amulets, photos of my dog, piles of antique lace, and paintings of my parents' country, Lithuania, scenes of fields, windmills, and the Baltic Sea. I was sensitive, quiet, and cried easily. I was shy, pulled my sleeves over my hands, and as I walked into the loft I was struck with a thought. I'll treat her like you would anyone else, with kindness, interest, and grace. I took a deep breath.

She was sitting at the kitchen table eating raw ravioli, the cat watching, poised over her shoulder on the windowsill. Rosemary's long black hair was shiny, and her pale, very round face reminded me of a beautiful cherub. The dogs sat at either side of her, and she fed them bread. She looked at me and smiled.

I instantly liked her. She had a happy, jolly way about her, large dark eyes that were sincere, and she was interested in everything about me. She wasn't the bone-thin girl I'd imagined. She was pudgy and didn't seem hung up on her weight.

We started talking hair. That's what I remember, hair, guys, school.

My therapist once told me I was stunted emotionally at seventeen. This proved it. Somehow Rosemary yanked something out of me, picked up something that had drifted off. I didn't have any girlfriends, and here was a girl that I couldn't get enough of. I wanted to know what face powder she used, which shampoo, what she ate, how many hours she slept, what movies she'd seen, books she'd read.

I'd forgotten about her father. Where was he? We'd talked for an hour. He'd disappeared. At one point I saw him way over at the other end of the loft, cleaning out his dog's ear.

I made up Rosemary's bed with my good linen European sheets and lent her my nightgown. "Wow, thanks," she said. She was polite and thanked me for the towels, lotion, for every little thing.

I can't explain it. I don't know if we got along because we came in without expectations or maybe in dread.

"She's nice," I told my then boyfriend.

"She's bubbly," he said.

"You'd scared me. She's not a bitch."

"She can be," he warned.

It then occurred to me that our history and backgrounds play into our present lives. Maybe Rosemary and I had a new, fresh relationship, something good. Maybe she and her father had old stuff going on—resentment, anger over the divorce, and all that spoiled and left bitterness.

WE WEREN'T MARRIED yet. He suggested we wait until afterward to call and tell her. Our plan was to drive to Virginia with the dogs and marry in the mountains. Neither of us was from Virginia, and I'm still not sure exactly why we went there. But in May we went, and afterward called Rosemary to tell her the news. She yelled. She cursed at Old Husband and hung up. He sulked. "She's pissed," he said. "We're in trouble."

Trouble. That word made me panic. I didn't want trouble. I was antitrouble. I called her back and spoke with her. My approach was always friendly, polite. I liked her. And she never, ever blew up at me. We eased into talk of school, then dogs. We loved dogs. Only mutts, though, and they had to be rescued or from shelters. She told me she was thinking of being a doctor. We spoke like you might with a roommate. We avoided Old Dad, Old Husband. He was her problem, now both our problem. She and I were not the problem.

I REMEMBER THIS. It was summer and we all drove upstate to go hiking. We stood at the car and got our stuff together. Her backpack was huge. Big enough for a European tour. "What's in there?" Old Husband asked her. She was carrying a hair dryer, science books, makeup, socks. He started yelling, the way a father might, telling her to lighten the load, what's wrong with her. I defended Rosemary. This is how it went. I tried to be neutral but ended up taking her side. No, not to gain love, because we still, years later, still don't have love, but I sided with her merely because I saw myself in her. Or at least saw the person I'd wanted to be at eighteen, nineteen, twenty. Confident and unstoppable.

FOR A WHILE, everything just kind of went along. Her short visits, chats on the phone, little presents that I'd send her. For me, the bitch never surfaced, but for Old Husband it was hell. When they spoke on the phone, he was quiet. She would scream accusations at him. He was the worst father. Never paid for anything. Selfish. I would go to sleep at night and leave them on the phone. He would be hunched over, cat in his lap, one hand on his dog's head, listening to Rosemary, his eyes cast down.

And then she graduated college. Her mother would be at the ceremony. I'd never met her, never spoken to her, but I had my approach. Polite, gracious, quiet. How could I go wrong?

I'd seen photos of Old Husband's ex-wife. I'd snoop in his dark-room and there she was. Black-and-white shots of her naked. She was sad looking. Droopy. I knew she gave him "a hard time," and yelled at him in public. But I was ready. I could handle this.

We went upstate. It was May, near our anniversary, cold, rainy, and I wore a suit. I don't know why I wore a suit. I never wore suits, and we met in the auditorium. I shook the ex-wife's skinny hand, then we went to sit far away. That night Rosemary insisted on going out with Old Husband and me. We were to take her to a vegetarian Indian restaurant. I perked up, relaxed, as we piled into the car and drove off. Her mother stayed behind, and I didn't think much of it. I thought maybe, just maybe, Rosemary wanted to be with us instead of her mother.

We ordered. We gave her gifts. A bracelet from me. A roll of cash from her father. She seemed happy for a minute, then put her things into her purse, snapped it, and said, "I'm going to med-ical school and I need you to pay for it."

She looked directly at Old Husband, the way a dog looks when it's about to attack. A stare, blank but evil.

For a few minutes neither of us said anything. Old Husband sipped his mango lasse. He looked like someone in a mental home, sad and helpless.

Was the "you" directed at both of us? I wanted to vomit. Why was she ruining our dinner? I hated Rosemary, fast, like you would a girlfriend who stole something. I had little money. Old Husband was in debt. I hated her for throwing this boomerang across the restaurant table. Our relationship was what kind of shampoo do you use, and have you read the lat-est Margaret Atwood book. Money was not our topic. The boomerang hit me hard and as usual, I had nothing to say. I had no answer.

"Well?" she said. She looked at us both, one at a time. The bitch had surfaced.

I've always had a hard time with feelings. I hide. But I was angry. She was my pop-o-matic stepdaughter. I met her when she was big. Older. Why did I have to pay for medical school?

I panicked. The night was ruined. Suddenly she was like the metal part of a snow plow, ramming her questions over and over and over. "Why can't you help? Where am I supposed to get that kind of money? Why can't you go into your retirement accounts?"

As if we had retirement accounts.

Everything about Rosemary made me sick—her nerve, her assumptions, the way she tore and shoved nan into her tiny mouth. That mouth with the perfect teeth, white and non–coffee stained.

Then came the deadly blow. The boomerang snapped against Old Husband's neck. Rosemary speared a samosa, held it in front of her face, and said, "You're a shit father."

I wanted to slap her. Instead, I pulled the sleeves farther over my hands. It's one thing to think hate, it's another to say it. I wanted to slap her, pull her hair back and set her straight. Instead, my hands in fabric fists, my posture slumped, I said something about the decor, which was pink.

A husband with a daughter wasn't all pajama and boy talk. There was financial responsibility. I guess I would stand in the way of her becoming a brain surgeon. Deep down I knew she could get loans. That's what all med students get, don't they? So in the end I knew her attack was an attempt at torture, an opportunity to ask and declare war on her father, and me too. We continued our dinner in silence, reminding me of how I'd get with my parents. How silence is sometimes the best way. We have this saying in Lithuanian, one my parents love to use: Once you have said hurtful words, they are out in the air like a bird. The bird will fly and will not come back.

WE DROVE HER back to campus and I walked her to the dorm room while Old Husband stayed in the car, parked in the emergency fire lane. I apologized. I told her, "I'm sorry." She knew I was talking about the money. "I'm sorry but we will not, cannot pay. We won't even try." She looked at me blankly, without expression, the way a cat would, where you don't know what they're thinking, or even if they're thinking. It was both chilling and comforting. I was free to go.

Soon after that, the phone calls began. Old Husband always answered the phone, because he was always sitting in the chair and thinking, and he would answer and then there would be long periods of silence as he listened. Rosemary was chewing him up, spitting him out. Then she would hang up on him. I stayed quiet, didn't get involved, and decided to let them work it out. Of course there would be loans. She could take out loans for medical school. Her old dad was now shit to her. Penniless. Worthless.

THE LAST TIME I would see her was the weekend before 9/11. We were upstate with our dogs, plus another dog we found abandoned and took on, and Rosemary came with us, and we stayed in our cottage in the mountains. She'd agreed to come up with us and spent most of the weekend sleeping. That Saturday night we were two hours late for a dinner party because of her hair. She had to dry it and brush it a long time. She then had to curl the ends, slowly, little clumps at a time. It went on and on. Old Husband yelled. I was upset with her, but she shrugged and said, "Hair is important."

Old Husband looked at my matted locks. "She doesn't do anything with her hair," he told Rosemary.

Again, I sided with her. "Exactly," I said. "I'm a mess and she's not." And though we arrived for the dinner party when everyone was already eating dessert, I felt grateful to have her with us. I instantly forgave her for things. She was a girl who worked on her priorities which were of the moment. Which then, days later, surfaced on that blue-sky morning in Washington Square Park. Old Husband and I were walking the dogs in the park when a plane appeared dangerously overhead. We watched as it headed downtown. The explosion, flames, and horror instantly followed, and hours later, Rosemary called to tell us she was going to help and disappeared.

I have not seen her since. In the past three years she has been in medical school and spending summers in India, helping the poor in hospitals, and she went on her path quietly, focused, lips over her jaws. On occasion, I ask Old Husband how she's paying for school, and he'll shrug and say, "Loans." Loans and my guess is her mother is helping along.

Every few months, Rosemary calls Old Husband, once even from India. Their conversations are short. Things have gone back to how they once were in terms of subjects. She wants to know how the dogs are doing, how her cat is doing, how I'm doing. For some reason she and I never speak. When she calls, I'm either out walking the dogs or at work. We are busy. We are doing our own thing.

ON OUR SEVEN-YEAR anniversary, Old Husband and I had to put down Rosemary's old cat. He was dying from lymph cancer and we had to make the decision. Old Husband called her and told her we had to put him to sleep. She cried. There was a long silence. Then she hung up.

"She hates me," he said. "She's blaming me. She said she would have come home to take care of him."

I called her back and listened to her cry. The cry was deep, sobbing, perhaps triggered by some faraway memory of something else, something lost or longing. Or perhaps it was the cat, perhaps it really was that simple. Somehow all of us were brought together and though we are quite separate, alone in thoughts and places we sit, we are part of something big, like a big store where you can find anything, or like a big shelter where you can wander, cage to cage, never knowing where you will find love.

OUR RELATIONSHIP IS something that comes up, then disappears. I think of Rosemary often and recently found stray kittens living on the street, which I took in and kept, and I like to think that perhaps in this way, Rosemary and I are joined. Although we are apart and not in touch that much, our love is fused through our attachment to animals. Often I sit on our fire escape overlooking the land of shoes on Eighth Street. The fire escape has bars like a cage. From out here, looking inside I can see Old Husband. He's sitting in his chair, kittens on his lap. Though they are wild and feral and hiss, they like to be on his lap, his hands petting them both, slow and sure of love.

Broken

S. KIRK WALSH

*It would be several years before I would truly understand and
feel the deep-seated pain of my parents' divorces.*

In January of 1988, I flew home to Ann Arbor for a week of
recovery. I was a senior at a small liberal arts college in the
northern reaches of New York State and had just spent the
month on the nearly abandoned campus among human-size
snowbanks, subzero temperatures, and a dozen or so seedy bars.
Virtually every night I found myself on a barstool in one of the
aforementioned bars, consuming Budweiser after Budweiser,
shot after shot. Rarely did an evening end with any sort of vivid
punctuation, say brushing my teeth or slipping into my worn
nightshirt. Instead, these intoxicated evenings were character-
ized by stretches of blackness dotted with blurry memories here
and there, wobbling home along the snow-covered railroad
tracks, barely able to feel the snowflakes melting against my face,
or ending up in some guy's tapestry-lined fraternity room, unable
to find my shoes or jacket in the dark.

One could argue that it was the isolation. Few students
remained on campus during January Term. Plus, my boyfriend
had dumped me for a frosty-haired, long-lashed freshman.
Admittedly, at the start of the month I had different designs on
our relationship: I was still a virgin at age twenty-one, feeling
something like a freak, and had decided that the lacrosse-playing,

brown-eyed boyfriend could be the one. (Of course, I overlooked the fact that Lacrosse Boy and I rarely had anything to talk about unless we were well lubricated; our favorite drink was Jack Daniel's and OJ.) One of my close friends coached me on the deflowering possibilities: "Suggest that the two of you go away for a weekend," she said excitedly. "Maybe Vermont. Skiing." Lacrosse Boy and I never made it to that romantic ski cabin in the woods. Instead, I spent most of the month attending my one class in contemporary literature (reading the likes of Jay McInerney and Bret Easton Ellis), and drinking every night and trying to figure out what was wrong with me.

Home was where Mom and my stepfather, Carl, lived. A highly respected architect by trade, Carl had designed every detail of our newly built house—from the two-sided granite-tiled fireplace that faced the living room and the master bedroom to the soaring twenty-one-foot ceilings and exposed beams—that sat on the wooded edge of the University of Michigan's arboretum. I was looking forward to the visit. I needed a break from the partying, a respite to regroup before returning to school for my final semester and stepping into the uncharted territory of "real life." But even before I returned home, something felt out of step with the visit: usually when I returned to Detroit, Mom greeted me at the gate at Metro Airport. This time, Mom told me over the phone in few words that she had a meeting and wouldn't be able to pick me up. That I should take a cab home instead.

As the taxi wound its way down our curved driveway, the windows of the house were darkened. My voice echoed when I yelled "Anyone home?" As I clicked on the lights, the house felt strangely empty. I wandered through the main space into the master bedroom and into the oversize walk-in closet (which we jokingly referred to as "the womb") to find the left side—Carl's side—empty except for the metal hangers dangling side by side.

Heat rushed into my cheeks and tears started to wet my eyes as I made my way around the house, searching for further evidence of Carl's departure. Within minutes, the wheels of Mom's car crunched down the graveled driveway. When I asked her what happened, Mom told me that they were getting divorced. When I asked why she didn't tell me before now, she asked "Are you really that surprised? Didn't you see it coming?"

THE FIRST TIME I experienced divorce I was five years old. As the story goes, Mom and Dad sat my three siblings and me down twice to break the news. To this day, I still don't recall either episode. Admittedly, I have few memories from this period of my life: the day that my three older siblings and I all came down with the chicken pox; the time when my foot got caught in the spokes of Mom's back wheel while I was sitting in the child's seat; the afternoon I earned my ducky patch at the country club for swimming a length of the pool's shallow end. There was also the woman who took care of me, Mary. She had soft, chocolate hands and smiling brown eyes. I remember sitting on a metal stool in the basement as she methodically ironed sheets, pillow-cases, and shirts. She gave me red-and-white-striped mints in exchange for being quiet.

There is only one family photo that remains as evidence of our original family of six. It was taken in our backyard circa 1968. The lawn was manicured with a few scattered dead leaves caught in between its blades. Mom and Dad sat in two white-painted wicker chairs with my older sister and me on their laps; my two brothers stood obediently on either side. Mom was dressed in a two-piece dress outfit reminiscent of Jackie Kennedy, a pink fitted skirt with a pale baby-blue top bordered with pink piping. Dad was clad in a slate gray suit and tie, ready for a day at the office. My older brother, Clune, wore a powder blue jacket, slate gray pants, and a tie, almost looking like a seven-year-old twin of Dad. Bennett was dressed in a white rounded-collar, short-sleeved shirt and navy blue overall shorts with a white fleur-de-lis stitched over his heart. And my sister, Ami, and I were dressed in our identical white dresses, lace-bordered socks, and white patent leather shoes. My small legs were still pudgy; my cheeks baby faced and round. Everyone was smiling except Mom, who was looking down at me. Within a year's time, Dad would be in and out of a three-year affair with one of Mom's friends. Eventually the other family moved to Cincinnati, Ohio, to save their marriage while Mom asked Dad for a divorce and moved the four of us to a ranch-style house in Ann Arbor. She was thirty-six years old at the time (two years younger than I am as I write this) with four children between the ages of five and twelve.

Not surprisingly, my siblings and I remained mostly in a post-divorce malaise after my parents' breakup. Being the youngest at five, I still didn't understand the nature of our new family setup. We all liked Dad, why didn't he live with us? Why were our visits relegated to Sundays only? Why couldn't we see him more? I can't remember if I posed these questions to Mom. My guess is not. Instead, each one of my siblings and I submerged ourselves into our own variations of silence. My older brother, Clune—the only one among us who truly understood what was going on—spent most of his afternoons after school alone at the nearby pond populated with crawfish and toads, sitting on its edge, skipping stones along its placid surface. I discovered a playground down the street, where there was a jungle gym in the shape of a tall giraffe: I climbed up its narrow neck, my legs on either side of its orange-spotted head, sitting up there for long stretches at a time. Ami and Bennett spent time at the various houses of their new friends, friends whom they would forget the names of later, only to describe them in vague terms like "the girl who was mean to me." Sure, there were times when all four of us played together: across the street from our house, there was an enormous field of straw grass that belonged to the church that sat on the opposite edge. Clune would cut a maze of paths through the tall grass with our electric push mower. There, my three siblings and I would run through the intricate paths of strawlike reeds, doing our best to hide from each other. I remember both the thrill and fear running through my veins as dusk pressed down from the nondescript, Midwestern sky, the grass snapping at my bare ankles as I ran faster, my lungs beginning to ache. A part of me wanted to be found so I wouldn't be alone; another part of me wanted to see how long I could make it on my own.

Aware of our unhappiness, Mom considered the possibility of moving to another town. She was hesitant to uproot her children yet again and took a vote among the four of us. Unanimously, we voted to move after Mom heard about a four-bedroom home for sale in Birmingham, a town about an hour away. For the next five years, both of my parents were single. And though they were officially divorced, it was never entirely clear to me the status of their relationship. Dad continued to pick us up every Sunday for church and dinner at the nearby hunt club. On occasion, he would come inside and have a couple of glasses of wine with Mom. Sometimes these visits ended amicably. Other times they didn't, like the time when Mom locked Dad out of the house after an exchange of sharp words; Dad ran around to the front, punching a doggy bag of leftovers through one of the small square windows bordering the door, shards of glass scattering onto the floor of the hallway like lost diamonds. Then there were the gifts, such as the white Chevy Blazer with the large red ribbon tied around its hood that arrived in our driveway on Mom's birthday. And the vacations we took together as a family—Aspen, Key Biscayne, and Nantucket. Mostly, what I remember from

these trips was being all together. I have no recollection if Mom
and Dad slept in the same hotel room or not. All I cared about
was the fact that we were a collective unit. *The Walsh Family.* I
never wanted to go home. I wanted to keep living in the warm
bubble of vacation, where we were once again a family like everyone else.

WHEN I WAS eleven years old, Dad married Karyn, a woman
fifteen years his junior. I remember when Dad told me the news:
Ami and I were sitting in the backseat of his car in the parking
lot of a yacht club that sat on the edge of the Detroit River. As
soon as he told us, both Ami and I broke down into tears. It
didn't seem possible. How could Dad do this to us? Weren't he
and Mom going to get back together? Mom also took the news
hard. At the time, she held a demanding job as manager of a
health food restaurant and threw herself into her work. She was
rarely home. Because of the lack of parental supervision, our
house became the party house of choice. At the time, my older
brothers attracted two distinctly different groups of friends. At
age fifteen, Bennett was a full-fledged burnout. He and his like-
minded friends congregated in the basement. The generic recre-
ation room felt like it was submerged in another world under the
eerie glow of an overhead red lightbulb. A drum kit sat in the corner collecting dust, and the thin baby-blue carpet reeked of
spilled bong water. Clune and his friends fell into the beer-
drinking, pseudo-jock category and spent most of their afternoons
parked on the threadbare couch and chairs in our den. Often
when I returned home from school, I would find them half passed
out, their glazed-over eyes fixed on Tom chasing Jerry on the television, empty Stroh's cans at their feet. After depositing my
textbook-laden backpack in the front hall, I retrieved beers for
them from the fridge, watched one or two television shows, usu-

ally *Gilligan's Island* and *M*A*S*H*, before retreating to my bedroom.

More specifically, to my closet. Often when I later talked about my closet to friends or my therapist, I described the closet more like a small room; after all, it had a narrow rectangular window overlooking the front lawn and an enormous V-shaped birch tree, its almond-shaped leaves sometimes fluttering against the pane. A wide wood counter sat underneath the sweater-filled shelves lining the far wall, making for a perfect hangout for a club of one. On the wall between shelves and counter, I taped up two large black-and-white photos of my parents on their wedding day in June of 1957. There was a smart-looking, younger version of Dad, dressed in tails with a pinned ascot. He held a lit cigarette by his side. In a formal posed shot, Mom looked something like a porcelain doll, her tear-shaped lips glistening with lipstick, her eyes serene and focused. A simple veil of lace traveled behind her back, her brown curls carefully pinned away from her beautiful, fragile-looking face.

In the closet: this was where my parents were still married. This was where I was part of a normal family, like the Whitelaws who lived down the street. Who ate dinner together every night at six o'clock. Who spent their Saturday afternoons together, playing football or softball. In the quiet universe of my closet I spent most hours drawing the same picture over and over again: an idyllic landscape of rolling hills, where the sun was always smiling, the seagulls bobbing overhead. A few cars drove on the two-lane highway that divided the hills from the sandy shoreline. Simple A-frame houses with white picket fences dotted the landscape. A rope swing hung still from one of the sturdy trees. The drawing always was given the same title—"Our Town." Again and again, this was what I drew, taping up the variations of it in between the two images of my just-to-be-married parents. Ironi-

cally, there were never any people in these landscapes. In retrospect, it was a safe place because there was no one who was
going to leave me.

WHEN I WAS thirteen, I met Carl for the first time. I distinctly
remember the day: I was riding my metallic green Schwinn bike
down our tree-lined street and spotted an enormous white motor
home parked in front of our house. Something inside me said
that this oversized vehicle belonged to the man who had been
mysteriously dating Mom for the past six months. When I
stepped inside the kitchen, Mom introduced me to Carl. He was
a striking white-haired man with sparkling brown eyes, small
apple-shaped cheeks, and a flush complexion. Carl smiled at me
as he shook my hand. I asked him if that was his motor home out
front. He said yes, and that maybe later he would take me for a
ride. I nodded, both excited and nervous at this stranger's presence. Mom was in a noticeably good mood as she busied herself
at the counter, slicing sausage and cheese for a plate of crackers.
What I remember most vividly was the moment when Carl asked
Mom if we had any mustard. Mom responded with a smile and
said, "Your mustard is in the fridge." *Your mustard*—two innocuous words, but they carried enough weight to make me realize
that maybe Carl was here to stay.

In June of 1979, Mom and Carl were married. A four-month
renovation of our house quickly followed. Our downtrodden
house was transformed into a beautiful, contemporary home
with state-of-the-art hardware and appliances. On the first floor,
the renovations were extensive. The garage was transformed into
a family room with a loft space above. A dense navy blue carpet
lined the floor; the walls, a pristine white. Carl's sectional couch,
a Knoll's prototype, bordered two walls. A bank of windows faced
the driveway and backyard. Here was Carl's work area—a draft-

ing table, a small library of architect and design books, sharpened pencils, and the essential slide rulers and other plastic rulers. Every night after dinner, I could find Carl here, the television news on mute, Bach playing over the stereo as Carl contemplated his next set of blueprints. For the first time in my memory, I was living with a father figure in our house. Carl made our house feel safe and comfortable. We often ate dinner together. He liked to make homemade soups and was constantly trying to perfect his vichyssoise recipe. He even let me borrow his sweaters—my favorite was a rust brown crewneck from Banana Republic—to wear to school. And most important, it always felt like somebody was home.

WHEN I RETURNED for my final college semester in February, I did my best to downplay Mom and Carl's pending divorce. I told my friends that I was fine. Everything was fine. At least Dad and Karyn are still married, I rationalized to myself. Things aren't that bad. I spent my final semester much as I spent that lost January Term—drinking, getting together with random guys, drinking some more. Two weeks before graduation, I was pulled over for a DWI. After I failed the Breathalyzer, the police chose not to arrest me. Instead, they drove me home and told me to retrieve my car in the morning. On graduation day, I mostly remember being hung over, the heat of the June sun making my stomach feel queasy. I don't remember who the commencement speaker was or the moment when I was handed my diploma with a firm handshake. I remember that Mom came by herself. By this time, Mom and Carl's divorce was final. A couple of weeks after graduation, I saw Carl for the first time since they had split up. He was living in a small one-story house a block away from the University of Michigan football stadium. It was a temporary arrangement, a friend's place, until he found something better.

We ate dinner, and Carl gave me my graduation present—a yellow waterproof Walkman and his Banana Republic sweater, still wrapped in its dry cleaner's tissue and plastic.

WITHIN THE YEAR, Dad and Karyn announced their divorce. By this time I was living in New York City and sharing a one-bedroom apartment with my older brother Bennett in Chelsea. Often we had dinner with Dad because he maintained several clients in Manhattan. So it didn't seem unusual when Dad invited Bennett and me to a fancy French restaurant on lower Fifth Avenue, saying he had some important news to share with us. We sat at a white-clothed, candlelit table for three on the second level overlooking the bustle of the bar and main eating area. After we ordered our meals, Dad proceeded to tell us that Karyn had asked for a divorce. For a man who rarely showed emotion, Dad was visibly saddened by this turn of events. "I tried," he said, listing the things he had done, such as seeing a therapist. "But her mind is made up. Karyn is not happy."

I did my best not to look at Dad as I stared into the flickering light of the candle, willing myself not to cry. I wanted to believe that it was their problem—they were the ones who couldn't stay married. What did that have to do with me? I wasn't the one going through another divorce. After all, I was twenty-two now, practically an adult. But that didn't stop the unidentifiable swell of pain from spreading into my chest. This isn't happening, I said to myself. This isn't happening again. I stared down at my plate of untouched food and then took another sip of white wine as Bennett questioned Dad about what happened. I remember trying to block their conversation out, glancing down at the strangers' heads below: at least two or three deep, they lined the long mahogany bar, chatting to each other and smoking cigarettes. Their lives seemed so much easier than mine.

———

IT WAS DAD and Karyn's divorce that ultimately did me in. The stability I perceived from both of my parents' second marriages had vanished—and the trauma of Mom and Dad's initial divorce tumbled into my emotional life with great force. Within a year, I would go into therapy and work with the same doctor for more than a decade, sifting through the details and emotions of my past. At age twenty-four, I stopped drinking. Admittedly, it would be several years before I would truly understand and feel the deep-seated pain of my parents' divorces. For a long time, I swung between the two ends of the psychological pendulum— thinking either that I needed to get over it or that I was forever damaged by the events of my child- and early adulthood. In retrospect, I recognized that unearthing my feelings of anger and sadness about the divorces was essential to getting to the other side. With time, something inside me started to shift: I started to see where I began and where my parents ended. And eventually, I learned to accept the traumatic events as part of my own personal history—and realized that I would always feel a little brokenhearted about everything that happened.

Diana's Child

MAURA RHODES

I feared that my son might love his stepmother's
child more than he loved mine.

My older son, Will, has just become a big brother for
the third time. He's thrilled. I wish I were as happy
about this new arrival as I was about the births of his
other siblings, my other children—five-year-old Eliza and two-
and-a-half-year-old Lucas. But this time I wasn't the one counting down the weeks, laying in a layette, living from OB visit to
OB visit, pouring over baby-naming books. The woman who had
those pleasures was my ex-husband's wife—Will's stepmother, if
you will.

But I won't. I don't accept that Will has another "mother." As
far as I'm concerned, Diana's just the thirty-something woman
who lives with my fifty-something ex, John, and is (apparently)
pretty nice to Will during his weekend visits. I think this is partly
a typical reaction, based on conversations I've had with other
divorced moms in my position. It's tough to acknowledge that
someone else might be placing her hand on your own child's
feverish forehead, or in possession of a recipe for lasagna that
he'll actually eat—when he won't touch your own version. It's
also somewhat personal: I've met Diana, and even had a mini-
run-in with her before she married John, when she had the gall
to leave a message on my answering machine reminding Will to

call his dad the next day to wish him a happy birthday. For the record, I've never forgotten John's birthday, or Father's Day or Christmas for that matter. An insightful friend surmised at the time that Diana's audacity was a sure sign that she was gunning for a wedding ring.

If that's what she wanted, she got it. John told me he and Diana were getting married the day I went through the egg-retrieval part of in vitro fertilization to have Lucas. I wasn't surprised—and I wasn't really bothered either. By this time, she and John had been together for a year or so, and while in the beginning I'd worried that Will might come to care more for her than for me (it was Diana, after all, who first gave him bubble gum and introduced him to Sprite—without checking with me first, of course), I told myself she wasn't really mom material. (Did I mention that she gave him bubble gum and Sprite without checking with me first?) I also knew that she was kind and loving toward Will—not at all a wicked stepmother–type—and more important I knew that she hadn't replaced me in Will's heart; all the soda in the world can't dissolve the bond between a mother and her son. And, being the fair-minded person I try to be, I knew I had to be a good sport about the marriage. Although John's reaction to my engagement to Michael had been, "You're just being selfish," he'd grown from suspicious to cordial to downright friendly toward Michael over the years. It was the least I could do to attempt to return the favor; besides, I rarely saw Diana, so I didn't have to try all that hard. She was a phantom limb on our kooky family tree, showing up once in a while for a performance at Will's school, riding along occasionally when John brought Will home from a weekend visit.

In fact, it was on such an evening that I got what should have been my first hint that there may one day be a baby in the picture. It was a warm spring evening and we were all out futzing in the yard when John drove up to drop off Will. Diana was in the car, and since I couldn't very well not say hello (and what reason would I have not to?), I went over to the passenger side with Lukey, still an infant, in my arms. As I was showing him off, Diana happened to say she'd been knitting baby clothes and putting them away. "I told John," she said, "'Hey, you never know.'"

I shrugged off the notion with just the teeniest bit of gleeful disdain. I didn't believe for an instant that John, with his record of marital instability and his erratic schedule (he's an actor), would agree to have another child—especially when he hadn't exactly agreed to have the first one. Will had been an accident—or, I prefer to say, a surprise, conceived during the only episode of unprotected sex I'd ever had in my life, just a few months after John and I got married. I'd let my Pill prescription lapse during our honeymoon (we were in Europe for a month) and had decided not to renew it when we got back. I knew that sometime down the road we'd want to have kids. Even if we didn't try to get pregnant for a year or two, I wanted to be drug-free, and for some reason had the notion that it took months for the body to rebalance itself after being chemically altered by hormones—in other words, I thought you couldn't get pregnant right after going off birth control pills, so I just didn't worry about it the night I got home from a business trip and there were no condoms or sponges in the house.

One missed period and two extremely sore breasts later, I found myself so distracted by the idea that I might have been totally wrong about the lasting power of the Pill (or a freak of nature) that I left my office in the middle of the afternoon, bought a home pregnancy test at the drugstore across the street, and did it in the ladies' room at my office. When the second pink line appeared, I didn't believe it. How could a splash of pee on a stick tell you something so life altering? On the way home that evening, I bought a different kind of test, one that seemed more scientific because it involved little vials and test sticks; I did it in the wee hours the next morning: positive. I went to work early and called my gynecologist—or rather, my obstetrician—who was able to see me that day. The blood test confirmed I was pregnant.

At this point, I hadn't told John anything—and I was afraid to. I thought he'd think I'd tricked him; I knew he'd freak out about the expense. And even though it was Valentine's Day and we were going out to dinner that night—the perfect setting, when you think about it, for telling your husband he's going to be a dad, I called him to break the news. (That alone speaks volumes about the future of our marriage.)

If John was at all suspicious that I'd duped him, he didn't let on. He was surprised by the news but seemed genuinely pleased, and we had a lovely dinner that night, celebrating not just our first Valentine's Day as husband and wife, but our first as parents-to-be.

It was a blissful beginning. My pregnancy was uneventful, until we discovered the baby was breech and I was probably heading for a C-section—a huge disappointment, because I'd romanticized the idea of giving birth so much that I couldn't stomach the thought of actually *scheduling* my baby's arrival. But of course as soon as the doctor tugged Will out of my body, I forgot all that, and John was as thrilled as I was to meet our little boy.

It was also the beginning of the end. John started rehearsals for a new play, a small-scale production about Florence Nightingale, while Will and I were still in the hospital; in those early photos, John has the mustache he had to grow for the role. Even though the job meant I'd be home alone with a brand-new baby, John had had my full support when he'd told me about the part. I was his biggest fan; I would never have stood in the way of his career. And he was a great partner during the run of the play; rather than go out with the cast after every performance—something I'd learned that actors need to do, to wind down, to rehash their mistakes, to stroke each other's egos—John came straight home. I assumed he was putting his family first, doing the right thing—and doing it because he wanted to.

But almost as soon as that play ended (a short run, just a few weeks), he landed another role. Things were fine during rehearsals, but once the show was up, John started going out with the cast every night—not coming home to his exhausted and lonely wife and to his baby, who was far from sleeping through the night. Because John had a day job, that meant that I was alone with Will all day every day, and every night, including weekends—with the exception of Monday nights, when the theater's dark.

It was on a Monday night, before dinner, while Will was miraculously sleeping during what was usually the witching hour for him, that I asked John to please come home some nights after the play, to spend time with me, to help with the baby. I didn't even say every night. And his response was, "I came home every night after *Nightingale*." It was a revelation: whether he meant it or not (and I can't say that he denied it later in marriage counseling), John was essentially saying that daddy duty was over for him. He'd paid his paternal dues, and now I was on my own. I knew we were through, even though it took several years to make it all official.

To be fair, during that time John wasn't an inattentive or unloving father. Together we weathered a stream of serious ear infections that culminated in minor surgery to put tubes in Will's ears. And John was the one who noticed that, at six months, Will's eyes didn't seem to be aligned—it turned out he had a condition that required major surgery and glasses. But more often than not, John's idea of spending time with Will was to prop him up on the sofa beside him while he watched the evening news.

As for spending time with me—well, let's just say that again the tube won out: apparently Ted Koppel had greater sex appeal than I did.

In the years since our marriage ended, I've never once felt that John doesn't love Will. He hasn't been a steady presence—his career won't allow that. There've been times when Will hasn't seen his dad for months. I've always imagined that must be as tough for John as it is for Will—maybe tougher. That's why it seemed improbable that John would ever have another child: he's not able to spend time with the one he already has.

And yet, when John left a message on my voice mail at work one evening more than a year after my driveway encounter with Diana, saying he was on his way to my house to pick up Will to take him to dinner, but wanted to talk to me first, an image of tiny booties and sweaters tucked away in a drawer sprang to mind. I knew he was going to tell me he and Diana were expecting a baby as surely as I'd known, fourteen years ago, that I was expecting Will before I slipped out on my lunch hour to buy a pregnancy test. I was so sure, in fact, that I didn't call him back. Because inexplicably, the idea mortified me.

But why? Why did it bother me so much? When Will came home from dinner with John, I asked him as casually as I could if the sushi had been good, how his dad was—if there was anything new going on? Will had nothing to report, and I was temporarily relieved. Maybe John had just wanted to ask about switching a weekend or to tell me he'd accepted a part in an out-of-town play. When I didn't hear from him again right away, I relaxed, figured I'd jumped to conclusions.

That's why I didn't hesitate to answer the phone a few evenings later. John was on the other line. "I just wanted to tell you before I talk to Will that Diana's pregnant. There's going to be a little baby soon," he said.

There was such excitement in his voice, it was as if he were telling his best friend, not his ex-wife, and was expecting enthusiastic congratulations. I dearly wished I could muster up such a reaction, but in my miserable pettiness all I could manage was, "Oh, OK, I see," call Will to the phone, and slink away.

IT GOT WORSE. If, during her pregnancy, Diana wrestled with morning sickness, hemorrhoids, sciatica, indigestion, or swollen ankles, I bet her pain didn't compare with mine. I'm not proud to say that I thought terrible things sometimes—not that anything bad would happen to Diana or the baby, but that maybe she and John would decide to move to the West Coast, or even that their marriage would break up. I was horrible, and yet I couldn't help myself. I never asked John how Diana was doing when I spoke to him on the phone or ran into him during a Will pick-up or drop-off. I wasn't sure when the baby was due, and didn't try to find out. (I'd thought June; it was actually March.) I groused to friends who probably were close to writing me off as a maniac. At the very least, I could tell they couldn't understand what I was so upset about. It wasn't like I didn't have my own kids. It wasn't like this kid was going to affect my life at all.

And I was dismissive about the baby with Will. He seemed genuinely excited about his new sibling-to-be, but his enthusiasm left me feeling deflated. When he said one day, "Well, pretty soon Eliza and Lucas are going to have a new baby brother or sister," I snapped, "The baby won't be related to Eliza and Lucas. It'll be your half-sibling, not theirs." Mind you, I've never referred to Eliza and Lukey as Will's half-siblings; I've never wanted to play up that distinction. How awful of me to try to set John's child apart from my own in Will's eyes, a child whose relationship to Will would be no different than his relationship to them.

Will said nothing more, but I'm sure my words had stung. It

wasn't my finest moment, but it was a seminal one: in that single, scathing response to Will—one I still regret—the reasons for
my discomfort about John and Diana's child gelled. Just as I'd
worried once that he might come to love his stepmother more
than he loved me, I feared that my son might love his stepmother's child more than he loved mine. This baby would represent one more lap in the inevitable race to be viewed as the
better parent that all divorced couples find themselves engaged
in—whether they want to be or not.

I wanted to marry the better stepparent, provide the cozier
home, bear the smartest, cutest, sweetest siblings. I suspect I've
been running a lot harder than John has. My prolonged and petty
obsession about his child was much more intense than any negative feelings he might have felt when Eliza and Lucas were
born. (Either that, or he's been better at covering them up.) In
fact, he's been as interested in and delighted by them as if he
were their uncle—never forgetting birthdays, taking Eliza for ice
cream, hugging them when he drops Will off. I've always appreciated that; now I saw how important it is that I respond in kind.

IT'S A SLOW ROAD. Baby Jack's birth took me by surprise:
Will told me he'd arrived one Friday when I got home from work.
I confess that I didn't act very interested. Nor did I ooh and aah
over the images of Jack that John proudly showed me on his dig-
ital camera a few days later. And when I finally saw the little boy,
when he was a few months old, all I could muster was, "Well, it
looks like he's all there. You did a good job!"

JACK IS SEVEN months old now. Will hasn't indicated in any
way that he thinks he's a niftier kid than Eliza or Lucas. My worst
fear hasn't been realized, and it's helped me to soften up. In an
e-mail to John I managed to tack on a line hoping Diana and Jack

were doing well. And when one day John picked Will up from my office in New York City to take him to lunch, I went down in the elevator with Will to meet him, figuring that Jack would be there. And he was, an adorable little guy strapped to his dad's chest in a Snugli. I grinned at him—and he grinned back. And in that brief exchange between strangers, one of us entirely innocent of the significance of the meeting, I turned a corner. Who knows where that will lead my son's little brother and me? I don't exactly see our families melding into one—but when we do meet, even if it's only in the driveway on a warm spring evening, at least I can offer him a smile.

My Fairy Stepmother

LESLIE MORGAN STEINER

My stepmother did something even my own blood relatives
didn't have the heart, the courage, or the emotional
intelligence to do: she helped me save my own life.

A s his thirty-two-year marriage to my mother unraveled,
my father called me every other day or so. His voice
sounded tired, lonely, and frustrated. I listened intently,
helpless and mesmerized, as he told me about the angry voice-
mail messages my mother left and the doors she slammed.

He was tall and handsome, with a slight pigeon-toed gait
inherited from his Cherokee grandmother. The second son of a
poor, fundamentalist Christian Texas family that had never sent
a child to college, my father had gone to Harvard (magna cum
laude) and Harvard Law School (head of the Law Review). Dad
then spent three decades at a large Washington, D.C., law firm.
He could leave my mom, but I knew he'd never leave the firm.
The place was his real home; family had never served as a haven
of any sort for him. His own father had died of a heart attack
when Dad was a teenager, and as my father left for college pre-
occupied that his carefully saved summer earnings would not
cover the train fare to Cambridge, much less books and food
once he got there, his mother told him he was joining the devil.

I'd always found him to be an affectionate, if absent and
absentminded, father. Dad came to visit no matter where I went
(Wyoming for a summer job as a horse wrangler; Madrid for a

semester in high school; college), even if he didn't have much to say once there. He was the kind of dad who ruffled my hair every time he passed through the TV room, but one who could never remember my boyfriend's first name or exactly when my birthday was.

MY OWN CINDERELLA story went like this: I was twenty-six, a student in graduate school, two years into a marriage to a man who beat me behind the locked door of our West Philadelphia apartment. He choked me when I made the coffee too bitter in the mornings, threw boiling pasta on the kitchen floor when I spoke on the phone with my best friend, threatened to kill our dog with one of his two unregistered handguns if I joined a study group with male students.

The pictures from our wedding belong in a fairy tale. I wore my mother's silk and lace wedding gown. Coming down the aisle, my father stood next to me, tanned and gray at the temples. My mother was on my other side, divinely gorgeous with her silver hair, tanned tennis legs, and sapphire mother-of-the-bride dress. Only our tight grimaces hint that something just might be wrong with this pretty picture.

SOON AFTER MY own wedding, my father fell in love with a small Jewish woman with long, fluttery dark hair. S. had three grown kids of her own and a twenty-five-year history of being a stay-at-home wife indulged and neglected by her workaholic doctor husband. Peeking out from under a gigantic, oversized red hat, she looked me straight in the eye when we met. Engulfing me with the fine silk of her patterned blouse and glorious French perfume, she proclaimed, "I'm *so* glad to finally meet you, Leslie," sounding as if she had been waiting for decades when she and Dad had known each other only a few months. "Your father loves you so much and is so proud of you."

Not words he had ever said himself, but I wasn't going to try to explain *that* to her quite yet. She was everything my mother wasn't—effusive, girlish, easy with compliments and laughter. I fell a bit in love with her too.

I visited Dad and S. quite often during their courtship, as they moved into a new house together and then waited for my father's divorce to be finalized. My mother refused to speak to me during this time, and perhaps in reaction, I clung to my sweet new friendship with S. I brought her books I loved, miniskirts from the Gap, and a pink mohair jacket from a trendy Manhattan boutique so our outfits could match; she called me "darling" and "babe" and ended every night with a perfumed kiss followed by "ciao, bella." We used to walk her poodle together on the quiet, safe streets of their neighborhood as she talked of clothes, motherhood, how to avoid treacherous men, and what a wonderful lover my father was (more than I wanted to know).

MY MOTHER HAD always believed my husband was not good enough for me. I thought she meant the fact that he had dropped out of school in eighth grade, then received his GED but never formally graduated from high school. I never imagined there might be darkness in him that I missed. I loved him. As pathetic as that sounds, it is true. For a long time, love was plenty enough reason to be with him. I told no one about his guns and tirades. I didn't want to admit the truth to myself or anyone else.

During one of our evening walks, my stepmother surprised me by saying, "If I had known you before, I'd never have let you marry him." I was touched by her protectiveness, and confused. Did she know what he was doing to me?

———————

SEVERAL MONTHS LATER, I found myself sitting beside her on the slippery black leather seat of a limousine. Like the cinder girl coming home from the ball at midnight, I was returning to graduate school after a trip to New York City. Instead of turning pumpkins and mice into a horse-drawn carriage, my stepmother had given me walks up Fifth Avenue, a hotel room with linen sheets and heavy damask curtains that blocked the light so I could sleep until 11:30, costly restaurant meals, and a slate blue Ferragamo suit that was easily six times what I could afford as a struggling grad student. I never imagined this cosseted waif in a Rodier pantsuit could grant other wishes.

The car idled outside our rundown Philadelphia brownstone. I could see the lights inside our shabby apartment. My husband was home.

As I prepared to get out of the limo, my stepmother dug in her enormous Chanel purse. She took out her checkbook. She starting writing a check. For $1,000.

"I want you to tell him to move out. Right now. Give him this money to find another apartment."

I sat up in surprise. I put my hand on hers and found it soft and warm.

"Why?" I asked.

"You know why," she said, her brown eyes kind. "He's hurting you. You didn't tell me but I know. Leave him now. You are young. You've got an incredible future ahead of you. In five years you will be married to someone else—someone kind, who loves you for the amazing woman you are. Now. Get out. Before you change your mind."

Numbed by surprise at hearing such candor, I didn't say anything. But I took the check, went inside, and before I'd unpacked my suitcase I told my husband to find his own apartment or that I would leave him and find my own.

IF ONLY THE end of my first marriage were that simple. But love, hope, and a wedding certificate make a brutal cocktail. In addition to my stepmother's confrontation, it took the Philadelphia police, generous financial support from my mother, a dozen relentlessly honest friends, a divorce lawyer, a therapist, and a locksmith to pry me out.

Nonetheless, within six months I had divorced, graduated from business school, and moved to Chicago to start life over, with $100,000 in student loans in my name for both our business school educations (my beloved had bad credit, poor thing). But I was safe. My stepmother did something even my own blood relatives didn't have the heart, the courage, or the emotional intelligence to do: she helped me save my own life.

PUZZLING THAT IT took a stranger to do that. And she is a stranger again to me now fifteen years later. True to her prediction, I am remarried to a lovely man with whom I have three children. She and I grew apart as we realized how little in common we had. As the distance grew, she took my father with her, no small price to make me pay.

But still, she is my fairy stepmother. I owe her a permanent place in my heart, gratitude as solid as a piece of petrified wood. She appeared in my desperate, dangerous life for a brief two years when my family could not help me and I could not help myself. I can never repay her directly; my brand of hardscrabble wisdom and cynical hope has no use in her life filled with her own kids' lives, charity fundraisers, and a closet lined with hatboxes.

I do try to pass on her gift, however.

————

I REMEMBER ONE night, soon after my divorce, driving home along a dark city street with the windows down to take in the fresh spring air. The road was empty, well lit by streetlamps, no cars on either side.

Except for one. A new gray Honda with the driver's door open, beeping "ping . . . ping . . . ping" because the keys were in the ignition. A nicely dressed black woman about twenty-five years old stalked away from the car, brushing off a tall, handsome young black man wearing a sports coat and jeans. Tears streamed down her face. The man walked close behind, alternately cajoling her and a second later raising his fists. As I slowed down she made a break for it. The man shoved her against a dirty storefront. Even from my window I could see the fear on her pretty face.

Without thinking, I jerked my car to the side and parked in front of the gray Honda.

"Hey, what's going on?" I yelled as I climbed out, jangling my keys like some kind of wand, rage shaking my arms.

The man let the woman go. She ran back to the car and slid behind the wheel. He stepped back as I approached. I knew exactly what he was doing and I knew he'd done it one hundred times before.

I didn't look at him. I went instead to the car and leaned in. She clutched the wheel, crying and staring straight ahead.

"I know what's happening here," I said to her. "I left a husband who beat me for three years. You know, you do not have to put up with this. You do not deserve to be treated like this."

"I know," she whispered. She wouldn't look at me. "I know you're right," she sobbed, and bent her head over the wheel. "It's just taking me longer than I thought."

I put my hand on her arm, which was tense and stiff and

clutching the wheel like a lifeline. Her eyes were rimmed with red. I saw resolve in them.

"You're going to be OK. I promise." I handed her a clean tissue from my pocket. "No one can treat you like this if you don't let them."

She nodded again and wiped the tears away. "Thank you," she whispered.

As I backed away from her car, I gave the man a long stare. The spell broken, his face was open, sorrowful, filled with hope and fear—a look I'd seen dozens of times on my own husband's face before my stepmother interfered and helped me to choose myself, my life, over his.

Suddenly, I felt as old and wise as my stepmother must have felt that night in the town car with me. I could almost measure the girl's determination. I knew she would be all right, that she'd forge her own happy ending, and that she'd now carry a piece of me in her heart too. I had helped her in a large and small way, although we were strangers who'd never see each other again and she was not my flesh and blood anymore than I am my stepmother's.

Step Shock

CANDY J. COOPER

They were family, I was interloper, and
I didn't know how to join.

My mother hatched our Thanksgivings from old Midwestern recipes that called for the canned, frozen, and boxed. I remember the last one she directed, when she artfully assembled her cranberry and mayonnaise salad, then her shrimp and vegetable casserole bathed in cream of celery soup. As molds jelled and birds roasted, all the men headed out for a rugged game of touch football, their exhales visible in puffs across the front lawn. Hours later, at a linen-covered table, my father spoke of his gratitude for family, sending my sister to the tissue box on behalf of my mother. My brother followed with the butter trick: I asked for it and he gladly obliged, jamming the yellow stick into my fingers.

I liked our ritual back then, full of subterranean furies and affections. It was all ours, down to the sibling flaps and bloody football injuries.

That family multiplied. In-laws and high chairs began to squeeze around the Thanksgiving table, and one by one, each newcomer learned to love the grapefruit salad and bright green crème de menthe pie. They even joined in the après-dinner towel snap, performed with soggy linens as we dried and placed the last silver serving fork into its zippered case.

One ritual hung darkly over us all: my mother's cigarette smoke curled above the holiday table through all those years, her pause between courses. I had pleaded with her when I was young, then fretted to myself as an adult. By age sixty-four she was gone, felled like the flowering dogwood we'd lost in our backyard, whose creamy petals and crimson leaves had once cascaded over everything.

In her last days, she gave me instructions. "I don't want you to change a thing, honey," she had said to me, resting her cold hand on my warmer one. I had tried to plan and stage my wedding before my mother died, and she was asking me to go forward without her. In tight-lipped agony, my father and I returned her sequined mother-of-the-bride dress to the boutique where I had found it.

According to her wishes, I changed nothing, but of course everything changed. After her death, our family's center spun away from us. It reconfigured only bit by bit, a giant creature of the modern age. I had helped to enlarge it. All at once, it seemed, I was a many-headed stepperson: stepmother, stepdaughter, stepdaughter-in-law, stepsister, stepaunt, and stepniece. Our contours were no longer defined by only blood, but by loss and then love, by present shading past, ritual meeting ritual.

Our tightly choreographed Thanksgivings also swelled—into giant step potlucks, like church socials, with so many crisscrossing relational possibilities they seemed to call for flow charts. I didn't greet the expansion with magnanimity. The turkey seemed drier, the day more chaotic, and I curdled the crème de menthe pie. I was in step shock.

My mother's passing led, inexplicably, to my intensely joyous wedding, part wake, part long-overdue celebration of love. At thirty-eight, it was my first try at matrimony, my husband's third. The wedding party included two of his children, ages four and six. All dressed up, they scattered rose petals along the wedding aisle and later argued fiercely over who had tossed too many too quickly, causing them to run out.

My slender stepdaughter, dressed in a flouncy communion dress I'd found, hugged me later in my sheathlike gown. I hugged her back, delighted by my insta-family. In my mind's eye, this was the beginning of something big and rangy, hip and lovely. I would be Mia Farrow, with arms wrapped around stepchildren, foster children, adopted children, and my own children, all under the roof of a big old house.

The vision fit nicely with truth—I loved children, I wanted a child, and I was a childish adult, full of goofy jokes, physicality, and sentiment. I had ridden a bicycle to my first meeting with my would-be stepchildren. We ran around a playground and tied my husband's leg to a tree. They liked me, he later said. I liked them; they were spirited and original.

Slowly, though, our whimsical outings turned more routine, squeezed into rushed Tuesday night dinners and cranky Friday night sleep-overs, an inviolable new schedule that amounted to torturous instability for all. We became a drive-through family. For all of my abstract affection for children, I had never lived among real ones. I didn't know they awoke at dawn, played and fought like wild cats, and ate only white food. What a shock to my single, childless life, cultivated to perfection over twenty years.

On Saturday mornings now, instead of sleeping until noon, I was awakened at daybreak to the siren sounds of a plastic fire truck that screamed "Warning! Warning! Building on fire! Building on fire!" It seemed an appropriate sound track to the visit-drills. They ended with my husband's voice, a mix of despair and court-ordered urgency, as he rounded up the children to take them to their other home. The Loud Family, I called us.

But I grew passive and voiceless, reluctant to assert that there might be a better way. In truth I felt apart; they were family, I was interloper, and I didn't know how to join. I retreated from the cacophony—to the movies, to the gym, or to long phone calls with friends.

I took refuge in my decades-old urban-hippie lifestyle, which was under assault, it seemed. Next to my brown rice, seaweed, and root vegetables sat white bread and Lucky Charms. Power Rangers silenced my jazz collection and prized alto saxophone. My husband, a literary critic and low-culture buff, gifted explicator of nineteenth-century poetry and modern series television, was turning our tasteful love nest into a junkified palace, it seemed.

Wicked Stepmother began to appear on my shoulder, and I brushed her away like dandruff. How shallow, I told her, I welcome the children. I played more board games and dropped more chocolate chips into pancakes. But expectation was crashing into reality. Where was our rhapsodic love affair, my breezy Mia Farrow family, the child of my own?

My husband and I passed through this stage in love and at odds—devoted to family but dunces on step relations. Books later told us that stepfamilies blend over a period of years. Expecting more is a trap. Well, I had fallen in. I had traveled the world, survived lice in Greece and a molester in France. I had lived in a house where crack cocaine was trafficked and viewed the wreckage of plane crashes and earthquakes. Being a stepmother, to my surprise, was harder than any of that.

AS I STRUGGLED with my new role, my father, on the other side of town, grasped at his. Handsome and young looking, with a full head of chestnut hair, he would be catnip to women, I

knew. He was witty, lively, and genuine, and the business he had
started on a farm parcel on the edge of town some forty years earlier had grown and prospered as a city expanded around it.

Even more attractive, perhaps, was his not knowing that he
was a catch—the most eligible bachelor in all the Midwest, I
would tell him. But after forty-five years with my mother, his
high-school sweetheart, he seemed to fear both dating and being
alone. The latter eventually weighed more heavily, and one day
he drove down to the old Main Street jeweler he knew and had
his wedding band cut off.

I worried about my father dating, the way he probably had
fretted all those years about me. My worry had to do with his
loneliness and good fortune. "I don't mind spoiling a woman," he
had told me when I cautioned him once. Anything more from me
would sound mercenary instead of caring. Still, I tried. "Dad, you
just want someone who loves you and makes you happy," I would
say. Or, "Don't forget the seven rule." That was my made-up rule
that said he had to date at least seven women before settling
down with any one.

Certain women seemed to scare him. He would report on
their daring necklines or snug-fitting clothing with a kind of awe.
One day downtown I ran into him with someone new. She was
graceful and interested, and looked in rough outline like a modern version of my mother—petite, with dark, pageboy hair and
tailored clothing. No décolletage, no lipstick.

I invited them to our home for dinner, a reversal of roles if ever
there was one. They held hands and stayed close. She was
younger, engaged in career, and active in the town's social and
charitable life. My father seemed entranced. He soon acquired a
cell phone and jumped when it rang.

They spent their weekends on long bicycle trips and began to
travel, and over the course of the next year or two, the seven rule

was broken. The wedding took place at Walt Disney World, in a stage set–like wedding pavilion with views of Cinderella Castle across the chapel stairs. Disney characters graced the reception. My new stepmother, a year older than my relatively new husband, looked radiant, and everyone celebrated in high spirits in the days that followed. I nursed a fever in my darkened hotel room. The hotel doctor prescribed antibiotics for an eye infection, but I suspected something else—step fever, a plague of unfinished grief for my mother.

I grew vigilant, seeking signs of my father's happiness. My new stepmother's considerable effort to include us all, her love and devotion to children, her attentiveness to my father's ills—these registered, but faintly. As for his happiness, there could be no right amount; if too little was a bad sign, too much meant betrayal.

My attentions lasered in on some postwedding real-estate deals, including the sale of one and reconstruction of another of my parents' two homes. It felt like our past had been shoved off a cliff and me with it. Yoohoo, Hey, Over Here, I wanted to say like a child. Don't forget about meeeeee, as my voice faded over the edge like a cartoon character.

I was brining, nearly pickled, in a salty mix of blended families. My brother had divorced and remarried a mother of one; my father-in-law had found a new wife after losing his to Alzheimer's. He was his second wife's fourth husband. Even my beloved maternal aunt, a widow, had remarried.

With everyone blending, I was trying to expand the family the old-fashioned way, with sperm and egg. Infertility became my central drama, with my stepchildren as animated reminders of what I couldn't have.

THE DAY AFTER my son was born, my bright-eyed stepchildren raced into the hospital room, eager to hold our swaddled dumpling. My husband and I passed him in turn from our arms to theirs and back again. This would be our unofficial ceremony. Now my blood and theirs resided within one plump soul.

It would hardly be just that simple, though. A big job with a high-powered panel of enthusiastic recruiters hounded my husband. We went to visit, flew first-class, and sat at a dinner where my infant son kicked and drooled over the pant legs of a venerated university president for an hour. What was not to love? Still, I didn't want to go.

My husband agonized, and in his soul-search regarding his children, thought magically. We would see one another less frequently, but for longer periods of time. We would take vacations together and have more adventures. In a better job, he would be a happier person, and thus a better father. It could not be worse than the fire drills, I reasoned.

We decided to try, and our little caravan took off for the East, with our stepfamily to follow. Now the Tuesday- and Friday-night visits became weekend and holiday visits here and there. Airplanes and snowstorms and lost baggage became our new ritual. One year the bags, filled with Christmas presents, vanished for good.

Instability inflated, with more separation, more intense togetherness, and bigger children and feelings. Now we were the time-warp family, thrown together to create family on deadline. Just as we would begin to know one another again, it would be time to split. Late into our last nights together, my stepdaughter and I would whip up extravagant desserts. She would sample the chocolate genoise cake on her next morning rush out the door.

But the rougher edges of family would remain behind with the cake and dirty dishes. Why take up precious visits with difficult feelings?

Of course those feelings enlarged, with one activating another like a circular game of Mouse Trap. My investment in motherhood bore the excesses of a forty-year-old with a first child, and my gigantic affections toward my sweet baby, demonstrated in infinite hugs and kisses, only pointed up my careful style as a stepmom. Everyone noticed but me, until my stepchildren began quietly taking their resentments out on their younger brother, whom they also adored.

That was when I first considered the interior lives of my stepchildren, though I never asked. I had thought of myself as an adult friend, fun at times, aloof at others, a calming presence in a mad-dash family. I knew my stepchildren needed my husband; it had never occurred to me that they might want or need me.

My increasingly unreadable stepson, meanwhile, was trying to express the pain of having a part-time dad. My husband, in response, tried to demonstrate his great affection—and guilt, for he had left their mother—by heaping attention and indulgences during visits. He was uber–Disney Dad. He hovered over his sprouting adolescents, offering a movie, a Broadway show, a trip to the electronics or shoe store, a driving lesson, a sushi dinner, a beach vacation. It gave them unusual power but not always a sense of gratitude. Could there ever be gratitude when a parent has left home, I wondered, no matter the demonstrations afterward?

Still, the excesses activated my censorious side. We enforced limits in our smaller family; the rules should not evaporate for our larger one. The thought summoned Wicked Stepmother and I'd retreat—Mouse Trap—bringing us back to the start of the circle.

I had seen a close colleague in a blended family walk away, and I knew the odds of success in such families were against us. But divorce was never for or within me. Even in my most cynical moments, I operated with a kind of Midwestern fortitude and

perhaps naïve hopefulness. And there was the matter of love—
mine for my literary junk-culture man.

"BLENDED FAMILY" SUGGESTS to me that we all dive
into an Osterizer, turn the setting on high, and liquefy into one
muted color. The implication is that we will transform and
become one. It's not like that, and I think we need a new step
language. The step words are practically unutterable to us all—
and handicap the relationships. "Stepmother" implies that I am
some version of my stepchildren's mother, when what I am is the
adult person married to their father. Nor do I feel like any sort of
daughter to the woman who married my father, as "stepdaughter"
seems to say. But with the assigned labels, we are left to compare
our step relationships to the flesh and blood ones supposedly
replaced. I have felt motherly toward my stepchildren and like a
daughter to my stepmother, but in the meantime, I have lived
with the failure of not living up to either role.

IF I COULD, I would offer up my one dramatic moment of
insight to help all steps that come after me. Or a computerized
service, StepQuest, which would lead stepfamilies from darkness
to light. Plug in current coordinates—intersection of Alienated
and About to Flee—and destination—Mia Farrow, etc.—and out
would spit a page of directions with map. I wish my own journey
had been so directional.

Instead, it has looped around, stalled, and herky-jerked along,
just like my hair-raising trip to work one day recently with my
sixteen-year-old stepdaughter gripping the wheel. Each lurch forward equals a sliver of progress, which, added to the ones before
and after, forms a pockmarked path to awakening.

I am in the backseat, drinking my white tea with soy milk,
breaking a sweat on an August morning. It is a day reminiscent

of a broiling August one of a few years back, when our air conditioner blew and our blended family sought relief that night on the basement floor with a fan and, in my stepdaughter's case, draped out a third-floor window. The next day we went rafting, down a drought-parched river so shallow that we walked the black raft across the rocky bottom, wearing life jackets.

"*Stop!*" my husband shouts from the front seat as his sports sedan heads for a pedestrian straight ahead.

"Hey, don't yell at her," I yell at my husband, feeling sorry for our driver, who is about to commit manslaughter.

It's genetic, I decide, recalling my husband's own terrible driving, this time in a snowstorm over Christmas at my sister's mountain cottage, where he lodged the car in a snowbank. That was the year the septic backed up and nine of us shared the master bath. My stepdaughter found her way there in the middle of the night, then got lost in the pitch black of the master bedroom. She felt around the room until she groped the slumbering shape of my sister, who awoke with a fright.

"This was not a good idea," my husband mutters, then blasts a "*Look out!*" as we approach the rear of a stopped car ahead. We heave forward, straining against seat belts.

"You're doing great, really, just relax, almost there," I say, wiping tea spots from my lap. I can't believe she's driving. I met her when she was three, about five minutes ago, or in reality about a dozen masterful, home-decorated birthday cakes ago. Now she is tall, athletic, and alluring with her angular face, hip-hugging jeans, and chatty knowingness.

It's heating up in the car, but I dare not suggest lowering the actual temperature. Our driver eases up on the clutch more gracefully than the time before. She is improving. We jerk forward, and I drift off to the previous week at the beach, where we cooled our toes in the titanic surf. Except for my stepson, who sat in a beach chair in his oversized hip-hop sweat gear listening to music, looking as if he wanted to be just about anywhere else but there, with us.

With my own son, I might have doused him in salt water, or hugged him impulsively, or coaxed him into jumping waves. As it was, my heart went out while the rest of me flopped back under my beach umbrella.

We lurch on, and somewhere during the whiplash forward I am thrown outside the car: not my body, but my angle of vision. From just outside, I can look in and see that this ride is us, strapped down, tossed together and at the mercy of not knowing how. We have, on occasion, nearly wiped out.

From out here it all adds up. Heat wave plus drought plus Christmas plus Thanksgiving plus Seder, beach, birthday and death-defying first driving lesson equals our clan, as close to joy or catastrophe as any family, maybe. Random moments realign into one inimitable arc.

My road-challenged stepdaughter, my inscrutable stepson, my unflappable stepmother—they have rerouted my path in life. It's the scenic route, perilous around the hairpin turns high above the craggy shore. It's the route I've always preferred.

The car pitches to a halt in front of my workplace. Great job, I say, I'm so very sorry I won't have the pleasure of this ride home with both of you. And out I tumble into the heat, drenched in sweat, and grateful beyond measure.

Learning to Pray

MIKE DOLAN

The longer I stay in Taos the more clearly I see the
fatal path of my father's second marriage and the
corrosive effect it has on him.

I never received what I asked for from my father. He did not
have much that I needed, but being a son I had to keep asking. I did get unexpected gifts, though. Gifts someone else
might not be able to see. His third wife was a gift like that.

Spring 1983, Taos, New Mexico
I am helping my father plaster an adobe house he shares with his
second wife, Bea, their eight-year-old daughter, Elizabeth, several drama-seeking dogs (porcupines, poison-happy neighbors,
truck tires), a cat that is always pregnant or trying to lose her kittens, and a trio of ducks that my father has named Thanksgiving,
Christmas, and Easter. Martin Fingernail, a Cheyenne Indian
from Oklahoma, sleeps in his truck in the driveway, but spends
most of his time at the kitchen table drinking coffee, smoking
cigarettes, and polishing his cowboy boots. Martin has recently
been in a bad truck wreck. My father and Bea have nursed him
back to health. I have known Martin since I was a boy and first
introduced to my father's world in New Mexico and the members
of the Native American Church. In the church, members take
each other as relatives. My father and Martin are brothers.

I am seventeen and have dropped out of high school. Too

often stoned, scared by my inability to concentrate, and betrayed by people preparing for college, I have escaped. I have taken a bus from Toronto to Taos. I am on my way to Hawaii to do a mother lode of stoned repetitive physical labor on a pot farm run by friends of my father.

My father and I have stripped the plaster from the house, pulling it off the adobe bricks in long crumbling swatches using hammers and crowbars. We are now rewrapping the entire structure in chicken wire. The chicken wire gives the new plaster something to hold on to. The house looks like it is snared in a chrome spiderweb. To attach the chicken wire to the adobe bricks you twist a ten-penny nail around the X in the wire and hammer it into a firm spot on a brick. I have never done this work before, and I struggle to find good holds for the nails. My father's mood is foul. He is impatient with me. He has perfected the head shake, the sigh. He barks instructions through gritted teeth. I cannot wait until he sparks the first joint of the day.

It comes around ten in the morning. I can see him mellow, his shoulders go slack, the caustic edge slips away. He stops barking. He admits the work is hard. He looks to the sky, talks about the weather, laughs at the dogs, playfully throws a hunk of adobe to scatter the ducks who are sitting in the dog bowl.

THE LONGER I stay in Taos the more clearly I see the fatal path of my father's second marriage and the corrosive effect it has on him. My father seems trapped, depleted by the poisonous undertow he and Bea have created. In the early morning I lie in the bed across the room from Elizabeth and listen to the bitter words they exchange. Money is low. Food stamps and welfare keep things afloat (the fridge holds big tubs of honey and blocks of crappy cheese from the federal food giveaways), but extras are a tense negotiation.

My own parents divorced when I was four. Although they made a striking pair—my mother, black Irish and Czech, tall and elegant; my father short and strong, a scratch golfer, a risk taker, a man's man—their marriage had no real chance. My mother got pregnant with my sister Colleen during her junior year at a Catholic college. I was born ten months after Colleen. The end of the marriage came fast.

I fantasize about saving my father. Making enough money in Hawaii to buy him his own house, to set him free. I have some money from working three jobs after I left high school. I buy groceries and take Elizabeth out for milkshakes. She is a quiet little girl, no doubt tucking into some pocket within herself to guard against the toxic vibes permeating her home. I use all of my tricks on her—the accents, the imitations. Thankfully she still laughs at me. We both get silent as we head back to the house.

Pot seems to be the only lubricant in my father and Bea's relationship. When they are holding, they take nightly drives onto the mesa and come back acting like high-school sweethearts. Bea stays up late baking him a chocolate cake. My father and Martin tie up a kettledrum and sing peyote songs deep into the night.

SINCE THEIR MARRIAGE, when I was nine, Bea has been my ally, a buffer from my father's relentless dissatisfaction and aggression toward me. In the past I appreciated this, but things have shifted. She has stopped taking care of herself. She talks to me about leaving my father, how he is stopping her from being the person she wants to be. "I used to be able to get groovy. I mean, I really could. But with him, it's just a nonstop bummer." She tells me odd intimate things about my father, he wishes he had the money for a face-lift, he is going to leave and live in a trailer in the Huerfano Valley in Colorado.

One night I get home late. I have been at a concert by a local band, The Mutz, and afterward a large group of us snuck into the pool at the San Geronimo Motel. I was jealous of the band and made a point of singing louder than anyone when songs started bouncing off the pool's plastic bubble roof. The bass player glided over to me and told me I was fucking up the harmony. Then the girl I wanted to kiss swam away with him. She whispered something in his ear, their limbs tangled, and they disappeared under the surface of the black water. Bea offers a game of Scrabble. She tells me a lengthy tale about how my father is cursed.

"It happened in Colombia. He went there to astral travel; take Yage and fly into a celestial plain. Yage is a powerful drug. It is used by a shaman as a gateway to the spirit world. Some call it the visionary vine, others call it the vine of death. It's the real deal. Your father was in a hut with a medicine man and his son and they had just taken the Yage when the son's wife came in. Your father was attracted to her and could not stop looking at her. He really wanted to fuck her."

She pulls a Camel filter, rips the filter off, and lights it. The tobacco is mellower than in the Camel straights.

"The son of the medicine man saw the way your father looked at his wife. His bullshit move; a slap in the face from a stranger whom they were sharing their strong medicine with. They left their bodies and went astral traveling, but when they were supposed to return the medicine man's son threatened to leave your father out there, in the stars. Your father was able to convince them to bring him back to earth, to his body, and they did. But when he was back in his body he looked down at his leg and there was a giant tarantula there. This was the sign of the curse. They told him he could never be happy with a woman in this lifetime."

THE NEXT DAY my father and I are plastering the walls. The sun is hot early. The pot has run out. My body feels distant, devoid of minerals, vitamins. I keep looking at my hands; the skin looks severely translucent. My breath is shallow and thin. I have never wielded a trowel. The sand/cement mixture is too heavy. I don't know how to leverage my strength. My arms burn, my shoulders scream. My father tells me to forget it, just run the mixer, bring him the plaster, and stop putting so much fucking sand in the mix. I plow the wheelbarrow loaded with plaster up the three slanted two-by-sixes to the low scaffolding where he is standing. I lose my balance, the plaster shifts, and the wheelbarrow rips itself from my hands. The plaster falls into the tall corn-colored grass of the yard.

"You gonna get your head out of your ass?"

His expression is one of total revulsion. Then something in him shifts. He shakes the expression off his face. He looks at me with something like compassion, or at least fraternity.

"You know what the good life would be? I mean, you know what it would really be? To live in a cave up in the mountains and just shoot heroin and read books, the Greeks. Think about that. Come down once a month and go to a prostitute."

SIX MONTHS LATER my father leaves. Instead of a cave in the mountains he moves to a small house in Arroyo Hondo. Martin abandons the truck and moves in, not just into the house, into Bea's bed. Some time later my father drives back to confront Martin, his brother, and Martin pulls a knife on him. The divorce is complicated by the fact that neither my father nor Bea can risk going before a judge. If anyone mentions the drug use, Elizabeth could be taken by the state.

Fall 1983, Haiku, Maui
I am trying to lose myself, but I don't fit in here. I look like a surfer but can't surf. I paddle out one day stoned on potent

purple-haired buds. I swerve away from the surfers. I imagine I
have discovered a new break. The waves pummel me into the
coral. I chase a girl to a party and end up having to fight a huge
man named Tosh. I spend most of my time farming. I love my
plants. I visit my female *Cannabis sativa* plants, hundreds of
them. I mulch them with guava leaves. I crush the fruit and grind
it into the soil with my fingers. I check their huge donkey dick
buds for balls, which some plants can throw. The females
become hermaphrodites to pollinate themselves. I find no balls.
I scrape the resin off my hands; it is a sticky hash oil I smoke in
a ceramic pipe. I secure the barbwire fence I have strung along
the creek to keep the roving cows away from my precious crop. I
dash back to the compound singing Stiff Little Fingers songs. I
run barefoot and practically naked—my OP shorts have been
shredded by the fence work. The man is standing stock-still in
the bamboo grove that slopes down to the well built by the Chinese at the turn of the century. He is wearing camouflage, reef
walker shoes, wraparound sunglasses, and has a .45 strapped to
his leg. He says he is digging bamboo for his yard, but we both
know he is scouting my plants. Days later he will return with
more men, more guns. They will discharge their weapons so we
will know not to try and rescue the tens of thousands of dollars
worth of Da Kine they are ripping out of the ground. A grower I
know talks about buying an AK-47 and sleeping with the plants.

I decide to go to New York and become an actor.

Spring 1989, New York City
My father visits and sees me in a play on Broadway, *A Few Good
Men*. He compliments the other actors, not me. He criticizes my
apartment and tells me I should relax; enjoy my success. I buy
him a Father's Day dinner in the Village. He says he would like
to try crack. I attack him about the kind of father he is: the peo-

ple he didn't protect me from, the drugs he let me use. He lifts the level of anger and tells me he would have killed anyone if he knew they had abused me. He insists that he is not responsible for my early drug use.

"You gave me acid when I was five," I rail.

"You always wanted to take the drugs. What the hell could I do?"

He leaves. We do not talk for many months.

Fall 1990, New York City

I am always alone in New York. I keep telling myself I need to find a "scene" to be part of, then I will be OK. I have worked a good deal as an actor. I am better then. I am comfortable being part of the falsely intimate family of a cast. But when the jobs end, there is no continuity to my life; casts scatter, find new temporary attachments. When I am not working I feel crazy. I question everything about my life, myself.

I FEEL BEST when drinking, but I am scared to drink. I have woken up with bruises all over my body, no memory, no keys. One night I come to in the middle of Amsterdam Avenue. I am swinging a garbage can and throwing trash into the street. I am trying to get homeless men to fight me.

MY FATHER CALLS with news, good and bad. Good. He has met a lady, Carol. She is a Navajo, he tells me, built close to the ground, sturdy; different from other women he has known. He has moved in with her and her two young children. The bad news is that he has prostate cancer. He doesn't want to have an operation and he doesn't want to do radiation. He tells me he is going to test his faith. He is going to have a peyote meeting for himself. He asks me to help him. I agree.

Fall 1990, Edgewood, New Mexico

I help my father and other members of the church raise the tepee. Three poles tethered together near the top go up first, forming a tripod. The other poles are fit in, forming the circle's perimeter. My father walks the edge of the poles, working the rope that secures each added pole, like a man training a horse. I carry the poles and lodge the ends against my boot as I lift and place them. I can feel that something has shifted between my father and me. His focus is no longer on me; his attention is elsewhere. He is generous with his thanks.

I MEET CAROL and her children, Myron and Leanne, at a trailer park where they are living with my father. Leanne is eight, shy and studious. Myron is four and all over me. He calls me brother and hangs on my arms, my legs. His mantra is "I'm big, huh?" Carol has a wide face and big brown eyes. She was raised on the Navajo reservation outside Gallup and was sent to schools where they washed her mouth out with soap if she spoke her language. The same language honored for use by code talkers during World War II. Her expression is stoic, but I learn that a playful smile comes easily to the corners of her mouth. She welcomes me and tells me how important it is to my father that I have come. When a growl inches into my father's voice, she laughs at him and tells him she won't talk to him if that is the way he communicates. He relents, and they make decisions and move on with the preparations for the meeting.

CAROL IS FULLY behind my father's decision to treat his cancer with a peyote meeting. She is not like the other women I have met in the peyote church; mostly Anglos coming to the church on the heels of the hippie daze. This meeting for my father's health is not a gambit for her, not a fad. She has no doubts.

She believes in the power of the medicine, of the prayers. My father has often told me how he found this church after much seeking. He grew up Catholic, studied philosophy, but he felt he found his true spiritual path in the tepees, the songs, the prayers, the feasts, the wise Indians, and the sacrament of peyote present in the Native American Church. In the past we have fought over this. I have called him a drug addict, seen the church as simply a convenient way to stay stoned, to mask his addiction in a spiritual quest. I am certain the meeting will fail to cure my father's cancer. Western medicine will be called in, but Carol's presence challenges these notions. She grew up in the church. Her parents were some of the first Navajos to participate. The church is real to her on a whole different level.

I HELP WITH the meeting any way I can. I offer money for a down payment on their new FHA home is Los Lunas. I help Carol and Myron and Leanne move from the trailer into a house. Most importantly to my father, I sit up all night in the tepee. I eat the fine-ground peyote that makes me gag. I swallow the metallic medicinal peyote tea that makes me gag. I roll tobacco in the corn husks and pray that the cancer will evaporate. I listen to the songs and rock to the speedy beat of the drum. My eyes lock onto the flames of the fire. I take breaks outside to breath mountain air free from the drench of cottonwood smoke. Outside under the mountain stars my father puts his arm around me, thanks me for being at his side. I sit as tall as I can all night. I give my father everything I have.

MY FATHER EATS a lot of peyote. He soldiers down handfuls of the powder, gulps of pulpy gravy, tin cups of the tea. I hear him retching outside. I listen to him sing, high pitched and fierce. Carol sits beside him, guarded from the fire with the eagle-feather fan she moves up and down to the thump of the drum. She wears beaded moccasins and has a Pendleton blanket wrapped around her waist. At midnight she brings in the water and says a prayer. She places the enamel tin pail between her and the fire, and asks the Great Spirit to remove my father's cancer so that he can live a long life, be a good father, a good husband. She says more prayers in Navajo before lifting the pail and drinking.

A WEEK LATER the doctors can find no tumor on my father's prostate. Soon after that my father and Carol are married in a traditional Navajo ceremony in her mother's hogan. There are no rings or vows. They share corn from a woven basket and water from a gourd. The elders offer advice and gifts. Some of the elders speak only Navajo, but they fully embrace my father.

"I don't know what it is," he tells me. "They are Old World. I feel like I have finally found people who understand me. They love me." With his vows to Carol I see that my father has finally found his place within a marriage, a family. This concentrates the sadness I have always felt around my father, the grief at his inability to be my father. But my father's devotion to Carol also inspires me and in some ways sets me free.

I decide that when I get back to New York I will ask an actor I know about rehab.

Spring 2005, Austin, Texas
I am part of many things now. I have not had a drink or used any drugs in over twelve years. I have found my own way of feeling connected to others, to myself, to my own understanding of God. I have gone back to college and graduated. I am living in the West for the first time in many years, working on a second master's degree. I am married to a beautiful and remarkable woman.

I have sought out and found the help I need to navigate the frightening miracle of our intimacy. I am a work in progress.

I SPEAK TO my father regularly, but we are not close. I know it is best to not need anything from him. But we have found an acceptable level of connection; we talk about driving routes between Austin and Albuquerque. He talks about his stepchildren. Leanne is now a doctor. Myron is struggling. He is set to fight six members of a Mexican gang, but my father is trying to walk him through this rough patch. My father tells me about the work he and Carol have done on their cabin in the wilderness above the Continental Divide. He calls it his paradise and explains the seasonal rotation of wildlife they witness. His life has not followed a standard trajectory, but I am happy that he and Carol are easing peacefully into the twilight of their days.

I FINISH MY first year of graduate school. I am trying to plan a trip to New Mexico to visit my father and Carol. An e-mail arrives. There is a change of plans. He has been to the doctor. His PSA numbers have jumped; his cancer is back. As before, he does not want to have an operation or radiation treatment. He writes that he is driving to the peyote gardens south of Laredo to gather medicine. He and Carol are going to have a meeting for him at Ben Eagle's land in Colorado. He tells me the dates, but we both know I will not be there. I have attended my last peyote meeting. I will find my own way to pray for him. I am praying for him right now.

The Mrs. Davises

SUSAN DAVIS

*I wish I could remember the rabbi's name because he's
responsible for one of the sweetest moments in the
history of first wife–second wife relations.*

H ere's what you should know about my father: he was an
ophthalmologist, a tinkerer, a surgeon, a craftsman, an
artist of the microscopic fix. He hoarded broken appliances and spent his leisure time repairing them. He brought
home prisms and crystals, regaling us with tricks of refracted
light. He kept a chart of the migratory habits of the Sephardic
Jews on the back of his home-office door. He ran the fifty-yard
dash in record time; invited all the neighborhood boys to join him
on our backyard basketball court; held an impromptu infirmary
on our front porch each sunny Sunday; and sent yellow roses to
all the women (or girls) in his life on their birthdays. He was my
source, my reference, guide and maker. I lived by the radiance of
his smile.

My mother, Edwina, and my stepmother, Jan, were bound by
my father's professional fortunes long before they ever shared his
name. Neither woman remembers their first meeting. But
they've each made up a story and agreed to accept their individual versions because their relationship requires a known (even
vaguely) beginning. My mother says it was a weekday, she had
taken me, her youngest, for a checkup that included a shot and
the reward of a visit to my much beloved daddy. She thinks Jan

was working at the reception desk. My mother notes Jan's "tarty" appearance and that she was surprised by Jan's "warmth" and "sweetness" toward me. Jan remembers my mother as imperious except when it came to me; with me, she was "sweet." Neither mentions my father at all.

My mother is tall and thin, with short, eye-catching salt-and-pepper hair. Her fashion sense is classic but colorful, stylish but subtle. In the late 1970s she was in her early forties, a Jewish doctor's wife in Detroit living the life those very words evoke—charmed old house on a tree-lined street; three healthy, precocious children; an American-made station wagon in the driveway; country club membership; a standing appointment with a manicurist; and a wardrobe that rotated with the seasons. She was also living a life that might surprise you, a life she worked and fought for—as the chief legislative aide to a Detroit city councilwoman; as a tireless activist for women's rights; marching in the streets for social justice; remaining in her integrated inner-city neighborhood after the infamous riots of 1967; sending her children to Detroit's embattled public schools.

Jan was in her late twenties, a single mother of three, having survived an abusive marriage. She never got to go to college, but she persevered through a nurse's aide program and was working in my father's office checking in patients, performing routine examinations, readying equipment and medicine. Jan is curvy, with teased-up, dyed-blond hair and makeup like a Vegas showgirl. Her clothes, including her nurse's uniform, were always tight.

NOT LONG AFTER that fabled day when my mother and Jan first met, my father began a pattern of inexplicable and increasingly important forgetting—first it was birthdays, appointments, then it was picking me up from dancing school and attending my brother's tennis matches. Eventually, it was forgetting to report a car accident and to pay his (our) taxes. We dismissed this with nervous giggles, saying "He's such an absentminded professor," or "He has too much on his mind." Within a year my mother got a phone call straight from the script of a made-for-TV movie. A man whose wife worked for my father was sure the two, his wife and my father, were having an affair. This man had evidence. My mother offered the man a few choice expletives and hung up. She confronted my father, and to her utter shock my father confessed. The woman wasn't Jan. Her name was Cheryl. Within weeks Cheryl was gone from my father's office and my father was gone from our house. My mother filed for divorce. My sister was twenty-one, living in Colorado, having graduated from college and begun her life as an adult. My brother was nineteen and away at college in Arizona. I was sixteen and miserable. My mother was forty-three, stunned and terrified, as she had yet to be without my father since she was fifteen.

After my parents' separation, my father's behavior went from bad to weird. He disowned the three of us, leaving me to fend for my own college tuition. He estranged himself, not returning our phone calls, not finding the time to see us. He refused any contact with my mother's family with whom he had been remarkably close, so close that my mother's younger brother Alan (who was thirteen when he met my father) followed my father to Harvard, lived in the same house as my father, wore his same jacket and tie to meals, and eventually shared his college ring. Indeed, the initials and date JDD 1957 are engraved just behind the crested "Veritas." Turning the ring slightly, you'll find ADC 1961 in the same italic script. Brothers. They were brothers. My relatives called me to cry and vent. Why won't he see them, what had they done wrong? I was trying to figure that out for myself, about myself.

Following his lawyer's advice, my father moved into a tiny,

empty, sad, sorry, gloomy apartment near his office. Jan offered to keep him company. He was desperate to be taken care of. My parents' divorce case showed up on the docket of a judge my mother knew well from her work in the feminist community. The judge offered to recuse herself. My father, fearing a long wait and lack of resolution, accepted the judge's bias. The day in September when I sat down in the front row of my first class as a college freshman, my parents were officially divorced. By Thanksgiving my father was married to Jan. I found this out after the fact. The wedding was quick and secretive. No one I knew had been there. When I told my mother about it, she asked blankly, "Which one was Jan?"

Then my father blacked out in the operating room (he was the assisting, not the primary, surgeon; no one was hurt). The neurologists who worked him up were stunned. His synapses were completely misfiring. They were amazed he could drive a car, let alone doctor. He had dementia at best, Alzheimer's at worst. He had to retire, immediately. The diagnosis was a gift, and soon he had slid all the way down the hill into oblivion. My family was truly grateful—at least we had an explanation for his erratic, sometimes mean, sometimes terrifying behavior: he was actually, literally, losing his mind.

I DEVELOPED A theory that my father had his affair so my mother would kick him out and he could then marry the care-giving Jan and spare my mother a protracted character-compromising, torturous life of watching him disappear and eventually die. I argued that he had married each of his wives because she was the right fit for what lay ahead. My mother was a bride of promise—a righteous companion, the perfect person to grow up with, to navigate adulthood, a professional life, and a family with. Jan was a wife for the worst of times—the steadfast, selfless, faithful nurse. And yes, I understand the implications of what I write. My mother was not a woman ready to sacrifice her own career, emotional wellness, and health to care for my father during his slow demise. As admirable a person as my mother was (and is), she was no saint. Jan was.

And Jan was a kind of mother to me as well in as much as she insulated me from the ugly truth of my father's illness. The arc of my father's illness corresponded with the end of my college career and years of wandering in the wilderness of early adulthood, trying out careers, boyfriends, hairstyles, apartments, even cities. But there was never a question that I would stop this ignoble but completely necessary pursuit and move back to Michigan to tend to my father. Like the mother who pushes a child out of the way of the oncoming train and gets caught on the tracks herself, Jan prevented my permanent derailment. She allowed me the freedom to travel my own arc uninterrupted.

ONE DAY MY mother was at the hairdresser, sitting under the dryer on the banquette with an array of tinfoil antennae and a magazine open in her lap. The woman next to her was staring. She too had a head full of tinfoil spikes and a magazine open on her lap. The woman whispered tentatively, "Are you Mrs. Davis?"

"Yes, yes I am."

"So am I," the woman giggled. "I'm Jan, Jerry's wife."

"Oh, Jan," my mother sighed. "I'm so sorry, so sorry. How are you doing?"

"OK, sort of. Well, not so well. He hardly recognizes anyone anymore. The book I'm reading about dementia says the short-term memory goes first. I wonder if you could help me. He keeps asking about Mary. Who is Mary? Do you think there's another woman in his life?"

My mother chuckled warmly. "Oh no, dear, Mary was his housekeeper growing up. She used to cut the crust off of his sandwiches. She took impeccable care of him."

"When he was growing up?"

"I bet he hasn't seen Mary in forty years."

"Well that's a relief."

"Here." My mother pressed a piece of paper into Jan's hand. "Take my number and call me anytime. I've known him since he was seventeen. I'm happy to help."

That was meeting number two.

From then on we lost count. It was a regular thing to find my mother on the phone conveying my father's history to Jan—his bar mitzvah portion, high-school basketball career, the agony of choosing a medical specialty. They met for lunch. My mother unearthed photographs of her wedding, our babyhoods, her in-laws, vacations and graduations. She gladly became my father's biographer, introducing his wife to his colorful life story. And when my father's disease made his otherwise strong body belligerent and dangerous and my brother had to sue Jan to share guardianship so we could remove him to a facility equipped to handle his condition (something she knew was necessary but did not have the heart to do), it was my mother who offered Jan absolution and the wisdom of experience. "It's OK," I heard her whisper into the phone, "he's sick, you've done what you can do, you've got to start to let him go." "Let him go," she repeated, "let him go."

MY FATHER DIED on December 1, 1992. He was one of the rare Alzheimer's patients who was actually killed by the disease. His brain simply forgot to tell his lungs to breathe, his heart to pump and beat. He was fifty-seven years old. It was my unspeakable heartbreak. For days I could not get the words to escape my throat. Literally, it was unspeakable. This was not just a buried reference, this was my severed chord.

He left the important, studyable parts of his body to the Alzheimer's unit at the University of Michigan. The rest he asked to have cremated. Jan decided to host a service at a funeral home she knew and liked, a Catholic funeral home in a part of town I'd never been to, a part of town where Jews did not tend to go. My mother offered to host a few nights of shiva. She declined the standard duration of eight nights, saying simply, "I am not his widow, he had a wife." At the last minute Jan called my brother and suggested he find a rabbi for the funeral; she thought my father would have wanted a rabbi. We all flew in the night before and converged on my mother's house. It was a slumber party of grief. My uncle and aunt camped out in the den. My mother slept on the living-room couch, my brother and sister-in-law in her room, my boyfriend and me in one of the guest rooms, my sister in the other. My brother spent hours calling down the phone book's list of Jewish organizations and agencies trying to find a rabbi willing to come to a Catholic funeral home, stand beneath a crucifix, and perform the funeral service for a Jewish man he never knew. It took the better part of the day and night, but my brother found one, a young man from a liberal temple in a remote suburb. I wish I could remember the rabbi's name because he's responsible for one of the sweetest moments in the history of first wife–second wife relations.

The day of the funeral was gray and cold, the sky a single cloud, the leafless trees of Michigan more bent and broken than ever. From my mother's house north of Detroit we drove in a long line of somber black cars to the funeral home an hour away. The place was solemn and hushed, as funeral homes are. While over a hundred people milled beside the closed coffin (we were sur-

prised by the turnout; so many of my father's friends and colleagues having given him up for dead when the disease overtook
him completely), "the family" gathered in the funeral director's
office. Jan's three children were there with their spouses, the
girls wore party dresses and glittery eye shadow, their husbands
wore three-piece suits. Jan's youngest, her son Billy, the football
star, the gentle young man who once got between my raging
father and his cowering wife, the police officer in training, wore
his church clothes and choked back tears. Jan stood alone in the
middle of the room wearing a clingy black dress with a cascade
of appliquéd, sequined flowers. Her jewelry was sparkly and
abundant and she teetered on four-inch stilettos. Across the
room from Jan's kids, slumped in chairs and leaning on each
other, sat my aunt and uncle wearing layers of dark wool, my sister in her purple if-you-hire-me-I'll-be-both-practical-and-
creative interview suit; my brother in his only suit, a versatile
gray; my sister-in-law in an unadorned blue dress and borrowed
hose; and me, in a black skirt and garnet silk blouse, one I would
hastily give away the next week so as not to be reminded of the
day I gave my father's eulogy. Around my neck I wore several
strands of beads that my father had given to my mother. I fid-
geted with them obsessively, fingering one round stone after the
other. All of us were slack jawed and numb with disbelief. Only
my mother was animated, pacing in her low-heeled navy suede
pumps, clutching the delicate white handkerchief with my
father's mother's initial "R" embroidered into the corner, thought-
lessly smoothing the front of her textured navy suit. Occasionally
she would spin the ring on her right pinky finger, the one my
father gave her for an early anniversary. It spelled "love" in gold
script. Not long before their separation he had "stolen" the ring
back and had an emerald and two diamonds added to the letters.
The rabbi, who had trouble finding the funeral home, stumbled

in adjusting his glasses and mumbling apologetically, "I'm sorry I'm late." Gazing around the room, confused by our motley assortment, he asked, "Who is Mrs. Davis?" In one long stride, my mother appeared by Jan's side, straightened up to her full height, took Jan's trembling hand in hers, faced the unknown rabbi, and said, "We are."

THAT WAS MORE than a decade ago. They still meet, usually at the hairdresser's where they coo at the photos of the other's grandchildren and exchange salient details of marriages, deaths, retirements, and breakups. They are both well, both single but happy, living full lives—Jan is working and taking classes, my mother volunteers in Africa with AIDS victims and for women's causes in Michigan. They both garden and take their grandkids to the zoo each spring. They both continue to use my father's name.

Stone Soup[*]

BARBARA KINGSOLVER

*To judge a family's value by its tidy symmetry is to
purchase a book for its cover.*

In the catalog of family values, where do we rank an occasion
like this? A curly-haired boy who wanted to run before he
walked, age seven now, a soccer player scoring a winning
goal. He turns to the bleachers with his fists in the air and a
smile wide as a gap-toothed galaxy. His own cheering section of
grown-ups and kids all leap to their feet and hug each other,
delirious with love for this boy. He's Andy, my best friend's son.
The cheering section includes his mother and her friends, his
brother, his father and stepmother, a stepbrother and stepsister,
and a grandparent. Lucky is the child with this many relatives on
hand to hail a proud accomplishment. I'm there too, witnessing
a family fortune. But in spite of myself, defensive words take
shape in my head. I am thinking: I dare *anybody* to call this a broken home.

Families change, and remain the same. Why are our names for
home so slow to catch up to the truth of where we live?

When I was a child, I had two parents who loved me without

cease. One of them attended every excuse for attention I ever contrived, and the other made it to the ones with higher production values, like piano recitals and appendicitis. So I was a lucky child too. I played with a set of paper dolls called "The Family of Dolls," four in number, who came with the factory-assigned names of Dad, Mom, Sis, and Junior. I think you know what they looked like, at least before I loved them to death and their heads fell off.

Now I've replaced the dolls with a life. I knit my days around my daughter's survival and happiness, and am proud to say her head is still on. But we aren't the Family of Dolls. Maybe you're not, either. And if not, even though you are statistically no oddity, it's probably been suggested to you in a hundred ways that yours isn't exactly a real family, but an impostor family, a harbinger of cultural ruin, a slapdash substitute—something like counterfeit money. . . . Most of us are up to our ears in the noisy business of trying to support and love a thing called family. But there's a current in the air with ferocious moral force that finds its way even into political campaigns, claiming there is only one right way to do it, the Way It Has Always Been.

In the face of a thriving, parti-colored world, this narrow view is so pickled and absurd I'm astonished that it gets airplay. And I'm astonished that it still stings.

Every parent has endured the arrogance of a child-unfriendly grump sitting in judgment, explaining what those kids of ours really need (for example, "a good licking"). If we're polite, we move our crew to another bench in the park. If we're forthright (as I am in my mind, only, for the rest of the day), we fix them with a sweet imperious stare and say, "Come back and let's talk about it after you've changed a thousand diapers."

But it's harder somehow to shrug off the Family-of-Dolls Family Values crew when they judge (from their safe distance) that divorced people, blended families, gay families and single parents are failures. That our children are at risk, and the whole arrangement is messy and embarrassing. A marriage that ends is not called "finished," it's called *failed*. The children of this family may have been born to a happy union, but now they are called *the children of divorce*.

I had no idea how thoroughly these assumptions overlaid my culture until I went through divorce myself. I wrote to a friend: "This might be worse than being widowed. Overnight I've suffered the same losses—companionship, financial and practical support, my identity as a wife and partner, the future I'd taken for granted. I am lonely, grieving, and hard-pressed to take care of my household alone. But instead of bringing casseroles, people are acting like I had a fit and broke up the family china."

Once upon a time I held these beliefs about divorce: that everyone who does it could have chosen not to do it. That it's a lazy way out of marital problems. That it selfishly puts personal happiness ahead of family integrity. Now I tremble for my ignorance. It's easy, in fortunate times, to forget about the ambush that could leave your head reeling: serious mental or physical illness, death in the family, abandonment, financial calamity, humiliation, violence, despair.

I started out like any child, intent on being the Family of Dolls. I set upon young womanhood believing in most of the doctrines of my generation: I wore my skirts four inches above the knee. I had that Barbie with her zebra-striped swimsuit and a figure unlike anything found in nature. And I understood the Prince Charming Theory of Marriage, a quest for Mr. Right that ends smack dab where you find him. I did not completely understand that another whole story *begins* there, and no fairy tale prepared me for the combination of bad luck and persistent hope that would interrupt my dream and lead me to other arrangements.

Like a cancer diagnosis, a dying marriage is a thing to fight, to deny, and finally, when there's no choice left, to dig in and survive. Casseroles would help. Likewise, I imagine it must be a painful reckoning in adolescence (or later on) to realize true love will never look like the soft-focus fragrance ads because Prince Charming (surprise!) is a princess. Or vice versa. Or has skin the color your parents didn't want you messing with, except in the Crayola box.

It's awfully easy to hold in contempt the straw broken home, and that mythical category of persons who toss away nuclear family for the sheer fun of it. Even the legal terms we use have a suggestion of caprice. I resent the phrase "irreconcilable differences," which suggests a stubborn refusal to accept a spouse's little quirks. This is specious. Every happily married couple I know has loads of irreconcilable differences. Negotiating where to set the thermostat is not the point. A nonfunctioning marriage is a slow asphyxiation. It is waking up despised each morning, listening to the pulse of your own loneliness before the radio begins to blare its raucous gospel that you're nothing if you aren't loved. It is sharing your airless house with the threat of suicide or other kinds of violence, while the ghost that whispers, "Leave here and destroy your children," has passed over every door and nailed it shut. Disassembling a marriage in these circumstances is as much *fun* as amputating your own gangrenous leg. You do it, if you can, to save a life—or two, or more.

I know of no one who really went looking to hoe the harder row, especially the daunting one of single parenthood. Yet it seems to be the most American of customs to blame the burdened for their destiny. We'd like so desperately to believe in freedom and justice for all, we can hardly name that rogue bad luck, even when he's a close enough snake to bite us. In the wake of my divorce, some friends (even a few close ones) chose to vanish, rather than linger within striking distance of misfortune.

But most stuck around, bless their hearts, and if I'm any the wiser for my trials, it's from having learned the worth of steadfast friendship. And also, what not to say. The least helpful question is: "Did you want the divorce, or didn't you?" Did I want to keep that gangrenous leg, or not? How to explain, in a culture that venerates choice: two terrifying options are much worse than none at all. Give me any day the quick hand of cruel fate that will leave me scarred but blameless. As it was, I kept thinking of that wicked third-grade joke in which some boy comes up behind you and grabs your ear, starts in with a prolonged tug, and asks, "Do you want this ear any longer?"

Still, the friend who holds your hand and says the wrong thing is made of dearer stuff than the one who stays away. And generally, through all of it, you live. My favorite fictional character, Kate Vaiden (in the novel by Reynolds Price), advises: "Strength just comes in one brand—you stand up at sunrise and meet what they send you and keep your hair combed."

Once you've weathered the straits, you get to cross the tricky juncture from casualty to survivor. If you're on your feet at the end of a year or two, and have begun putting together a happy new existence, those friends who were kind enough to feel sorry for you when you needed it must now accept you back to the ranks of the living. If you're truly blessed, they will dance at your second wedding. Everybody else, for heaven's sake, should stop throwing stones.

ARGUING ABOUT WHETHER nontraditional families deserve pity or tolerance is a little like the medieval debate about left-handedness as a mark of the devil. Divorce, remarriage, single parenthood, gay parents, and blended families simply are. They're facts of our time. Some of the reasons listed by sociologists for these family reconstructions are: the idea of marriage as a romantic partnership rather than a pragmatic one; a shift in women's expectations, from servility to self-respect and independence; and longevity (prior to antibiotics no marriage was expected to last many decades—in Colonial days the average couple lived to be married less than twelve years). Add to all this our growing sense of entitlement to happiness and safety from abuse. Most would agree these are all good things. Yet their result—a culture in which serial monogamy and the consequent reshaping of families are the norm—gets diagnosed as "failing."

For many of us, once we have put ourselves Humpty-Dumpty-wise back together again, the main problem with our reorganized family is that other people think we have a problem. My daughter tells me the only time she's uncomfortable about being the child of divorced parents is when her friends say they feel sorry for her. It's a bizarre sympathy, given that half the kids in her school and nation are in the same boat, pursuing childish happiness with the same energy as their married-parent peers. When anyone asks how *she* feels about it, she spontaneously lists the benefits: our house is in the country and we have a dog, but she can go to her dad's neighborhood for the urban thrills of a pool and sidewalks for roller-skating. What's more, she has three sets of grandparents!

Why is it surprising that a child would revel in a widened family and the right to feel at home in more than one house? Isn't it the opposite that should worry us—a child with no home at all, or too few resources to feel safe? The child at risk is the one whose parents are too immature themselves to guide wisely; too diminished by poverty to nurture; too far from opportunity to offer hope. The number of children in the U.S. living in poverty at this moment is almost unfathomably large: twenty percent. There are families among us that need help all right, and by no means are they new on the landscape. The rate at which teenage girls had babies in 1957 (ninety-six per thousand) was twice what it is now. That remarkable statistic is ignored by the religious right—probably because the teen birth rate was cut in half mainly by legalized abortion. In fact, the policy gatekeepers who coined the phrase "family values" have steadfastly ignored the desperation of too-small families, and since 1979 have steadily reduced the amount of financial support available to a single parent. But, this camp's most outspoken attacks seem aimed at the notion of families getting too complex, with add-ons and extras such as a gay parent's partner, or a remarried mother's new husband and his children.

To judge a family's value by its tidy symmetry is to purchase a book for its cover. There's no moral authority there. The famous family comprised of Dad, Mom, Sis, and Junior living as an isolated economic unit is not built on historical bedrock. In *The Way We Never Were*, Stephanie Coontz writes, "Whenever people propose that we go back to the traditional family, I always suggest that they pick a ballpark date for the family they have in mind." Colonial families were tidily disciplined, but their members (meaning everyone but infants) labored incessantly and died young. Then the Victorian family adopted a new division of labor, in which women's role was domestic and allowed time for study and play, but this was an upper-class construct supported by myriad slaves. Coontz writes, "For every nineteenth-century middle-class family that protected its wife and child within the family circle, there was an Irish or German girl scrubbing floors . . . a Welsh boy mining coal to keep the home-baked goodies warm, a black girl doing the family laundry, a black mother and child picking cotton to be made into clothes for the family, and a

Jewish or an Italian daughter in a sweatshop making 'ladies'
dresses or artificial flowers for the family to purchase."

The abolition of slavery brought slightly more democratic
arrangements, in which extended families were harnessed together
in cottage industries; at the turn of the century came a steep rise
in child labor in mines and sweatshops. Twenty percent of American children lived in orphanages at the time; their parents were
not necessarily dead, but couldn't afford to keep them.

During the Depression and up to the end of World War II,
many millions of U.S. households were more multigenerational
than nuclear. Women my grandmother's age were likely to live
with a fluid assortment of elderly relatives, in-laws, siblings, and
children. In many cases they spent virtually every waking hour
working in the company of other women—a companionable scenario in which it would be easier, I imagine, to tolerate an
estranged or difficult spouse. I'm reluctant to idealize a life of so
much hard work and so little spousal intimacy, but its advantage
may have been resilience. A family so large and varied would not
easily be brought down by a single blow: it could absorb a death,
long illness, an abandonment here or there, and any number of
irreconcilable differences.

The Family of Dolls came along midcentury as a great American experiment. A booming economy required a mobile labor
force and demanded that women surrender jobs to returning soldiers. Families came to be defined by a single breadwinner. They
struck out for single-family homes at an earlier age than ever
before, and in unprecedented numbers they raised children in
urban isolation. The nuclear family was launched to sink or swim.

More than a few sank. Social historians corroborate that the
suburban family of the postwar economic boom, which we have
recently selected as our definition of "traditional," was no panacea.

Twenty-five percent of Americans were poor in the mid-1950s, and as yet there were no food stamps. Sixty percent of the elderly lived on less than $1,000 a year, and most had no medical insurance. In the sequestered suburbs, alcoholism and sexual abuse of children were far more widespread than anyone imagined.

Expectations soared, and the economy sagged. It's hard to depend on one other adult for everything, come what may. In the last three decades, that amorphous, adaptable structure we call "family" has been reshaped once more by economic tides. Compared with fifties families, mothers are far more likely now to be employed. We are statistically more likely to divorce, and to live in blended families or other extranuclear arrangements. We are also more likely to plan and space our children, and to rate our marriages as "happy." We are less likely to suffer abuse without recourse or to stare out at our lives through a glaze of prescription tranquilizers. Our aged parents are less likely to be destitute, and we're half as likely to have a teenage daughter turn up a mother herself. All in all, I would say that if "intact" in modern family-values jargon means living quietly desperate in the bell jar, then hip-hip-hooray for "broken." A neat family model constructed to service the Baby Boom economy seems to be returning gradually to a grand, lumpy shape that human families apparently have tended toward since they first took root in Olduvai Gorge. We're social animals, deeply fond of companionship, and children love best to run in packs. If there is a *normal* for humans, at all, I expect it looks like two or three Families of Dolls, connected variously by kinship and passion, shuffled like cards and strewn over several shoeboxes.

The sooner we can let go the fairy tale of families functioning perfectly in isolation, the better we might embrace the relief of community. Even the admirable parents who've stayed married through thick and thin are very likely, at present, to incorporate other adults into their families—household help and baby-sitters if they can afford them, or neighbors and grandparents if they can't. For single parents, this support is the rock-bottom definition of family. And most parents who have split apart, however painfully, still manage to maintain family continuity for their children, creating in many cases a boisterous phenomenon that Constance Ahrons in her book *The Good Divorce* calls the "binuclear family." Call it what you will—when ex-spouses beat swords into plowshares and jump up and down at a soccer game together, it makes for happy kids.

CINDERELLA, LOOK, WHO needs her? All those evil stepsisters? That story always seemed like too much cotton-picking fuss over clothes. A childhood tale that fascinated me more was the one called "Stone Soup," and the gist of it is this: Once upon a time, a pair of beleaguered soldiers straggled home to a village empty-handed, in a land ruined by war. They were famished, but the villagers had so little they shouted evil words and slammed their doors. So the soldiers dragged out a big kettle, filled it with water, and put it on a fire to boil. They rolled a clean round stone into the pot, while the villagers peered through their curtains in amazement.

"What kind of soup is that?" they hooted.

"Stone soup," the soldiers replied. "Everybody can have some when it's done."

"Well, thanks," one matron grumbled, coming out with a shriveled carrot. "But it'd be better if you threw this in."

And so on, of course, a vegetable at a time, until the whole suspicious village managed to feed itself grandly.

Any family is a big empty pot, save for what gets thrown in.

Each stew turns out different. Generosity, a resolve to turn bad luck into good, and respect for variety—these things will nourish a nation of children. Name-calling and suspicion will not. My soup contains a rock or two of hard times, and maybe yours does too. I expect it's a heck of a bouillabaisse.

Contributor Biographies

LINDA PHILLIPS ASHOUR is the author of four novels: *Speaking in Tongues, Joy Baby, Sweet Remedy*, and *A Comforting Lie*. Her short stories have been published in *The Paris Review* and *North American Review*, and she has written for the *New York Times Book Review*. She has taught writing at the UCLA Extension and has been a fellow at Yaddo. She lives in New York City.

SUSAN CHEEVER is the best-selling author of twelve books, including five novels and the memoirs *As Good as I Could Be: A Memoir of Raising Wonderful Children in Difficult Times, Note Found in a Bottle*, and *Home Before Dark*. Her work has been nominated for the National Book Critics Circle Award and won the *Boston Globe* Winship Medal. She is a Guggenheim Fellow, a member of the Corporation of Yaddo, and a member of the Author's Guild Council. She lives in New York City with her family.

KATE CHRISTENSEN grew up in California and Arizona. She is the author of three novels: *In the Drink, Jeremy Thrane*, and *The Epicure's Lament*. She has published essays and articles in various publications, including *Salon, Elle, Mademoiselle*, and the *Hartford Courant*. She lives in Brooklyn with her husband.

CANDY J. COOPER is a Pulitzer Prize finalist and winner of the Selden Ring Award for Investigative Reporting. She has written for the *New York Times, Detroit Free Press, San Francisco Examiner*, and *Parenting* magazine. She currently writes about social issues among young people.

ALICE ELLIOTT DARK is the author of one novel, *Think of England*, and two collections of short stories. Her story "In the Gloaming" was included in *Best American Stories of the Century*, edited by John Updike and made into an HBO movie starring Glenn Close and directed by Christopher Reeve.

SUSAN DAVIS is senior producer for talk programming at the public radio station WUNC in Chapel Hill, North Carolina. Her poetry has appeared in *The Paris Review, Boston Review, Antioch Review,* and *Western Humanities Review* among other literary publications, and was selected as a Poetry Daily feature in 2003. She has worked as a producer for National Public Radio's *Talk of the Nation* and edited and produced the NPR series *Along for the Ride*, the radio documentary series *Soundprint*, and the public radio program *Marketplace*. At work on a collection of poetry, Susan Davis lives in Chapel Hill, North Carolina, with her husband and two children.

MIKE DOLAN is a writer, actor, and filmmaker. As an actor he has starred in films, including *Biloxi Blues, Hamburger Hill*, and *The Light of Day*. He also worked on Broadway in *A Few Good Men* and *Breaking the Code* and has had leading roles in the television series *I'll Fly Away* and *Law and Order*. A short film he wrote and directed, *Arrow Shot*, premiered at the Sundance Film Festival and was broadcast on the Independent Film Channel. He is currently attending the James A. Michener Center for Writers at the University of Texas. He lives in Austin with his wife, S. Kirk Walsh.

DAVID GOODWILLIE has been a minor league baseball player, private investigator, Sotheby's auction house expert, and Internet entrepreneur—none of which turned out too well. He has also written fiction and non-fiction for several magazines and journals, including *Swink, Black Book,* and *Cover.* His first book, a memoir titled *Seemed Like a Good Idea at the Time,* is being published by Algonquin in June 2006. He is a graduate of Kenyon College and lives in New York City.

BARBARA KINGSOLVER is the best-selling author of five novels: *The Bean Trees, Pigs in Heaven, Animal Dreams, The Poisonwood Bible,* and *Prodigal Summer* (all from HarperCollins), as well as two collections each of essays and poetry. *The Poisonwood Bible* was named one of the top ten notable books of 1998 by the *New York Times* and *Los Angeles Times* and was selected by the Oprah Winfrey Book Club. She lives outside Tucson, Arizona, with her husband and two children.

DANA KINSTLER won *The Missouri Review* editors' prize in fiction in 2000. Her fiction has also appeared in *The Mississippi Review,* guest edited by Rick Moody. Her stories have been nominated for Scribner's Best of the Fiction Workshops and for a Pushcart Prize. Residencies include the Vermont Studio Center and Dorset Colony House. She is currently finishing a collection of linked stories and novellas and is also writing a novel. She lives in Tivoli, New York, with her husband and two daughters.

SHEILA KOHLER is the author of five novels: *The Perfect Place, The House on R Street, Cracks, Children of Pithiviers,* and the forthcoming *Crossways,* and three collections of short stories: *Miracles in America, One Girl,* and *Stories from Another World. Cracks* was chosen by *Library Journal* and *Newsday* as one of the best books of 1999. Kohler has been short-listed three times for the O. Henry Awards (1999, 2001, 2002) and awarded the O. Henry Award (1988), Open Voice Award (1991), Smart Family Foundation Prize (October 2000), and Willa Cather Prize (1999). Her story "Africans" was recorded and read at Symphony Space and on National Public Radio. She is currently a fellow at the New York Public Library's Dorothy and Lewis B. Cullman Center for Scholars and Writers.

SANDRA TSING LOH is a writer-performer whose off-Broadway solo shows have included *Aliens in America* and *Bad Sex with Bud Kemp*. Her latest shows include *Sugar Plum Fairy* (San Jose Rep, the Geffen Playhouse, and Seattle Rep), and *I Worry* at The Kennedy Center. Loh's books include *A Year in Van Nuys, Aliens in America, Depth Takes a Holiday*, and a novel, *If You Lived Here, You'd Be Home By Now*, which was named by the *Los Angeles Times* as one of the 100 best fiction books of 1998. She has been a recipient of the Pushcart Prize in short fiction and a MacDowell Fellow. She has been a regular commentator on National Public Radio's *Morning Edition* and on Ira Glass's *This American Life*; currently, her weekly segment *The Loh Life* is heard on KPCC, and her monthly segment *The Loh Down* is heard on American Public Media's *Marketplace*. She is a contributing editor for *The Atlantic Monthly*.

JACQUELYN MITCHARD is the author of six novels, including *New York Times* best-sellers *The Deep End of the Ocean* (the first novel chosen for the Oprah Winfrey Book Club) and *Twelve Times Blessed*. Her first children's novel, *Starring Prima! The Mouse of the Ballet Jolie* was published in 2004 by HarperCollins. A longtime journalist, Mitchard writes a syndicated column, "The Rest of Us," that appears in 120 newspapers nationwide. She lives near Madison, Wisconsin, with her husband and their six children.

LUCIA NEVAI's first novel, *Seriously*, was published by Little, Brown in 2004. Her short fiction has appeared in *The New Yorker, Zoetrope: All-Story, The Iowa Review*, and other literary magazines, as well as in two collections, *Normal*, published by Algonquin Books of Chapel Hill, and *Star Game*, which won the Iowa Short Fiction Award. She lives in upstate New York.

STEPHANIE STOKES OLIVER is the author of *Song for My Father: Memoir of an All-American Family*, published by Atria in 2004, as well as *Seven Soulful Secrets for Minding Your Body and Finding Your Mission* and *Daily Cornbread: 365 Secrets for a Healthy Mind, Body, and Spirit*, both from Doubleday. She is deputy editor of *Essence* magazine.

ELIZABETH POWELL is the author of *The Republic of Self*, winner of the 2000 New Issues First Book of Poetry Prize, chosen by C. K. Williams. Her work has appeared in *The Harvard Review, North American Review, Hunger Mountain Review, Black Warrior Review*, and other journals. She is the recipient of fellowships from the Vermont Council on the Arts, Arts Vermont Endowment, and Yaddo. She teaches at the University of Vermont, the New England Young Writers' Conference, and serves on the staff of *New England Review*.

MAURA RHODES has been a senior editor at *Parenting* magazine for seven years. Prior to that, she was an editor at other publications, including *Self, Longevity*, and *Health*. As a freelance writer, she has published work in those magazines, as well as in *Redbook, Good Housekeeping, McCall's, Family Circle, Fitness*, and *Women's Health and Fitness*. She is the author of two career guides in the series *Careers Without College* and is the coauthor of *Radu's Simply Fit: Get the Workout of Your Life with America's Leading Fitness Coach*.

ROXANA ROBINSON has received fellowships from the Guggenheim Foundation, the National Endowment for the Arts, and the MacDowell Colony. She is a critically acclaimed fiction writer, author of three novels and two collections of short stories. Her biography of Georgia O'Keeffe was short-listed for the National Book Critics Circle Award and was named one of the *New York Times*'s most notable books of the year. Her work has appeared in *The New Yorker, Harper's, The Atlantic Monthly*, and *Best American Short Stories* and has been widely anthologized and broadcast on National Public Radio. She has been named a Literary Lion by the New York Public Library.

PHYLLIS ROSE is a distinguished critic, biographer, and memoirist. Among her books are a critical biography of Virginia Woolf, *A Woman of Letters*, which was a National Book Award finalist; a portrait of Victorian marriages, *Parallel Lives*; a life of Josephine Baker, *Jazz Cleopatra*; and a memoir, *My Year of Reading Proust*. She teaches at Wesleyan University in Connecticut.

TED ROSE is a journalist and former television producer whose articles and essays have appeared in the *New York Times, Washington Post, Newsweek International, Talk Magazine,* and on National Public Radio's *All Things Considered*. He is at work on a book about his year at a Buddhist retreat in the Rocky Mountains. He lives in Boulder, Colorado.

LISA SHEA is a novelist and freelance writer. Her first novel, *Hula*, won a Whiting Writer's Award and was a regional best-seller. She is at work on a second novel (*The Free World*), a book of linked stories (*Offspring*), and a nonfiction book on the migraine. Her essays, features, and book reviews have appeared in the *New York Times, Elle, Interview, O, The Oprah Magazine,* and *Esquire*. She has taught creative writing at the University of Massachusetts, Barnard College, Mount Holyoke, the University of the South, Bennington College, and New York University.

ANDREW SOLOMON is the author of *The Irony Tower: Soviet Artists in a Time of Glasnost*; the novel *A Stone Boat*; and *The Noonday Demon: An Atlas of Depression*, which won the 2001 National Book Award and has been published in twenty-two languages. He is currently working on a book called *Ten Kinds of Love: Parenting Traumatic Children*, and also completing a Ph.D. in psychology at Cambridge University. He writes regularly for *The New Yorker* and lives in New York and London.

LESLIE MORGAN STEINER works at the *Washington Post Magazine*. She is the editor of an essay collection, *The Mommy Wars* (Random House, March 2006). She lives in Washington, D.C., with her husband and three children.

D. S. SULAITIS's short stories have appeared in *The Quarterly, Painted Bride Quarterly, New York Stories*, and *Inkwell*, and in *Boston Review* as winner of its 2003 fiction contest. She has received two New York Foundation for the Arts fiction fellowships, for 1996 and 2004. She is currently working on a collection of stories and a novel.

SASHA TROYAN's first novel, *Angels in the Morning*, was published by Permanent Press in 2003. It was a *Book Sense 76* pick. Her second novel, *The Forgotten Island*, was published by Bloomsbury/Tin House in 2004. She was born in America but raised and educated in France. She now lives in New Jersey with her husband and their two sons.

S. KIRK WALSH's essays and articles have been published in the *New York Times, Christian Science Monitor,* and *Rolling Stone,* among other national publications. Her poems have appeared in *Mid-American Poetry Review* and *Mirror, Mirror,* an anthology. Residencies include The Ragdale Foundation and Virginia Center for the Creative Arts. She is working on a novel and lives in Austin, Texas, with her husband, Mike Dolan.

306.874   My father married
M   your mother.

$24.95

DATE			